A Journey into
Steinbeck's California

THIRD EDITION

Susan Shillinglaw

With photographs by
Nancy Burnett

<u>ARTPLACE SERIES</u>

Roaring Forties Press
Berkeley, California

Roaring Forties Press
1053 Santa Fe Avenue
Berkeley, CA 94706

Copyright © 2006, 2011, 2019 by Susan Shillinglaw

Printed in China.

ISBN: 978-1-938901-82-9 (print)
ISBN: 978-1-938901-83-6 (ebook)

Library of Congress Cataloging-in-Publication Data

Names: Shillinglaw, Susan, author. | Burnett, Nancy, photographer.
Title: A journey into Steinbeck's California / Susan Shillinglaw ; with
 photographs by Nancy Burnett.
Description: Third edition. | Berkeley, California : Roaring Forties Press,
 [2019] | Series: ArtPlace series | Includes bibliographical references and
 index.
Identifiers: LCCN 2018057799 (print) | LCCN 2018058922 (ebook) | ISBN
 9781938901836 (ebook) | ISBN 9781938901829 (paperback : alk. paper)
Subjects: LCSH: Steinbeck, John, 1902-1968--Homes and haunts--California. |
 Steinbeck, John, 1902-1968--Knowledge--California. | Novelists,
 American--Homes and haunts--California. | Novelists, American--20th
 century--Biography. | California--In literature. | California--Biography.
Classification: LCC PS3537.T3234 (ebook) | LCC PS3537.T3234 Z86646 2019
 (print) | DDC 813/.52 [B] --dc23
LC record available at https://lccn.loc.gov/2018057799

For Bill Gilly,
who most certainly knows why

Contents

COVER ART: *Landscape from Laguna Seca,* David Ligare

David Ligare was drawn to Monterey County by the writing of John Steinbeck and Robinson Jeffers. In Steinbeck's fiction, Ligare finds a "compelling dissonance between the loveliness of this landscape and the longings and sufferings of its inhabitants." Stories in *The Pastures of Heaven* and *The Long Valley* tell about inhabitants' loneliness, isolation, and lack of fulfillment.

Ligare's own Salinas Valley landscapes are less about dissonance and more about pastoral serenity. As paintings such as *Landscape with Red Pony* attest, central to his work is the notion that the gentle beauty evoked at a particular time is a fleeting moment of serenity, peace, and escape. Correct light is essential—fading daylight, approaching night, golden light, or what Virgil called the "mortal serenity of evening." Clouds are low in the sky, as they often are in Monterey County. Grasses and flowers convey a particular time of year, as is true in Steinbeck's work: seed heads ready to burst, lupin in bloom, oak leaves bright green.

Both Steinbeck's and Ligare's landscapes possess a mythic quality. Archetypes are envisioned as part of a place—like Joseph the seeker in *To a God Unknown* or Ma the earth mother in *The Grapes of Wrath* or Samuel the prophet in *East of Eden*.

Preface to the Third Edition

John Steinbeck was a traveling man, restless and curious throughout his sixty-six years. Born in the Central California farming community of Salinas in 1902, he fled hometown proprieties at age seventeen and enrolled in Stanford University, although he "went to college almost frantically unenthusiastic," he later admitted. When his student budget permitted, he took off for San Francisco, where "he savored his first independence . . . living where he chose, doing as he wanted, eating at random when and where and what he liked." As an under-graduate, he envisioned even greater freedom—he planned a voyage to China on a merchant ship (nixed because he had no sailing experience), then considered riding horseback to Mexico picking his way through the desert (no money for that), and finally booked a trip through the Panama Canal in 1925.

The itch to travel was constant. While California remained Steinbeck's lodestar, the world beckoned. In late 1935, he and his wife Carol drove from Pacific Grove to Mexico City; a year and a half later, they booked a freighter to Scandinavia and ventured into Russia, where, he bragged on his return, they didn't meet a single "worthwhile" person. In California and beyond, Steinbeck connected to ordinary people—no surprise that he and Carol hung out with seamen on their ship across the Atlantic. The couple went to Baja in 1940 with Steinbeck's best friend, marine biologist Edward Flanders Ricketts, to collect invertebrates (resulting in the publication of *Sea of Cortez* in 1941), and Steinbeck was planning another collecting trip with Ricketts, this time to British Columbia, the year Ed died, 1948.

For a few months during World War II, Steinbeck was a correspondent covering England, South Africa, and the Italian coast, and in 1947 he and photographer Robert Capa toured Soviet Russia, assessing the survival strategies of a country and people blasted by war. The 1950s were devoted to travel. He and his third wife, Elaine, sailed to Europe in the summers and flew to the Virgin Islands in January; he often covered expenses by writing journalistic pieces for popular magazines such as *Collier's, Holiday,* and *Esquire.* In 1960, he drove across

America with his dog Charley, circling back to his California roots. And in 1966–67, his health declining, he accepted an assignment to cover the Vietnam War, which would turn out to be his final journey.

As Steinbeck lived, so he wrote. Three of his most important books were travel narratives, *Sea of Cortez*, *A Russian Journal* (1948), and *Travels with Charley* (1962). Several journalistic series focus on travel, in one way or another, from his first, "The Harvest Gypsies," written in 1936, to his final series about Vietnam, "Letters to Alicia," syndicated in American newspapers in 1966 and 1967. And many of his books are about characters as restless as he: Lennie and George, Tom Joad, Jim Casy, Adam Trask. Elaine Steinbeck reported to a friend that in 1958 John was putting the final touches to a new short novel, "The Marshal of Manchou," a "Don Quixote-ish story of a man in a small western town who gets so enthralled in 'adult westerns' on TV that he goes out into the world to do Good. Very charming, funny, and touching."

That book was never published, but there surely was a bit of Steinbeck himself in the idealistic Marshal, out to "do Good," to nudge readers into fuller understanding of others, whether marginalized Californians, fellow Americans (his last book, *America and Americans*, a jeremiad, assessed our values), Soviet citizens, or Mexican revolutionaries such as Emiliano Zapata (in *Viva Zapata!* which came out in 1952). Travelers like Steinbeck are adventurers. They are curious. Some, like Steinbeck, want to burrow into the marrow of a place, to be an eyewitness to unfolding contemporary events. Some, like Steinbeck's malcontents in *The Wayward Bus*, learn important lessons. And some, like Steinbeck, travel in order to better understand themselves and others as Citizens of the World. For Steinbeck, who inhabited each region he traveled to as fully as possible—delving into history, geography, culture, and politics— to travel was to live fully, deeply, truly.

His personal stamp, which he settled on in the late 1930s, was a flying pig, "Pigasus," and beneath he wrote his motto in Latin: "To the stars on the wings of a pig." In other words, as Elaine later explained, "go as high as you can on the equipment you've got!" That phrase suggests both his creative yearnings and his wanderlust.

But it's also true that he was a homebody, and the paradox of flight from and return to California was the story of his life. Although he left his home state in the early 1940s, and settled in New York City in 1945, John Steinbeck never truly left California at all. "You look like a Californian," an Okie boy told him in the 1930s—rugged, square-shouldered, intense, free- thinking, broad-humored. The West nurtured his soul, even when he was three thousand miles away, living in a New York apartment and finding watery solace at a summer cottage on Bluff Point in Sag Harbor, Long Island, a place not so very different from the one his father had built in Pacific Grove in 1904, two blocks from Monterey Bay.

California was, quite simply, home. In 1948, for example, he was living in New York City with his second wife, Gwyn Conger, and his world was falling apart. His health was bad, his nerves shredded, his stomach tight. He was being sued for breach of contract on a film of *Cannery Row*. His marriage was crumbling. He was taking antidepressants and felt himself in a "kingdom of despondency" after the death of Ed Ricketts, who had been hit by a train in Monterey. What buoyed him during these grim months were thoughts of the book he had envisioned since 1930 or before, the opus to his birthplace, *East of Eden*. He decided he should live in the Salinas Valley and considered buying property in Corral di Tierra, where his beloved Aunt Mollie had lived: "My hunger for there is very great," he wrote in his journal.

That hunger marked his life and work. His love of California informed story after story, those written during his years at Stanford through 1955, when a musical called *Pipe Dream* opened on Broadway. It was based on a little-known sequel to *Cannery Row*, *Sweet Thursday*. The musical was one of Rodgers and

Hammerstein's few flops. Steinbeck complained that they didn't understand the material, his delicate touch that made brothels homelike, madams decent, a marine scientist a gentle sage, and bums endearingly rough-edged, lonely like everyone else. Steinbeck's West was an egalitarian place, where ordinary folks needed to be understood and heard. Steinbeck's California fiction invites readers to the human carnival, where migrants and bums, strike organizers and bindlestiffs, ranchers and blacksmiths rub elbows, all yearning for something promised in the West, in California, the state where dreams are supposed to come true, where wanderlust is supposed to be satiated.

Steinbeck's final book, *America and Americans* (1966), is threaded with stories of his Salinas childhood and his California youth. Two years after that book was published, John Steinbeck died in New York City. As he wished, he was buried in Salinas after a memorial service at Point Lobos. He also requested that his Nobel Prize be donated to Stanford University. There is only one home, he told Elaine—Central California.

Out from, return to. In *Sea of Cortez*, Steinbeck writes: "a man looking at reality brings his own limitations to the world. If he has strength and energy of mind the tide pool stretches both ways, digs back to the electrons and leaps space into the universe and fights out of the moment into non-conceptual time. Then ecology has a synonym which is ALL."

For "tide pool," read any place one examines with full participation. In this book, that place is largely focused on Steinbeck's California, rich with associations that are multilayered: personal, historical, ecological, cultural, and spiritual. This book captures Steinbeck's holistic vision of the place that was always the place of his heart, Central California, his home—ALL of it.

FROM THE TIDE POOL TO THE STARS

ALL THINGS ARE ONE THING, ONE THING IS ALL THINGS

Mandala by Ray Troll, with a quotation from *Sea of Cortez*. This art was created for the Western Flyer Foundation, which is restoring the boat that Steinbeck and Ricketts chartered to the Sea of Cortez in 1940.

Acknowledgments

A career spent in Steinbeck's company has been a delightful journey, taking me from California to states across the United States, and also to Japan, Mexico, England, the Soviet Union, the Republic of Georgia, Austria, and Sicily. I warmly thank the legions of librarians, government officials, and scholars across the globe who asked me to speak about John Steinbeck's writing and career, making these journeys possible and helping to inspire this book. Because he connects with readers worldwide, I have connected through his works. My life, as well as theirs, I trust, has been deeply enriched by Steinbeck's empathy, political vision, and environmental sensibilities. This book celebrates his open-hearted gaze upon the world.

My Steinbeck sojourn began with a nudge. Without my own Ma Joad—former English Department chair Lou Lewandowski—I would never have been swept into Steinbeck's orbit. When I was a newly minted Ph.D. and a lecturer at San Jose State University in 1987, Lou appointed me director of what was then the Steinbeck Research Center and thus opened the road to Steinbeck's world. Journeys are enhanced by wise counselors. Without my own Jim Casys—scholars Robert DeMott and Jackson Benson—I would hardly have found my path. Others provided steady direction, including my dissertation advisor, the late, great John Seelye, former general editor of Penguin Classics, who asked me to write introductions to *Cannery Row* and *Of Mice and Men* in 1992. Penguin editors Michael Millman and Elda Rotor have been beacons for years. Scholarly roadmaps and fine friendships have sustained me in the ever-gracious world of Steinbeck scholars, editors, and teachers. He connects. We connect.

Inspiration for this book came in the early 1990s, when I first prepared lectures on "Steinbeck and Place" for Stanford University's Knight Fellows. Thank you Jims—Risser and Bettinger—and Dawn Garcia for a quarter century of invitations and heartwarming support.

I have been fortunate to know many of Steinbeck's friends and family, and each has generously shared stories of Steinbeck the man, all of which enrich this book. They have brought him to life for me: Elaine Steinbeck, Toni and David Heyler, Jean Boone, Ed Ricketts Jr., Nancy Ricketts, Toni Volconi, Jean and Bruce Ariss, Sharon Brown Bacon, Nada Berry, Margaret Ringnalda, Virginia St. Jean, Virginia Scardigli, Thom and John Steinbeck, Arthur Miller. And many, many others. Steinbeck's embrace was immense, his connections to family and friends adamantine.

Since 1987, I have taught a Steinbeck class every semester at San Jose State University—students help one see texts anew, and I am grateful for their insights. And with my husband, Bill Gilly, I have taught a cross-disciplinary course, Holistic Biology, at Stanford's Hopkins Marine Station, which has deepened my appreciation of Steinbeck's ecological vision. My thanks go to Gilly, Chuck Baxter, John and Vicki Pearse, and Nancy Burnett.

Any author scrounging around in archives must be in equal measure delighted by resources snagged and by the ever-cheerful assistance of librarians, historians, booksellers, and collectors. None of Melville's sub-subs here. This book would not have been possible without the guidance and invaluable resources provided by librarians at Stanford University libraries, the Monterey and Pacific Grove Public Libraries, Pacific Grove Heritage Society, Pebble Beach archives, and San Jose State University's Steinbeck Center, as well as the National Steinbeck Center in Salinas. Pat Hathaway's photo archive of Monterey County is a local treasure trove. I am also grateful to Don Kohrs, librarian at Hopkins Marine Station, for help researching the third edition.

Colleagues and friends listened and fully participated (Steinbeck's word) in my frantic year writing the first edition and my more leisurely months implementing changes for the second and third. Thanks to all. By now, you know Steinbeck very well.

My children—Ian and Nora—have lived with John Steinbeck all their lives and have forgiven my motherly lapses. And I'll never forget the beaming faces of my stepson, Clayton Gilly, and his partner Amanda at my first reading of this book in San Francisco in 2005, with Steinbeck's Stanford friend, Bob

Cathcart, age ninety-four, also in the audience. My husband has taught me about science, life, and love. His fine-tuned editorial sensibilities erased blemishes in the first, second, and third editions of this book.

From all of this, it should be clear that a phalanx of creative people stand behind this book. I began writing the first edition in 2004, with the blithe notion that I could quickly write up years of slide presentations. Publishers Deirdre Greene and Nigel Quinney sustained my year of writing by holding me to a scheduled chapter a month, editing each as I wrote. What a gift. In an era of rising costs for full-color books, this third edition would have been a chimera without the generous financial support of Bruce Taylor and Taylor Farms. I am deeply appreciative of his steady kindness and unparalleled Salinas Valley generosity.

A Journey into
Steinbeck's California

THIRD EDITION

Chapter 1
Steinbeck's California
The Valley of the World

Near San Juan Grade Road,
Salinas, California.

In 1979, a U.S. postal
stamp was issued
in John Steinbeck's honor.

In 1951, when John Steinbeck had been a resident of New York City for about a year, he sat down at his desk to write *East of Eden* (1952), his ode to California. Nearly twenty years earlier, he had declared his intention to tell "the story of this whole valley . . . so that it would be the valley of the world." Epics take time to incubate. Certain forces coalesced when he moved East and ended a cycle of personal despair: a new marriage, a new home, distance from California. As he worked on his manuscript, he wrote in his journal, "My wish is that when my reader has finished with this book, he will have a sense of belonging in it. He will actually be a native of that Valley." John Steinbeck was ready to unravel his intertwined heritage of place, history, and people—and to retie it with a knot of his own invention.

Steinbeck's "valley of the world" is an enticing notion, particularly irresistible for anyone concerned with marketing the pleasures of the Salinas Valley. But, for the writer, the words undoubtedly suggested something closer to what D. H. Lawrence proposed when he tackled the subject of American writing in 1923: "Different places on the face of the earth have different vital effluence, different vibration, different chemical exhalation, different polarity with different stars: call it what you like. But the spirit of place is a great reality," he wrote in the introduction to *Classic American Writers*. John Steinbeck grew up sensing that spirit of place, feeling that the whole of

"On the level vegetable lands are the mile-long rows of pale green lettuce and the spindly little cauliflowers."

Monterey County ran through his blood. From age fourteen on, his passion was to set it down right and true. "My country is different from the rest of the world," he wrote to his publisher in late 1932.

> *It seems to be one of those pregnant places from which come wonders . . . I was born to it and my father was. Our bodies came from this soil—our bones came . . . from the limestone of our own mountains and our blood is distilled from the juices of this earth. I tell you now that my country— a hundred miles long and about fifty wide—is unique in the world.*

Steinbeck spent a long career shaping the contours of that unique land in words. His Monterey County is not Faulkner's Yoknapatawpha County, more fabricated than real, but the landscape of his childhood, often more real than fabricated. His valley of the world is historically rich, beautiful, and peopled with migrants. Steinbeck wanted to carve prose so exacting that the places of his heart—the bronze hills of the Salinas Valley and the churning Pacific Ocean nearby— would be fully rendered for any reader. But it's not just his descriptions that bring forth the spirit of place. His authorial grasp was ambitious and holistic. He wrote about nature's impact on the eye and the heart.

that would strike the symphonic chords of Steinbeck's life and birthplace. He considered the novel his *War and Peace*, written with "the great word sounds of speech not writing," with "song" in it. "I will make my country as great in the literature of the world as any place in existence," he wrote.

A Journey into Steinbeck's California is about Steinbeck Country and beyond, to places in California where he lived or which he reimagined. This book's intent is akin to Steinbeck's own—to capture the whole picture of landscapes close to his heart. Each place where he lived and wrote about shaped him differently because each had its own "vibration." He in turn shaped those places. Visitors to twenty-first-century Cannery Row expect to see Mack and the boys and are disappointed to find curio shops and luxury hotels. Time alters a street like Cannery Row. But its vibration persists.

John Adolph Steinbeck, Steinbeck's grandfather, arrived in Hollister, California in 1872 and established a small dairy and orchards on seventy acres.

He wrote about the history and geography of place. He wrote about the people who lived in the towns and valleys of Monterey County. He showed how each place he loved—Soledad, Jolon, and King City to the south of his birthplace, Salinas; and Pacific Grove, Monterey, and Carmel to the west—had a different energy. Steinbeck's fiction is a rich tapestry of land, history, and human experience.

East of Eden, part autobiography, part myth, part historical survey, part pure creation, was the "big book"

A Holistic Sense of Place

John Steinbeck said repeatedly that his books were written in layers: *The Grapes of Wrath* (1939) has five, *Cannery Row* (1945) has four, and *Sea of Cortez* (1941) has four, "and I think very few will follow it down to the fourth," he wrote his editor. That notion of multiple layers seems perplexing because Steinbeck, like most writers, resisted textual explications. Although his comments on layers provide no keys, they do suggest that each book may be approached from different perspectives. And, in fact, holism begins here, understanding the importance of increasingly complex layers, different "peepholes," as he notes in *Cannery Row*. To appreciate Steinbeck's spirit of place—as well as his holistic sensibilities—is to consider what layering might mean for him (although this book is hardly concerned with strict constructions): first is the wonder of the surface; second, human interactions; third, historical shadows; and fourth, the universality of life.

"The floor of the Salinas Valley, between the ranges and below the foothills, is level because this valley used to be the bottom of a hundred-mile inlet from the sea."

For John Steinbeck, surface texture encompasses the names of plants, weeds, birds, and trees, human eccentricities, and the contours of place. He asks readers to see with precision. Numerous examples could be given of his rapt attention to the external world. In a tide pool, "orange and speckled and fluted nudibranchs slide gracefully over the rocks, their skirts waving like the dresses of Spanish dancers." Salinas hills are "gold and saffron and red" in June and, as summer wears on, become "umber." California poppies are "a burning color—not orange, not gold, but if pure gold were liquid and could raise a cream, that golden cream might be like the color of the poppies," he writes in *East of Eden*, and deep purple lupins have petals "edged with white, so that a field of lupins is more blue than you can imagine." Steinbeck's prose gives readers

a human heart in contact with the land, to paraphrase nature writer Barry Lopez.

Steinbeck's holistic sweep includes human interaction with nature, as he declared in a notebook while writing *To a God Unknown* (1933): "Each figure is a population, and the stones, the trees, the muscled mountains are the world—but not the world apart from man—the world and man—the one inseparable unit man and his environment. Why they should ever have been understood as being separate I do not know." In Steinbeck's hands, the Salinas Valley becomes a template for human struggles. As the opening chapter of *East of Eden* shows, the valley is a land of contrasts seen and felt: drought and rain; rich years and scrappy years; aching natural beauty—tawny hills, springtime mustard, "round comfortable oaks"—colliding with menacing shadows—"high grey fog," afternoon winds, dark blue mountains to the West, and turbulent waters on the Big Sur coast (and, these days, unavoidable traffic). Chiaroscuro of the land tallies with his characters' own light and shadow.

California poppies.

Perhaps the mountain ranges bordering the Salinas Valley shouted "contrast" to Steinbeck most loudly—and those contrasts mean things deep in the psyche. The Gabilan Mountains to the East are "light gay mountains full of sun and loveliness and a kind of invitation," he writes in *East of Eden*. In *The Red Pony* (1937), the Gabilans are "jolly mountains, with hill ranches in their creases, and with pine trees growing on the crests. People lived there, and battles had been fought against the Mexicans on the slopes." But to the West lay the Santa Lucias, coastal mountains with stands of redwoods, deep ravines, hot springs, and scrub-covered hills. These are the unexplored, mysterious places in Steinbeck's fiction. Like Jody, his protagonist in *The Red Pony*, the young Steinbeck must have wondered about these "curious secret mountains" to the West and thought how "little he knew about them." Jody's father tells him that "I've read there's more unexplored country in the mountains of Monterey County than any place in the United States," a snippet of dialogue that might well have come from Steinbeck's own father.

Lupins in the San Antonio Valley.

These landscapes, resonant with human energies, are quite different from those of another renowned Californian, John Muir. Whereas Muir's is a triumphant wilderness, Steinbeck's is a peopled land, space with a human imprint. Even at its darkest, Steinbeck's nature is a place where people experience joy as well as pain. Nature offers a refuge. In *Of Mice and Men* (1937), George and Lennie find a protective clearing by the Salinas River; in *The Grapes of Wrath*, Tom Joad hides from pursuers in a cave; Jody in *The Red Pony* finds

A California oak, depicted in Anne B. Fisher's *The Salinas, Upside-Down River*.

comfort in a grassy spot near the water tank. In *Cannery Row*, Mack and the boys' home is under the protective shadow of a black cypress tree whose "limbs folded down and made a canopy under which a man could lie and look out at the flow and vitality of Cannery Row." Land shelters restless spirits.

A Sense of History

Steinbeck's holism also embraces what he called a necessary "wall of background" in each work. That meant getting the atmosphere right for each story. History and culture are as much a part of place in Steinbeck's work as is nature, all carefully rendered and symbolically evoked.

Human histories crowd California. Settlement came from all directions: Spaniards and Mexicans from the south; Chinese, Japanese, and Filipinos from the west; and German, Swedish, and English pioneers across the prairie or seaboard from the eastern United States. Steinbeck includes this historical diversity. His Salinas Valley is, in fact, a region roughly outlined by Spanish missions: Mission San Juan Bautista in the north, Missions Soledad and San Antonio de Padua to the south, the Carmel Mission to the west. These romantic, brooding ruins and restored churches stand sentry over Steinbeck Country and serve as fitting symbols of his holistic sensibility, for the history of the Salinas Valley shaped Steinbeck's prose as fully as did the valley's natural features. That rugged history is etched in mission grounds, where from the 1770s to the

Dark Watchers

To the Spanish, *Big Sur* was "El Pais Grande del Sur," or "the big land to the south." For Steinbeck, as for his Carmel neighbor, poet Robinson Jeffers, the Big Sur coast was a land of mystery: dark mountains, churning sea, silent redwood groves. Perhaps his 1920 stint on a road construction crew in the area stamped him with the region's turbulent appeal.

Highway 1 along the wild coast opened to much fanfare on June 27, 1937. Since then, the road has been compared to two of the loveliest and most precipitous drives in the western world, the Cornich in France and the Amalfi Coast in Italy.

One of Steinbeck's most anthologized stories, "Flight," is set in this region: "About 15 miles below Monterey, the Torres family had their farm, a few sloping acres above a cliff that dropped to the brown reefs and to the hissing white waters." When young Pepe Torres must flee into the mountains, "Dark watchers" haunt him—as they seem to

haunt the gnarly mountains today. "I don't know who the dark watchers are," Steinbeck responded to a 1953 query about the meaning of the story, "but I know they are there. I've seen them and felt them. I guess they are whatever you want them to be."

1830s padres converted Indian souls and cultivated rich soils—slowly eroding the native people's sovereignty (a history that opens his 1932 novel, *The Pastures of Heaven*). It is apparent in adobes that "seemed to have grown out of the earth," Steinbeck wrote, built on Spanish and Mexican land grants, many melting back into the ground during Steinbeck's childhood. It is recorded in the Spanish and English names of places Steinbeck knew well:

> *After the valleys were settled the names of places refer more to things which happened there, and these to me are the most fascinating of all names because each name suggests a story that has been forgotten. I think of Bolsa Nueva, a new purse; Morocojo, a lame Moor (who was he and how did he get there?); Wild Horse Canyon and Mustang Grade and Shirt Tail Canyon. The names of places carry a charge of the people who named them, reverent or irreverent, descriptive, either poetic or disparaging.*

That history is also Chinese Lee's mother in *East of Eden*, brutally raped in a Sierra gold camp, or the Japanese boy who is teased in *The Pastures of Heaven* (1932), or the rough Filipino migrant workers in

"Fingers of Cloud," one of Steinbeck's first stories, written when he was at Stanford.

Borderland

Steinbeck's West is also a borderland, something first identified by Wilbur Needham, reviewing the 1938 collection of stories, *The Long Valley*, for the *Los Angeles Times*. "Behind each story, inside it, and surrounding it, there is a presence . . . a fragile presence but with surprising strength in that borderland story of this world and the mind's world

Chinatown in Pacific Grove, early 1900s.

Working on irrigation in the Salinas Valley near Spreckels, circa 1908.

and maybe another world." Steinbeck crosses borders between place and spirit.

Appreciating what he calls "ALL" in *Sea of Cortez* is recognizing that humans are indeed connected to the land and its creatures, to other human histories—and to something larger than any particular place or vibration or historical moment: "Most of the feeling we call religious, most of the mystical outcrying which is one of the most prized and used and desired reactions of our species, is really the understanding and the attempt to say that man is related to the whole thing, related inextricably to all reality, known and unknowable." Steinbeck meant the same thing when he noted that his was a valley "from which come wonders." He meant it when he explained moments of full connection in his life:

> *You know the big pine tree beside this house [his family's cottage in Pacific Grove]? I planted it when it and I were very little; I've watched it*

grow. It has always been known as "John's tree." Years ago, in mental playfulness I used to think of it as my brother and then later, still playfully, I thought of it as something rather closer, a kind of repository of my destiny . . . if the tree should die, I am pretty sure I should be ill. This feeling I have planted in myself and quite deliberately I guess, but it is none the less strong for all that.

For Steinbeck, "ALL" is also suggested in what he called a "child's vision," a sensibility he wanted to capture in *East of Eden*, *The Red Pony*, *Of Mice and Men*, and even in the stately *Sea of Cortez*. "Adults haven't the clean fine judgment of children," he wrote to a friend. In *Of Mice and Men* he wanted "colors more clear than they are to adults, of tastes more sharp. I want to put down the way 'afternoon felt' and of the feeling about a bird that sang in a tree in the evening." Children see the world unmitigated. They participate fully. A child's vision of nature—universal, sharply observed, deeply

Cannery Row, by Bruce Ariss.

felt, and complete—is a part of Steinbeck's enduring legacy. As an adult, he wrote down the awe of his childhood spent in the lovely Salinas Valley and on the shore of the sweeping Pacific coast.

Another Peephole

The heart of the man John Steinbeck beats steadily in *Travels with Charley* (1962), a book not about California but about a quest for something broader: an appreciation of America itself. This late book says something about Steinbeck's holistic sensibilities. In it, most certainly, is Steinbeck the man—charming, curious, affable, lifelong dog owner, lover of all things mechanical, creator of gadgets. In 1960, Steinbeck decided to drive a camper truck around America on a 10,000-mile trek from his home in Sag Harbor, New York, to California and back. Long road trips are taken by restless souls—and that Steinbeck was. Books about road trips are often written by optimists and dreamers —and John Steinbeck had long studied that part of the human spirit. Like the Joads, Lennie and George, Joseph Wayne, and the grandfather in *The Red Pony*, Steinbeck was "westering," chasing an idea. Steinbeck's idea was America as a place. His goal was, as he says in *Travels with Charley*, to rediscover this "monster land" by understanding a country of diverse people, places, and histories.

When he reached California, at the midpoint of the book, Steinbeck was coming home—as Thomas Wolfe says we must not and cannot. He looked mournfully at places altered—Monterey, Cannery Row, Salinas. But he ended his stay in Monterey County on top of his

John Steinbeck, 1961.
Photograph by Hans Namuth.

beloved Fremont Peak, with an elegy to an unaltered panorama. Roll back the years and the fields still spread out and his father is still carving his mother's name on a tree near Big Sur. As Steinbeck left Monterey County, he rediscovered his own sense of place in a vista that still gives tourists and natives alike something akin to a chill: the sight of California's gentle golden hills, groomed valleys, and the churning sea beyond. In that panorama, Steinbeck may have found the America he was seeking. For him, America is a place in the heart, a deep connection to the land and to the traditions of one's people. Steinbeck Country is indeed the valley of the world if we look at it with Steinbeck's holistic sensibilities—the place, the people, the histories, the spirit.

A Journey into Steinbeck's California assumes another road trip—the reader's own—to discover some of what Steinbeck was after: the "exhalation" and "vibration" of California. With Steinbeck, we can pay attention to the slant of afternoon light, catch some of the region's layered past, and get a glimpse of small human stories tucked in valleys and Monterey streets. These elements are essential to Steinbeck's sense of place, a panorama of human stories that play out on California's inland valleys and Pacific coast.

Chapter 2
Salinas
A Remembered Symphony

Mural in downtown Salinas.

John Steinbeck as a high school senior, June 1919.

When John Steinbeck was born there in 1902, Salinas was a bustling town of 3,300, the county seat of Monterey County, "a true, enterprising, progressive, permanent American city," declared an 1881 promotional brochure. The rich land and cool weather supported ranchers and farmers, attracting "Portuguese and Swiss and Scandinavians," said Steinbeck, and Germans and English and Irish. Ranches were often large, the California pattern since Spanish and Mexican land grants divided much of the nascent state into gigantic plots. By the mid-1930s, the entrepreneurial Shippers and Growers Association controlled agribusiness in a valley whose population had grown rapidly since World War I. "It was the biggest town between San Jose and San Luis Obispo," Steinbeck writes in *East of Eden,* "and everyone felt that a brilliant future was in store for it."

The same would not have been said of young John Steinbeck, a restless and often indolent child. His parents were not farmers or ranchers—the Salinas elite—but middle class, with a respectable standing in town. His father was a businessman. His mother, a former schoolteacher, firmly guided her four children—three girls and John—toward promising futures. As often as not, John resisted her firm hand. He was an uneven, mostly uninspired student (in high school earning mostly 2s—a solid B—with lower grades, 3s and 4s, in Spanish and Latin and "Fair" in "Application"). He was a loving, if not always dutiful, son. Young John was something of a rebel, with a gang of three or four friends who joined him in childhood mischief. Mr. Steinbeck apparently asked nine-year-old John daily if he'd been whipped at school. And he was something of a loner as well, feeling since his fifth

13

birthday, he once wrote, that he didn't fit in with stolid hometown ways. At age fourteen he decided that he would be a writer, a calling that would shape his adolescence and determine his life's course.

Independence of thought, restlessness of spirit, empathy for those who, like him, felt socially marginalized, and a deep, abiding love of the land would define Steinbeck's life and art. That was his Salinas heritage and, more broadly, the heritage of the American West.

Steinbeck's Salinas

Incorporated on March 4, 1874, Salinas is a western boomtown that never went bust. The land created great wealth, "the richest community per capita, we were told, in the entire world," writes Steinbeck. "Certainly we Salinians never questioned it even when we were broke." This had first been cattle country. But in the mid-1860s, herds were decimated by a year of flooding that drowned cattle, followed by two years of drought that starved them. Grains—mostly wheat—became increasingly lucrative, and with grains came settlers to the newly plotted town of Salinas City. When lots priced from $100 to $1,000 were first offered for sale in 1868, they sold at a good clip. Steinbeck's maternal grandfather, Sam Hamilton, purchased a swath of Salinas City land in 1871 and another parcel on Central and Main in 1875; he also signed the city's 1872 charter. By the time the Southern Pacific Railroad came chugging through on November 7, 1872, the town's fortunes were set. Ranching and farming, and later the Spreckels Sugar Factory, made it the economic hub of the valley. The "green gold" of the 1920s—lettuce shipped out of the valley—made the town even wealthier. When Steinbeck was growing up, Main Street stretched for three prosperous blocks.

A parade in downtown Salinas, early 1900s.

Although John Steinbeck loved the valley's tawny hills and his own family, he didn't embrace his birthplace. Indeed, much of his career can be defined as a rebellion against this prosperous town, smug with its successes. The same man who kept the tone of the Salinas Valley in his head throughout his life resisted the town's perceived materialism, insularity, and snobbery. As a child, he relished the gossip he heard from his mother's friends, and one of his earliest extant writings, a short poem, satirizes the women's chatter. As a teenager, sensitive and awkward, he felt the sting of rejection when his father experienced business failures; townspeople, he later remarked, had been "merciless" toward his worried father. Asked to write a

The Salinas Rodeo

Salinas, an agricultural town, was also a ranch town. Cattle roamed the valley in the nineteenth century, and still do today. Cowboys roped steers and branded calves in hill ranches, in Carmel Valley, and up the Old Stage Road—and still do today. Many of the area's original Spanish and Mexican land grants were passed to ranching families; a few families still hold thousands of acres, running cattle as did their grandparents and great-grandparents.

The California Rodeo, one of the biggest in the nation, honors that heritage. Held annually in mid-July, the rodeo (pronounced roh-DAY-oh) began as a horse race in 1897, was envisioned in 1909 as a "Wild West Show," and in 1911 officially opened in its present location at Sherwood Park during what became known as the "Big Week." It was "a kind of local competition," Steinbeck wrote. "One's uncles and even athletic aunts entered the roping contests. The ranchmen from the valley in the foothills rode in on saddles decorated with silver, and their sons demonstrated their skill with unbroken horses. Then gradually the professionals moved in and it became 'show business.'"

In 1912, Japanese lanterns were strung across Main Street for the festivities—Steinbeck was ten, and Japanese lanterns became a lifelong symbol of celebration for him. Four thousand people attended "Big Week" in 1913—it was standing room only from the first day. A popular "Big Hat" barbecue was introduced that year, as were the Saturday night parade and daily horse parades in the street. Years later, writing letters home from Lake Tahoe, Steinbeck longed to come home for the rodeo (although he could not make it home for his sister Mary's spring wedding).

"I can remember my mother sitting in our family box," he wrote to a childhood friend, "with bull dust gradually settling over her and refusing to leave until the last of the wild horses crossed the finish line . . . she always seemed to me a little bit like Queen Victoria sitting in that box . . . Queen Victoria slightly dusted over with bull dust."

In March 1982, the community dedicated *Hat in Three Stages of Landing*, a sculpture of three hats flying through space by Claes Oldenburg and Coosje van Bruggen. The bright yellow hats, weighing 3,500 pounds each, are in ❶ **Sherwood Park** on North Main Street. At the dedication, it was reported that van Bruggen said, "My husband has read Steinbeck; his inspiration came from reading Steinbeck's description of the farm-worker attire."

One of the hats by Claes Oldenburg and Coosje van Bruggen near the rodeo grounds.

piece about his hometown for *Holiday* magazine in 1955, he noted that Salinas's

social structure was a strange and progressive one. First there were the Cattle People, the First Families of the Salinas Valley, gentry by right of being horsemen and dealing in gentry's goods, land and cattle. Theirs was an unassailable position, a little like that of English royalty. Then Claus Spreckels came from Holland and built a Sugar Factory (in capitals) and the flatlands of the valley around Salinas were planted to sugar beets and the Sugar People prospered. They were upstarts, of course, but they were solvent. The Cattle People sneered at them, but learned as every aristocracy does that not blood but money is the final authority. Sugar People might never have got any place socially if lettuce had not become the green gold of the Valley. Now we had a new set of upstarts: Lettuce People. Sugar People joined Cattle People in looking down their noses. These Lettuce People had Carrot People to look down on and these in turn felt odd about associating with Cauliflower People.

Beneath the smiling façade of the social hierarchy, however, Steinbeck sensed an uncertainty and pain that tallied with his own, a "blackness—the feeling of violence just below the surface. . . . It was a blackness that seemed to rise out of the swamps, a kind of whispered brooding that never came into the open—a subsurface violence that bubbled silently like the decaying vegetation under the black water of the Tule Swamps."

Salinas was a town of sloughs and dead-end streets, and for this sensitive young man, many

residents' lives seemed similarly mired, blocked, and dark. He empathized with their woes. Out of these feelings of oppression, both personal and environmental, he found his fictional voice.

Japanese Internment

During World War II, the Salinas rodeo grounds were commandeered by the U.S. government. From April to July 1942, 3,856 Japanese Americans, or Nisei, were confined here before being sent to permanent internment camps. John Steinbeck was perhaps the first American writer to protest Japanese internment. Indeed, he went to Washington, D.C., in the fall of 1941—before Pearl Harbor—and discussed the loyalty of California Japanese with Coordinator of Information director Bill Donovan. On December 15, 1941, Donovan sent a memorandum to President Roosevelt that summarized Steinbeck's recommendations: the Nisei "have condemned the action of Japan and have reiterated their loyalty," Steinbeck had told Donovan. Steinbeck recommended that these Japanese citizens should help local civilian-defense authorities keep up to date on "unknown or strange Japanese." Steinbeck noted that "such evidence of trust would be likely to cement the loyalty of inherently loyal citizens." Although Steinbeck's suggestions did, in effect, constitute a loyalty oath, nonetheless his was a far more humane solution than internment.

In December 1942, Steinbeck began work on a film, *A Medal for Benny* (1943), that protested discrimination against a Hispanic war hero. Indirectly, that film also protested treatment of Japanese Americans during World War II.

Public orders, such as this one, posted on April 11, 1942, in San Francisco, directed the removal of persons of Japanese ancestry.

1. **Sherwood Park:** Rodeo Grounds
2. **132 Central Avenue:** Steinbeck Home
3. **134 Central Avenue:** Griffin House
4. **147 Central Avenue:** Graves House
5. **153 Central Avenue:** Wagner House
6. **120 Capitol Avenue:** Roosevelt School
7. **240 Church Street:** Monterey County Courthouse
8. **66 Capitol Avenue:** Nesbitt House
9. **402 Cayuga Street:** Dr. Murphy's House
10. **350 Lincoln Avenue:** John Steinbeck Library
11. **1 Main Street:** National Steinbeck Center
12. **11 Station Place:** Railroad Depot and Harvey Baker House museum
13. **201 Main Street:** Kate's Bank
14. **210–14 Main Street:** Porter and Irvine's Department Store
15. **247 Main Street:** Farmer's Mercantile
16. **242 Main Street:** Bell's Candy Store
17. **332–34 Main Street:** Mr. Steinbeck's Feed Store
18. **12 West Gabilan Street:** Old Post Office
19. **269 Main Street:** Hotel Jeffrey
20. **726 Main Street:** Salinas High School
21. **Willow and Pajaro Streets:** Granger Railway Station
22. **768 Abbott Street:** Garden of Memories Cemetery

When questioned why he wrote so much about people's loneliness and isolation and despair, Steinbeck responded that he wrote about everyone, not simply lonely and isolated people.

The Steinbeck Family Home

John Steinbeck grew up in an imposing house at ❷ 132 Central Avenue, on Salinas's premier street. He had three sisters: taciturn Esther, ten years older; lively Beth, eight years older; and his favorite sister when growing up, Mary, three years younger, "a tough little monkey with wild eyes looking out of tangled yellow hair."

The family was close-knit and supportive. "He loved a sense of home," said Steinbeck's second wife, Gwyn. "He used to from his childhood . . . they were a very clannish family."

The sensibilities of Steinbeck's family remained with him throughout his life. Although he resisted his mother's bossiness and doting attention from his two older sisters, the firm contours of his family life provided lifelong ballast. "I think no one ever had more loyalty than I had from my parents," he told a biographer in 1953. He wrote his family long and regular letters. When he went to Sweden to accept the Nobel Prize in 1962, he bought each sister an engraved silver box. Lionized by the world, he remembered gifts for his family. Nearly all his books can be read in one sense as his characters' searches for homes, however ragtag, or families, however stitched together.

Much is known about Steinbeck's parents, and the outlines seem to follow that of several other prominent early twentieth-century male authors

(Hemingway, Fitzgerald, and Faulkner, for example)—a silent, disappointed father and an engaged mother with intellectual pretensions. Steadiness of employment was not Mr. Steinbeck's lot in life. Until 1911, he managed Salinas's Sperry Flour Mill, the largest flour mill in Northern California and producer of some of the finest flour in the state, "Drifted Snow." Although grains remained the valley's major crop until 1920, sugar beets replaced much of the barley, alfalfa, and wheat, and mill operations gradually declined. "Wish I had a good farm and a sure crop every year," a wistful Mr. Steinbeck wrote to one of his daughters as the mill business was failing. He then opened a feed and grain store, but that venture failed as well, and in 1918 he filed for bankruptcy. That same year a friend and fellow Mason found him steady employment as a bookkeeper with Spreckels Sugar Company. And on February 26, 1923, he was appointed Monterey County treasurer and paid a steady salary of $250 per month. Re-elected in 1926, he held the position until January 1935, a few months before his death. Nonetheless, John Steinbeck would always remember the painful, cash-poor years of his adolescence.

The Steinbecks' house today.

The experience of living with a father who had missed his calling shaped Steinbeck's iron will to write. Indeed, his determination to be a writer was formed about the same time that his father's grain store was going under.

In my struggle to be a writer, it was he who
supported and backed me and explained me—
not my mother . . . my father wanted me to be
myself. . . . He admired anyone who laid down
his line and followed it undeflected to the end. I
think this was because he abandoned his star in
little duties and let his head go under in the swirl of
family, money, and responsibility. To be anything
pure requires an arrogance he did not have, and a
selfishness he could not bring himself to assume.

In many ways Mr. Steinbeck was the family's bedrock. He was a thoughtful man—in 1888, before marrying Olive, he'd enrolled in the Home Library Association, something like a book-of-the-month club. Like Mr. Tiflin in *The Red Pony*, he was stern and exacting: to teach John responsibility, he gave him chores such as stacking firewood in the wood box and sweeping the porch and steps. Mr. Steinbeck also loved gardening, and he grew vegetables at a lot near the mill, where he also raised chickens and boarded horses—his own, Doxology, as well as John's and Mary's ponies, Jill and Sperry. One of his chief hobbies was mending and binding books in the basement. In the public sphere, he was committed to one group—the Masons—for fifty-two years.

Olive joined the Eastern Star, the women's Masonic club, and was no doubt one of its most indomitable members. In 1905, she was a charter member of the first social club in Salinas, the Wanderers Club, a group of local women who met every other Wednesday evening to discuss the countries of the world. Each meeting had an ambitious agenda, with members assigned various topics. Olive presented on "Architecture of the Missions" in 1914; "Chile—Its History" in 1916; "Darjeeling" in 1917; and "Newfoundland: A British Possession" in 1922.

Intellectually curious, Olive could also be overbearing, far too busy with social matters, and "never knows when to quit," as her husband wrote in a 1910 letter. She bossed her children as well as her husband and arranged everyone's lives—and yet was an invaluable assistant to Mr. Steinbeck when he was county treasurer.

Her energy could be invigorating. "Mother stated to the skies," Steinbeck wrote in a 1926 letter, "that she was

Olive and John Ernst Steinbeck at home, circa 1918.

John and Mary in front of their house with the red pony, circa 1908.

Mr. Steinbeck's feed store.

Summer Is Here
:: Also Fleas and Flies ::
Don't you want to rid
yourself of these pests?
Our disinfectants are the
best. Ask for CONKEY'S,
LEE'S or PRATT'S.

LET US SEND YOU A
SACK OF OUR FLOUR.
EVERY SACK IS GUAR-
ANTEED.

Call Up Main 60
When in need of Feed,
Grain, Hay, Seeds, Poul-
try Supplies, etc.

MONTEREY CO. FEED CO.

J. E. STEINBECK
Proprietor

glad of just twenty-six things in the space of a page and a half." She had a fierce devotion to her own and her children's betterment. Sensitive to art, she read aloud to her children and nurtured Steinbeck's love of language with her Irish love of storytelling. She insisted that both John and Mary take piano lessons. She listened to opera on records and on the radio, and took the children to San Francisco on "enrichment trips" to attend the opera and musicals; John remembered hearing Al Jolson sing "Mammy" in his first musical, which played at the Geary Theater. "I had a cloth hat and my shoes hurt because I thought my feet were too big and I bought shoes that were too small for me," he wrote Esther years later. Olive loved staying at the Clift Hotel, loved being pampered in elegant San Francisco. She made sure all her children were educated: the two older sisters went to Mills College in Oakland (Esther also spent a year at Berkeley), and John and Mary went to Stanford University.

Today, Olive Steinbeck's respectable air lingers about the imposing, Queen Anne–style family home, which has been the Steinbeck House restaurant since 1974. John's grandparents purchased the home on March 28, 1901, three years after it was built, and John's father was able to buy the home from his parents in 1908. Although the 4,000-square-foot dwelling suggests familial wealth, the Steinbecks were at best moderately prosperous.

The redecorated home retains its Victorian style. In the front parlor, young Steinbeck pounded piano keys from fifth to twelfth grade (a very good piano player, his

Writing *East of Eden*

When Steinbeck first mentioned writing "the novel of Salinas" in 1930, he said that it "should be left for a few years yet because I hate too many people there."

The gestation of this "long slow piece of work" did take years. Prepared to begin in late 1947, he wrote to the editor of the Salinas newspaper, requesting old papers and historical records, and came to

John Steinbeck in 1948, reading files of the Salinas *Californian* while doing research for *East of Eden*.

California early in 1948 to conduct research. His plan was to complete a first draft of "The Salinas Valley" and then accompany friend Edward F. Ricketts on a trip to the Vancouver Islands. The two would write a scientific book (on the model of *Sea of Cortez* and called "The Outer Shores"), while the "The Salinas Valley," John said, would sink into his unconscious. Then he would rewrite. "The Outer Shores," he stated, would be "practice poetry" for "The Salinas Valley."

That plan was crushed with the May 11, 1948, death of Ricketts and Steinbeck's divorce from his second wife, Gwyn, the same year. Not until 1951 would he begin writing "The Salinas Valley," a manuscript that contains the pain of a bitter divorce, fatherhood circumscribed, and friendship cut short. Published as *East of Eden*, this novel is tempered by woe.

Family dynamics are a central concern in the novel—Steinbeck's young sons, Thom and John, were very much on his mind as he began work. "[W]hile I am talking to the boys actually," he wrote in his journal, "I am relating every reader to the story as though he were reading about his own background. . . . Everyone wants to have a family. Maybe I can create a universal family living next to a universal neighbor."

teacher reported). On the stair landing, his older sister Esther was married. Until 1912, when a furnace was installed, the home's only heat source was the living-room fireplace. Family photos line the walls.

Steinbeck's two older sisters—one of whom dined at the restaurant regularly until the early 1990s—donated pieces of family china, John's harmonica and baby cup, and Mrs. Steinbeck's silver teapot, all of which are on display in a former bedroom. The Valley Guild operates

the Steinbeck House restaurant for lunches, teas and "first Friday" dinners. Proceeds are donated to charity.

Although John left Salinas in 1919 to attend Stanford University, he made periodic visits home. In 1933, after his mother had a debilitating stroke, he and his wife Carol returned to nurse her—and, as it turned out, to discover the power of his mature fictional voice. In his childhood home, he wrote the first Red Pony stories about a child's growing awareness of death. He also wrote parts of *Tortilla Flat* (1935) here, the rollicking stories cutting against the gloom of the house.

Old Town Salinas—Steinbeck's Neighborhood

The meaning of the town's motto, "Salinas is," may be as elusive as the soul of modern Salinas, a town of enclaves. Although today's Salinas lacks the polish of nearby peninsula towns, there's a gritty energy to the place, a slight underdog edge that can be sensed while walking its streets, nosing out the charms of Old Town, or walking to the Harvey Baker House by the railroad tracks (near where the Sperry Flour Mill once stood). Twenty-first-century Salinas, nearly 65 percent of its population Mexican, must meet the challenges of a socioeconomic spectrum ranging from growers with great wealth to impoverished migrant workers. Housing remains a pressing concern. Pride in traditions runs strong: the Asian Festival, July's Rodeo week, September's California International Air Show.

Salinas City Center is being revitalized. The first four blocks of Main Street are lined with former banks turned into antique stalls, a stately old movie theater, cafés, and boutiques. The 100 block includes CSUMB@ Salinas City Center, Maya Cinemas, and the National Steinbeck Center. Taylor Farms, "North America's favorite maker of salads and healthy fresh foods," has its world headquarters where the Caminos Hotel once stood.

On the east side of town, Market Street is lined with Mexican restaurants and shops. The old Chinatown, Cal's haunt in *East of Eden*—and young Steinbeck's as well—

sidestepped redevelopment until recently. Long a place of broken windows, abandoned buildings, and Dorothy's Kitchen, which serves meals to the homeless, the area is now the focus of a group committed to rescuing the histories of Salinas's Asian communities.

To stroll the Salinas streets with Steinbeck's books in mind—particularly the highly autobiographical *East of Eden*—is to feel cast back nearly one hundred years, to see the town and its denizens as Steinbeck saw them. The vulnerable, the revered, and the foolish appear in the pages of *East of Eden*, Steinbeck's *Vanity Fair*. Steinbeck's sprawling novel blends fact and fiction: vignettes of his mother's family are true, and portraits of Salinas businessmen and brothel owners are accurate.

At one time, palms grew along Central Avenue, sure signs of wealth and status in early Northern California. Near the corner of Salinas Street and Central Avenue, Dessie Hamilton, Steinbeck's beloved aunt, had a "nice

Salinas's Chinatown on Soledad Street was founded in 1893, after the first burned. The area drew diverse populations—Chinese, Japanese, Filipinos, and later Mexicans—and was a thriving community hub for generations.

little house" that the Trasks purchase in *East of Eden*. Dessie functions as a kind of feminine center in the book, her enclave of women in sharp contrast to manipulative Kate's brothel.

> *[Dessie's] shop was a unique institution in Salinas. It was a woman's world. Here all the rules, and the fears that created the iron rules, went down. The door was closed to men. It was a sanctuary where women could be themselves—smelly, wanton, mystic, conceited, truthful, and interested…. At Dessie's they were women who went to the toilet and overate and scratched and farted. And from this freedom came laughter, roars of laughter.*

The Graves house, 147 Central Avenue, where scenes from *East of Eden* were filmed.

It is wise to keep this passage in mind when reading Steinbeck's books—he came from a family of women, his literary agents were women, and many of his friends were women. Although his fictional women may assume stereotypical roles, their status says more about social mores than about authorial inclination.

The house next door to the Steinbecks', at ❸ 134 Central Avenue, is the oldest on the street, dating to 1890. In 1918, a year before Steinbeck left for college, the Griffin family rented the home; Mr. Griffin is mentioned in *East of Eden* as the saloon owner who "didn't like anything about liquor" and "on a Saturday night he might refuse to serve twenty men he thought had had enough."

One of Steinbeck's closest childhood friends, Glenn Graves, lived in the house at ❹ 147 Central Avenue. In a 1969 interview, Glenn remembered that John "was a very good listener, especially to old timers who had stories to tell. . . . He would visit the Williams sisters quite often." Those two unmarried sisters, eccentric and rich, characters in *East of Eden* and possibly "Johnny Bear," knew all the history of Salinas, as did Glenn's mother. "Anyone who had a story to tell, he was ready to listen. A lot of them came out in later books, and people didn't like it around here." The interior of the Graves's house was used during shooting of the 1955 film *East of Eden*.

Another friend, Max Wagner, often stayed with his grandparents at ❺ 153 Central Avenue. The Wagner family had lived in Mexico, and Mrs. Wagner had been a correspondent for the *Christian Science Monitor* during the Mexican Revolution. Steinbeck would sometimes read her his stories. Max's uncle owned a ranch north of Salinas off San Juan Grade Road, where Max lived from 1912 to 1914. John frequently rode his pony out there and later used this ranch, in part, as the setting for stories about Jody, a boy probably modeled on himself and Max. Max later worked in Hollywood, and in 1939 he introduced John to the woman who would become his second wife, Gwyn Conger. Steinbeck cowrote *A Medal for Benny* with Max's older brother, Jack.

At the corner of Central and Capitol, at ❻ 120 Capitol Street, is the Roosevelt School, the site of the former West End School, where Olive Steinbeck went to high school and John attended classes in grades three through eight. "Salinas had two grammar schools," Steinbeck writes in *East of Eden*, "big yellow structures with tall windows, and the windows were baleful and the doors did not smile. . . . The West End, a huge building of two stories, fronted with gnarled poplars, divided the play yards called girlside and boyside." Young Steinbeck, usually edging in on trouble, bringing home mediocre grades, was a solidly boyside sort. The building was torn down in 1925, but a

few poplars remain, as does a World War I memorial, with Martin Hopps's name at the top—the first of the town's servicemen to be killed. The Hopps's house once stood precisely where the memorial now stands. Steinbeck memorializes him in *East of Eden*:

> *Martin Hopps lived around the corner from us. He was wide, short, red-haired. His mouth was wide, and he had red eyes. He was almost the shyest boy in Salinas. To say good morning to him was to make him itch with self-consciousness. He belonged to Troop C because the armory had a basketball court.*

Martin Hopps's name is the first on this World War I memorial.

Olive rides in an army airplane, 1918.

The Nesbitt house, 66 Capitol Avenue.

If the Germans had known Olive and had been sensible they would have gone out of their way not to anger her. But they didn't know or they were stupid. When they killed Martin Hopps they lost the war because that made my mother mad and she took out after them. She had liked Martin Hopps.

He had never hurt anyone. When they killed him Olive declared war on the German empire.

. . . She found her weapon in Liberty bonds . . . . [and] began to sell bonds by the bale. She brought ferocity to her work. I think she made people afraid not to buy them.

Monterey County Courthouse

The present ❼ **Monterey County Courthouse,** at **240 Church Street**, was built around an older structure where Steinbeck's father worked as treasurer of Monterey County. The courtyard is a serene place to sit.

Today's imposing courthouse is on the National Register of Historic Places. The proposal for historic status describes it as "a perfect example, inside and out, of the Works Projects Administration Moderne style of the 1930s and also an excellent example of a concrete building whose surface is articulated by the pattern of form boards."

Artist Jo Mora's work is seen on the courthouse exterior. Born in Uruguay in 1876 to a Spanish father, also a sculptor, and a French mother, Mora traveled throughout the southwestern United States early in the twentieth century, living for a time with Hopi Indians. The

painter Frederick Remington encouraged Mora's work in clay models of cowboys, Indians, and animals. From 1920 on, Mora lived in Carmel; he designed the sarcophagus of Father Junipero Serra at the Carmel Mission—"the supreme professional effort of my life," he wrote—and a wooden sculpture of Serra in the Carmel woods.

The Monterey County Courthouse, 240 Church Street.

Mora's work for the courthouse is a fitting counterpart to Steinbeck's, an artistic rendering of Monterey County's diverse history. His sixty-one concrete heads represent dramatis personae of the county's history, real and symbolic. Doors on the building's west section depict a rich historical pageant: Native Americans; the coming of the Spanish represented by Juan Rodriguez Cabrillo's and Sebastian Vizcaíno's ships, by Gaspar de Portolá on his horse, and by soldiers; the Mission period, with a Franciscan friar surrounded by neophyte reapers of grain and the missions of San Carlos and San Antonio; and the American period, with a trapper on horseback, a wagon train, a bather, an angler, a hunter, a football player, and a golfer.

25

For her patriotism, Olive Steinbeck earned a terrifying (to her) ride in an army airplane to Spreckels, a true and hilarious story that found its way into *East of Eden*.

At ❽ 66 Capitol Avenue is the Nesbitt house, built in 1881. Salinas Town Marshall William Nesbitt, sheriff during Steinbeck's childhood and youth, lived here from 1902 to 1923. In *East of Eden*, Sheriff Quinn is modeled on Nesbitt, as Steinbeck notes in *Journal of a Novel* (1969), his *East of Eden* notebook: "When we first see Nesbitt (Sheriff Quinn) he will be Chief Deputy . . . I remember him well. He lived just around the corner from us." And in the novel he writes, "He

What Hometown Monument to Steinbeck?

In 1987, the retired managing editor of the local paper summarized Steinbeck's reputation in Salinas: Old-timers "hate him," he said. In book after book, it seemed, Steinbeck exposed denizens' weaknesses, unlocked their secrets, and seemingly ridiculed the good and the proper —and to make matters worse, sided not with growers but with workers.

But, a couple of decades after public burnings of *The Grapes of Wrath* in Salinas, the town began to reconsider Steinbeck's stature, ready to bestow some local honor. One of the first proposals was a 1957 suggestion for a John Steinbeck High School. The author declined that honor, writing that the town might "name a bowling alley after me or a dog track—but a school! The results might be disastrous not only to me but to the future generations of young people of the city of Salinas." He added, "Consider, if you will, the disastrous result if some innocent and talented student should look into my own scholastic record, seeking perhaps for inspiration. Why his whole ambition might crash in flames." The John Steinbeck High School did not materialize.

Shortly after declining the honor, he wrote to his sister, Esther, that the people who asked to name a Salinas school after him were the "same people [who] were merciless to [Dad]." Steinbeck's teenage resentment of Salinas denizens was deeply etched.

In 1959, a proposal was sent to the author for a John Steinbeck "browsing room" in the soon-to-be-constructed Salinas Library. He replied, "Your charming suggestion . . . is very pleasing to me, if my name would not drive people out. I must say that in the old library where Mrs. (Carry) Striening, for so many years presided over the stacks, I've browsed the product practically to the roots." The room became a reality.

Salinas honored Steinbeck again with a special Rodeo edition of the paper in July 1963—this time not bothering to ask permission. Recovering from an eye operation, the author responded with wry appreciation:

No town celebrates a writer before he's dead. It just isn't done. And if it's true that Salinas has done this—then Salinas has broken the rules again. It's hard to believe that you have done this and I must admit it makes me feel a little dead. I'm not yet permitted to read, so I don't know what you said, but you sure said it big! . . .

Now that was a pleasant thing for you all to do, . . . this Salinas edition . . . makes me feel very good and warm.

For many Salinas residents, a browsing room and a newspaper edition were simply not enough. For others, his legacy still rankled. "Council Cool to Idea of Creating 'Steinbeck Square'" noted the local paper on April 2, 1963. Monterey County citizens rejected the notion of renaming the Salinas/Monterey highway the Steinbeck Highway. A proposal to make the Steinbeck home a state monument fizzled in 1967.

was an institution, as much a part of the Salinas Valley as its mountains."

If a stray dog wanders by, imagine seeing Bob Ford, Salinas's dogcatcher for a time, who would dress in full cowboy duds and rope stray mutts. He is "Long Bob on his white horse carrying the flag" in the July 4th parade

The John Steinbeck Library, 350 Lincoln Avenue.

After Steinbeck's death in 1968, consideration was given to renaming Central Avenue or Main Street as Steinbeck Calle, naming the library or the municipal auditorium after Steinbeck, or revisiting the idea of a John Steinbeck High School. Other proposals were a subdivision of low-income houses, a mountain peak, and Central Park, where Steinbeck played as a boy (an honor favored by his widow, Elaine, and his sister Esther).

With many in the community still protesting, renaming the library prevailed, by a four-to-one vote of the library board. "I voted against it," Reverend Jo Wright of the Alisal Assembly of God told local papers. "In examining this gentleman's life and the type of life he lived, it's not a very exemplary one for young people coming into a library. He roamed quite a bit." San Francisco columnist Herb Caen was amused. "Latest from Lettuceland," he wrote: "In Salinas even Shakespeare would have trouble getting a unanimous vote."

in *Cannery Row*—as he carried the flag in every Salinas horse parade—and Tall Bob Smoke in *Tortilla Flat*.

The Steinbeck family doctor, Dr. Murphy, lived at ❾ 402 Cayuga Street, a house owned by the Murphy family from 1901 to 1950. Dr. Murphy saved Steinbeck's life when he had pneumonia in 1917 by performing surgery in the family home, removing a rib. Murphy's grandsons, Dennis and Michael Murphy, may well have been Steinbeck's models for the two boys in *East of Eden*, tormented Cal and Aron. (The Murphy family also owned Esalen, hot springs valued by Native Americans and now a high-end retreat near Big Sur.) Steinbeck wrote several letters to Dennis Murphy and to Dr. Murphy when Dennis decided to become an author. "Your only weapon is your work," he wrote Dennis.

On the same block, at 418 Cayuga Street, once stood St. Paul's Episcopal Church Rectory, where Aron Trask in *East of Eden* goes to study after school with quiet Mr. Rolf, "unmarried and simple in his tastes." The Steinbeck family attended St. Paul's when it was on 80 West Alisal Street. As an altar boy, Steinbeck once "set the cross in its socket at the end of processional and forgot to throw the brass latch that held it in. At the reading of the second lesson I saw with horror the heavy brass cross sway and crash on that holy hairless head. The bishop went down like a pole-axed cow." He relates this vivid memory in *The Winter of Our Discontent*.

John Steinbeck Library

❿ The John Steinbeck Library at 350 Lincoln Avenue housed the city's Steinbeck archives until 1998. In 2004–05 the library made the national news when it and two other Salinas libraries were threatened with closure because of insufficient funding. Had that

National Steinbeck Center, 1 Main Street.

happened, Salinas would have been the country's largest city without a public library. The American Library Association sent a delegation to Salinas in February 2005. An April 2005 read-in, drawing authors and citizens, was covered nationally. A private fundraising drive helped keep the library open, and a 2005 funding initiative passed. Its plight highlighted the importance of libraries to small towns.

When John Steinbeck walked to "Baby School," today Clay Street Park, he picked up his friend Herb Hinrichs, who lived in the six-gable house at 338 Church Street, across the street from what is now the John Steinbeck Library. Hinrichs insisted that he was the model for Andy in *Cannery Row*, the boy who mocked the old Chinese man.

The National Steinbeck Center

Open since 1998, ⓫ the National Steinbeck Center (NSC), at 1 Main Street, houses the city's Steinbeck archives as well as what may be the world's only museum dedicated to scenes from

a writer's work and artifacts from his life. Re-created are the Red Pony's stall, George and Lennie's bunkhouse (with a mouse in Lennie's coat pocket), Mrs. Malloy's boiler home on Cannery Row, and a replica of Steinbeck's Sag Harbor writing house, Joyous Garde. The museum features Steinbeck films, as well as video clips of Elaine Steinbeck and actors reading his work. The crown jewel is Rocinante, the 1960 GMC $3/4$-ton truck that Steinbeck drove around America with his dog Charley. The forest green pickup has a specially designed cabin on the back, built to Steinbeck's plan. Curtains made by wife Elaine Steinbeck still hang on the windows. Motor silent, back door open, parked at the top of Salinas's Main Street, the truck signifies much that Steinbeck represents: his restlessness, his many road narratives, his abiding love for America and for Americans' quest for dream landscapes.

The *Travels with Charley* trip, a broad sweep from New York to California and back, suggests the pattern of his life and his work. Steinbeck gave voice to the American myth of "westering," the hope of renewal in California; and he articulated with empathy and intense detail the failure of

Rocinante, now located at the National Steinbeck Center.

the arc westward, the shattered dreams of so many California patriarchs and farmers. In *Travels with Charley*, "eastering" is a personal retreat from the visionary West.

In 2015, the NSC building was purchased by California State University, Monterey Bay; two galleries now house changing art exhibits.

Behind the NSC, Market Street was once Castroville Street, the road to Castroville. In *East of Eden*, the unpaved road is "deep in sticky mud, and Chinatown was so flooded that its inhabitants had laid planks across the narrow street that separated their hutches. The clouds against the evening sky were the gray of rats, and the air was not damp but dank." Across Market Street are ⓬ **11 Station Place and the Harvey Baker House.** Nearby was the Sperry Flour Mill that Mr. Steinbeck managed from 1900 to 1911.

Chinatown flooded. "And do you remember how an easterly breeze brought odors in from Chinatown, roasting pork and punk and black tobacco and yen shi? And do you remember the deep blatting stroke of the great gong in the Joss House, and how its tone hung in the air so long?"

Main Street—Kate's Walk

Main Street retains much of its nineteenth-century flavor. This is the street that sinister brothel madam Kate walks in *East of Eden*, making weekly bank deposits. The steamy red-light district was near Salinas's Chinatown, a few blocks east, where the Long Green, the Elite, and the Arno were located. At the corner of Alisal and California Streets was the Palace, Jenny's place in *East of Eden*. (Jenny's real name was Mary Jane Reynolds; she died in 1922 and is buried in the Garden of Memories Cemetery.)

Kate "always went to the same places—first to the Monterey County Bank where she was admitted behind the shining bars that defended the safe-deposit vault." Kate's bank was at ⓭ 201 Main Street, built in 1907 by architect William Weeks. Kate crossed the street and "stepped into Porter and Irvine's" old department store at ⓮ 210–14 Main Street "and looked at dresses." At 3:30 she climbed the stairs to the offices over the Farmers' Mercantile, at ⓯ 247 Main Street, and went to the doctor's office, and then stopped at Bell's Candy, at ⓰ 242 Main Street, "and bought a two-pound box of mixed chocolates. She never varied her route." Because the real owner of Bell's Candy hated houses of ill repute, Steinbeck, turning the screw ever so slightly, had the fictional madam enter the store.

Near Main and San Luis Streets, Steinbeck's books were burned in the late 1930s—certainly *The Grapes of Wrath*, probably *In Dubious Battle* (1936) as well. Mr. Steinbeck's feed store, purchased in 1911, was at ⓱ 332–34 Main Street. The Masonic Temple was above.

A couple of other sites show up in *East of Eden*. At ⓲ 12 West Gabilan Street, between Main and

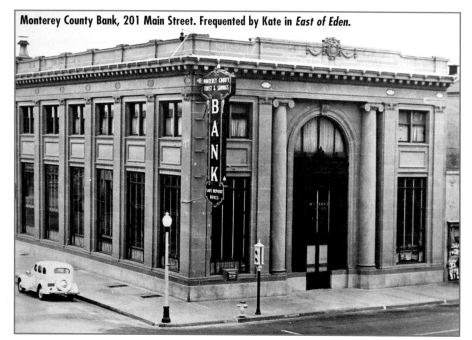

Monterey County Bank, 201 Main Street. Frequented by Kate in *East of Eden*.

At ❷⓿ 726 Main Street is Salinas High School, its cornerstone still in place and scheduled to be opened in 2020, one hundred years after the stone was set down. In 1920, Mr. Steinbeck was on the committee to prepare a dedication ceremony for the new high school, and he asked John and his visiting college roommate, George Mors, to gather local products to place in the cornerstone. The two young men allegedly included a handful of dried beans, corn, and sugar— and a vial of red wine. Although Mr. Steinbeck protested—these were Prohibition years—John and George prevailed, arguing that there was no more fitting local product than "Dago Red."

Salinas Streets, is the Old Post Office, where Adam Trask has a stroke. In the little alley at the side of the building, Cal Trask learns that his mother was a notorious brothel madam. The iron post office bars are still on the side windows. 14 East Gabilan Street, now an alley, was the site of Henry Fenchel's tailor shop, mentioned in *East of Eden*, where Fenchel is taunted during World War I for being German.

At ❶❾ 269 Main Street was the Hotel Jeffrey, headquarters of the self-appointed vigilante "General" during the 1936 lettuce packers' strike: "He set armed guards over his suite and he put Salinas in a state of siege," Steinbeck recalls in "Always Something to Do in Salinas." 405 Main Street was the sit of the Salinas Public Library Carnegie Building, which stood here from 1909 to 1960. Steinbeck often went there.

The railway station for the first Granger railroad, a narrow gauge built with private funds, was one block east of Salinas High School on ❷❶ Willow and Pajaro Streets. To save on the steep shipping costs of grain charged by the "octopus," the Southern Pacific Railroad, the community built the line, which ended at a wharf in Monterey. Built using Chinese labor, the little railroad operated from 1874 to 1879 before being bought out by the powerful Southern Pacific Railroad. It is from this station that a little girl takes a "free train" to Monterey in Steinbeck's story "How Edith McGillicuddy Met RLS," a true tale about Max Wagner's mother's meeting with Robert Louis

Stevenson that was published in *Harper's Magazine* in August 1941.

Two blocks past the high school and left off Main, Romie Lane leads to ❷ the Garden of Memories Cemetery at 768 Abbott. In *East of Eden*, Adam Trask walks to town in the "cold wind" after the burial of Sam Hamilton: "The cemetery was deserted and the dark crooning of the wind bowed the heavy cypress trees. The rain droplets grew larger and drove stinging along." Sam Hamilton's grave is in the Hamilton plot (near the mausoleum), while Steinbeck's is across a

road. When his ashes were placed here in 1969, Steinbeck's grave was marked with calla lilies, his favorite flower. His third wife, Elaine, was buried here in 2004.

Despite the lifelong tension between Steinbeck and his hometown, he asked to be buried in Salinas. This was his home, the place one always returns to in the end— the final act of westering. "It seems good to mark and to remember for a little while the place where a man died," he writes in *Sea of Cortez*. "This is his one whole lonely act in all his life."

Chapter 3

Beyond Salinas
Salad Bowl of the World

Sugar beet wagons, circa 1908.

Young John Steinbeck broke out of Salinas whenever he could. Roaming the land awakened his senses as the town of Salinas most certainly did not. Sometimes his tomboy younger sister, Mary, was his companion on long rambles into the hills; sometimes he explored with friends; sometimes he went alone. He swam in the Salinas River; hunted rabbits; rode ponies to the ranch owned by Max Wagner's uncle; took the little Spreckels train to Alisal Canyon, where wild azaleas bloomed; and visited Aunt Mollie's farm in Corral de Tierra. With his family, he traveled to the Steinbeck grandparents' home in Hollister or to Hamilton ranch near King City. The result of excursions away from Salinas was twofold: leaving him with an abiding love for the land and nurturing an equally compelling empathy for those who toil on the land.

Red Pony Ranch.

In California, field-workers once harvested sugar beets; now they pick strawberries and lettuce, artichokes and grapes. The valley's agricultural history is a complex mix of growers, shippers, and workers, each with a notion of how the land should be used, how temporary workers should be housed, and what crops should go to market when. To be the world's "salad bowl" is a demanding venture, one Steinbeck wrote about with a clear preference for those on the margins of profit.

Agriculture

The Salinas Valley is a fairly narrow 100-mile swath of rich land between the Santa Lucia Range and the Gabilan Mountains, running roughly from King City in the south to Castroville in the north. This region was settled, in succession, by peaceful Indians, visionary Spanish padres building missions, bold Spanish and Mexican ranchers claiming vast land grants, and energetic American ranchers and farmers who grabbed land as eagerly as the Spaniards and Mexicans had before them.

In the moderate climate and black soil of the Salinas Valley, many found the full measure of California's promise. Because the northern end of the valley cuts through the coastal mountains and opens onto the sea, high summer fog, generated by cool ocean air meeting the sunny inland heat, streams into the valley around Salinas. This misty blanket protects crops from the desiccating power of the direct sun. In the winter, the

The road to Red Pony Ranch.

Working beet fields, circa 1908.

temperature gradient reverses and the warmer coastal fog buffers the inland fields from wintry frost.

Until World War I, grains and sugar beets were the dominant crops. Beginning in the 1920s, acres were planted with lettuce, strawberries, celery, and broccoli —and some sweet peas (as in Steinbeck's 1934 story "The Harness"). Salinas soon named itself the "Salad Bowl of the World," an epithet that boldly suggests the region's agricultural wealth and assertiveness. Nearly a century later, the Salinas Valley remains the nation's top producer of leaf lettuce and strawberries, and yields large crops of broccoli, cauliflower, artichokes, and wine grapes. Central Coast wineries are flourishing.

The Salinas Valley before Agriculture

Prior to 1848, native grasses covered the hills around the Salinas Valley: Oregon hair grass, Idaho fescue, and California oat grass—all bunchgrasses—grew two to three feet in height. Even before Spanish mission settlement in the 1770s, native grasses were being replaced by wild oat, brought in on ships by early Spanish explorers.

One story has it that the padres brought wild mustard seed to California to mark the mission trail. By the mid-nineteenth century, mustard carpeted the valley in the spring. "When my grandfather came into the valley," Steinbeck writes in *East of Eden*, "the mustard was so tall that a man on horseback showed only his head above the yellow flowers."

In fields and orchards, mustard roots helped break up the soil. By the 1870s, up to 400,000 pounds of mustard seed was harvested by Chinese workers each fall. Mr. Steinbeck brought mustard seed when he visited John at Tahoe in 1927, and the two made mustard in John's tiny cabin.

For early travelers, the Salinas Valley could be forbidding, a place of sloughs, cut through by an often-dry riverbed, whipped by wind. In 1872, one traveler, Stephen Powers, found it

an execrable place at best. Everyday for seven months there rises, about ten o'clock, a wind which blows at a furious rate till nearly midnight. The dry bed of the river yields so much sand that it constitutes what is called "dry fog." The live oaks . . . look like old men leaning on their hands, with their coat-tails blown over their heads. Such a blast I had to face for fifty miles.

Migrant Labor

The history of California field-workers is a rich and varied one, reflecting repeated attempts by landowners to encourage—and then contain and curtail—the influx of immigrant labor. Although bindlestiffs like George and Lennie often toiled in the fields, the vast majority of workers in the Salinas Valley's rapidly growing agribusiness were temporary workers brought in to help plant and build California.

After California attained statehood, Chinese laborers came to California to work in the goldfields and to build railroads. In *East of Eden*, Lee tells Adam something about the sad history of Chinese workers:

> The herds of men went like animals into the black hold of a ship, there to stay until they reached San Francisco six weeks later . . . my people have learned through the ages to live close together, to keep clean and fed under intolerable conditions. . . . These human cattle were imported for one thing only—to work. When the work was done, those who were not dead were to be shipped back.

Beginning in the late 1860s, Salinas landowners contracted Chinese workers to harvest wheat, the dominant crop; in the 1870s, Chinese workers cleared sloughs surrounding the new town, reclaiming land for agriculture. Well into the twentieth century, Chinese crews dug drainage ditches and slogged through waist-deep water to clear brush and trees. Their adaptability and resilience made them essential to Salinas Valley agriculture—but, throughout California, waves of anti-Chinese sentiment resulted in the 1882 Chinese Exclusion Act, in force until 1943, which restricted immigration to merchants, scholars, and students.

Although Chinese field-workers remained dominant until the late nineteenth century, Japanese workers gradually filled gaps created by the Chinese Exclusion Act. Until about 1910, Japanese workers thinned, topped, and harvested sugar beets in the Salinas fields. But hostility toward "Asiatics" ran high in California. A 1908 agreement between Japan and the United States curtailed immigration, and the Immigration Act of 1924 cut it off entirely.

In the 1920s, single Filipino men, or "stoups," filled the gap left by limiting Japanese immigration. A story Steinbeck wrote at Stanford, "Fingers of Cloud," is set in a Filipino work camp, where "the howling wind came through the cracks" in the bunkhouse and the pockmarked men had only "a few boxes to sit on." Mexican laborers started crossing the border early in the twentieth century to work the California fields. Greater numbers came during the Mexican Revolution and after, particularly from 1917 to 1920, when Congress waived immigration requirements for agricultural workers.

Harvesting broccoli rabe.

During World War II, another wave of Mexican laborers filled the gap left when the Southwest migrants Steinbeck depicted in *The Grapes of Wrath* found jobs in the defense industry or fought overseas. Numbers of Mexican workers increased during the postwar period with the implementation of the Bracero Program, in force from 1942 to 1964, which brought workers temporarily into the United States.

Field-Workers

If F. Scott Fitzgerald is the American novelist who best captures our fascination with money, John Steinbeck is our troubadour of work, the writer who captures the value and dignity of laboring with one's hands. Characters in Steinbeck's fiction fiddle with Hudson Super-Six engines, dig ditches and graves, work in canneries, pump gas, and pick apples. Eliza Allen in "The Chrysanthemums" has "planting hands," her fingers burrowing deep in the soil. Steinbeck could not have known what that meant without a love of

"The surges of the new restless, needy, and strong—grudgingly brought in for the purposes of hard labor and cheap wages—were resisted, resented, and accepted only when a new and different wave came in. On the West Coast the Chinese ceased to be enemies only when the Japanese arrived, and they in the face of the invasion of Hindus, Filipinos, and Mexicans."

gardening, passed on to him by his father, and without having spent hours working in the fields around Salinas, witnessing the toil of others.

In the 1930s, a decade when most California field-workers came from the American Southwest, John Steinbeck became the voice for Okie despair. Although his fictional workers in *Of Mice and Men*, *In Dubious Battle*, and *The Grapes of Wrath* are largely white, he certainly knew of and wrote about other histories. Themes of immigrant isolation and social ostracism are threaded throughout Steinbeck's novels and stories. He had long been aware that some people profited from the valley's abundance while others lived "east of Eden," exiles from paradise. The man who would tell the tales of the world's dispossessed developed his commitment to those on the edges when he was very young.

Working at Spreckels during his frequent absences from college, the young John Steinbeck expanded his sensibilities, discovering stories that intrigued him far more than those of wealthy growers and shippers in Salinas. The plight of Indians in the missions, the dignity of old paisanos, the toil of migrant workers, the isolation and loneliness of people living on little ranches and farms—these were the tales he would tell.

Northeast from Salinas: Fremont Peak

Steinbeck loved ❶ Fremont Peak, a view of it caught from attic windows of his Salinas home. "The peak used to be the habitation of the shadow for me," he wrote a friend in the 1920s. "When I had some fancy too light, and too delicate to trust to the guffaws of my own townsmen I put them up on that smooth peak.

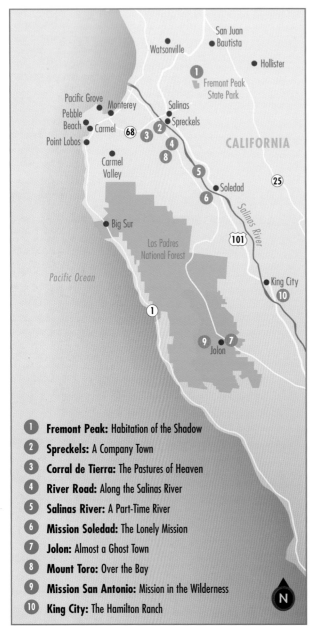

San Juan
Bautista

Watsonville

Hollister

1
Fremont Peak
State Park

Pacific Grove

Monterey

Salinas

Pebble
Beach

Carmel

Spreckels

2

Point Lobos

68

3

CALIFORNIA

4

Carmel
Valley

8

5

Soledad

25

6

Salinas River

Big Sur

Los Padres
National Forest

101

Pacific Ocean

King City

10

1

9 **7**
Jolon

N

1 Fremont Peak: Habitation of the Shadow

2 Spreckels: A Company Town

3 Corral de Tierra: The Pastures of Heaven

4 River Road: Along the Salinas River

5 Salinas River: A Part-Time River

6 Mission Soledad: The Lonely Mission

7 Jolon: Almost a Ghost Town

8 Mount Toro: Over the Bay

9 Mission San Antonio: Mission in the Wilderness

10 King City: The Hamilton Ranch

And all the helpless desires and thrusting hopes which rose in all parts of me were on the peak."

Fremont Peak (elevation 3,169 feet) remained in sight when Steinbeck rode his pony, Jill, north of town to his friend Max's ranch, his trail roughly paralleling San Juan Grade Road. (Roads out of Salinas were named for destinations: Castroville Road, San Juan Grade Road, Monterey Highway.)

He undoubtedly rode by a little one-room school like the one Jody attends in *The Red Pony*, a replica of which is located at the junction of San Juan Grade and Crazy Horse Canyon roads. Across from the school is a historical marker recounting Lt. Col. John Frémont's Battle of Natividad, a skirmish Steinbeck mentions in *The Red Pony*. On March 6, 1846, Frémont marched up

Fremont Peak.

Old Stage Road.

the peak that now bears his name with his band of irregulars, mostly backwoodsmen from Tennessee and Missouri; erected a log fort; and raised the U.S. flag. For three days Frémont claimed for the United States what was then Mexican territory.

Nearby, Old Stage Road winds over the steep hills north to San Juan Bautista. The Steinbeck family bounced over this narrow track when they visited the Steinbeck grandparents in Hollister, and Steinbeck traveled it on his 1948 trip to gather material for *East of Eden*, writing to his wife, Gwyn:

> [I] found the old stage road which I haven't been over since I was about ten years old and we went to Hollister that way in the surrey. Went over it to San Juan and do you know there were hundreds of places that I remembered. Kids do retain all right. Stopped in San Juan a while and then drove back over the old San Juan Grade which in the memory of most people is the only one. They have completely forgotten that which was once called the Royal Road and it is now just a country dirt road, which is what it always was, of course.

San Juan Grade Road remains the loveliest auto route between Salinas

Worker Unrest and the Short-Handled Hoe

The July 4, 1969, cover of *Time* magazine featured Cesar Chavez with a banner stating, "The Grapes of Wrath, 1969: Mexican-Americans on the March." Like the agricultural strikes of the 1930s, the movement called *la causa* protested inhumane working conditions

A short-handled hoe.

for 384,100 agricultural workers in California: inadequate housing, long hours, and low wages (and, later, indiscriminate use of pesticides). More broadly, Chavez and the United Farmworkers Union (UFW) wanted to better the lot of Mexican Americans. By 1969, Chavez's call for a nationwide boycott of table grapes was embraced by Edward Kennedy; folksingers Peter, Paul, and Mary; and Chicago mayor Richard Daley, along with other prominent Democrats. In California, Governor Ronald Reagan called the table grape boycott "immoral" and "attempted blackmail."

Largely fueled by Chavez's crusade, in September 1972 the California Rural Legal Assistance presented a petition to the Safety Board regarding use of the short-handled hoe to weed and thin crops. Public hearings were held in March and May 1973 to determine whether the short-handled hoe was an "unsafe hand tool" that caused damage to workers' backs. Growers argued that use of the longer hoe would cause "inefficiency." According to court documents, "Some workers testified that the short hoe really wasn't much faster, but that the field bosses favored them as a means of knowing at a glance if the crew was working (the assumption being that an upright person might be resting whereas a bent-over person was working)." The short-handled hoe was banned from use in the fields shortly thereafter.

Chavez led the 1960s grape boycott, working tirelessly for workers' rights.

and San Juan Bautista, and Old Stage Road, now closed to cars after three miles, is a splendid and accessible dirt track, a four-mile hilly walk past the road's terminus.

The summit of Fremont Peak is accessed by a well-marked road near San Juan Bautista. The view from the top is, as Steinbeck promises in *Travels with Charley*, panoramic.

South from Salinas: Spreckels and Sugar Beets

In 1896, Claus Spreckels, who had operated sugar plants in Hawaii and in nearby Watsonville, gave a rousing speech to Salinas farmers and businessmen, urging them to switch from growing wheat to growing sugar beets:

Now if you farmers will guarantee to grow the beets, I'll guarantee to turn 'em into sugar. I propose to build here at your door the greatest sugar factory and refinery in the world. . . . It will eat up 3,000 tons of beets every day and turn out every day 450 tons of refined sugar. . . . That means the distribution among the farmers of $12,000 every day and $5,000 more paid to workmen and for other materials in the manufacturing. . . . I shall buy and pay for the site and put up the factory myself.

And that he did. Acres devoted to grains became sugar beet fields. Irrigation ditches were dug. Water was pumped from the Salinas River. A few deep well pumps were sunk on company ranches; by 1924, well pumps were in general use around the valley. When ❷ the Spreckels factory opened in April 1899, the *Salinas Index* compared the five-story redbrick factory to the Brooklyn Bridge and the Eiffel Tower: "the greatest of all undertakings . . . will stand pre-eminent as one of the wonders of modern achievement." Claus Spreckels transformed the valley.

The Spreckels Sugar Factory, (Largest in the World) Spreckels, California

One farmer recalled, "You'd soak the ground in March or April by building borders all around the field and flooding it. Then when it got dry enough to work, you'd knock those levies down and you'd work it all real nice. Then you got your seed, beet seeds, from Spreckels. It came from Germany, most of it. Then you'd plant it and you'd cultivate it a little bit. But you'd never water it no more."

The Spreckels plant closed in the mid-1980s. Although without its redbrick factory since 1992, the well-groomed company town, population 673 in the 2010 census, looks much as it did when Steinbeck worked at the plant. In 2016, the agricultural company Tanimura and Antle completed a worker housing project, Spreckels Crossing, consisting of 100 two-bedroom units.

Claus Spreckels, the West's foremost patron of the sugar beet.

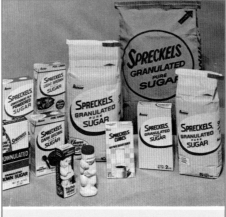

The Sweetest Story Ever Told

For two decades, Spreckels Sugar Company, the largest sugar factory in the world, employed most of the valley's agricultural workers. "Year round" employees settled in the little company town, still tidy today, community spirit still running high. Seasonal workers, "sugar tramps," drifted in for the beet processing season, which ran for sixty to ninety days, from July through September every year. Planting, thinning, and topping the beets began earlier, and called for scores of agricultural workers, nearly six times the number needed for beans and twenty times the number needed for barley. When the factory opened in 1899, mostly Japanese toiled in the fields. But, by 1918, when John Steinbeck came to work at the Spreckels plant, Mexican field-workers had replaced Japanese field-workers. East of town, "Little Tijuana" housed these Mexican workers, only a handful of whom were allowed to work inside the factory.

Steinbeck and his father spent long hours working for the Spreckels Sugar Company, traveling on the little narrow-gauge railroad—called the "dinky" because of the small engines—that connected Salinas to Spreckels. The Parajo Valley Narrow Gauge connected Salinas to the limestone quarries near the Alisal picnic grounds (where Cal Trask takes Abra to see the wild azaleas).

After his feed and grain store failed in 1918, the senior Steinbeck secured a job there as bookkeeper. Charles Pioda, plant manager and a brother Mason, hired Mr. Steinbeck, saving the family from certain economic ruin (the kind gesture echoed in *East of Eden* when Pioda helps Adam Trask). John worked as a carpenter's assistant; later he was an assistant chief chemist and a night chemist, assessing the sugar content of beet samples from various fields to determine harvest schedules. During time off from Stanford, he was a field laborer or "straw boss," overseeing day laborers on company ranches from Spreckels to distant Manteca in the Central Valley.

Of Mice and Men came out of his time working at Spreckels ranches. In a 1937 interview, Steinbeck said that he had "worked alongside" his model for Lennie, who didn't kill a girl but "killed a ranch foreman" with a pitchfork.

As a young man, Steinbeck came to know just what it meant to be a "have-not" in the midst of "haves." "Guys like us, that work on ranches, are the loneliest guys in the world," George tells Lennie in *Of Mice and Men*. "They got no family. They don't belong no place. They come to a ranch an' work up a stake and then they go inta town and blow their stake." Working side by side with young Steinbeck were men who made less than the thirty-two cents an hour he made as a bench chemist;

who dreamed only of living "off the fatta the lan'"; whose identity was stamped by poverty; who knew being marginalized meant long before the word became a familiar one. This perception of the sharp distinction between those who maintained power and those who never had it influenced Steinbeck greatly, and its acknowledgment became his lifelong subject.

Beyond Salinas: Corral de Tierra

John Steinbeck loved ❸ Corral de Tierra. His cherished Aunt Mollie, Olive's sister, lived on a farm in the valley, where most farmers raised chickens or grew tomatoes to sell to Monterey canneries. "They raise good vegetables" says the bus driver to his passengers at the end of *The Pastures of Heaven*, "good berries and fruit earlier than any place else." At the lower end of the valley, sandstone cliffs rise up, and to a young, impressionable Steinbeck they were King Arthur's keep (Aunt Mollie gave him a copy of the Arthurian tales, a treasured volume, when he was nine). He set one of his most puzzling stories, "The Murder," at the base of those lofty cliffs, in what is now the Markham Ranch development.

In Steinbeck's hands, Corral de Tierra becomes the Pastures of Heaven, a place both real and mythic, a valley of hazy beauty and dreams derailed. In 1939, he wrote to biographer Harry Thornton Moore:

I have usually avoided using actual places to avoid hurting feelings for although I rarely use a person

"He saw the quail come down to eat with the chickens when he threw out the grain. For some reason his father was proud to have them come. He never allowed any shooting near the house for fear the quail might go away." (Needlepoint by women of the Church of the Good Shepherd, Corral de Tierra)

or story as it is—neighbors love only too well to attribute them to someone. Thus you will find that the Pastures of Heaven does not look very much like Corral de Tierra. You'll find no pine forest in Jolon and as for the valley in In Dubious Battle—it is a composite valley as it is a composite strike. If it has the characteristics of Pajaro nevertheless there was no strike there.

At the end of *The Pastures of Heaven*, a busload of tourists looks into the valley from Laureles Grade Road: "the air was as golden gauze in the last of the sun. The land below them was plotted in squares of green orchard trees and in squares of yellow grain and in squares of violet earth."

Beyond Salinas: River Road to South County

❹ **River Road,** Elisa and Henry Allen's route in "The Chrysanthemums," runs along the Salinas River, still a pastoral stretch of highway. The road hugs the base of the Santa Lucias, passing old barns, ranch houses, a

The Salinas River

❺ The Salinas River, 155 miles long, is the third longest river in California and the largest subterranean river in the United States—until dams built in the 1950s and early 1960s kept water above ground most of the year. It flows from south to northwest, emptying into two man-made channels that carry water into Monterey Bay. For Steinbeck it was a "part-time river," a bed that filled in the spring and dried up in the summer. As he began writing *East of Eden*, he thought that the Salinas River would be his principal symbol, water running above ground and beneath the surface—so much like the virtue and hidden vices of his characters. Although he abandoned the river as an organizing motif, he makes frequent references to water and the river in the novel.

John Steinbeck and Glenn Graves by the Salinas River. "And then the summer came, and the water in the Salinas River went down until there were only pools against the bank. The Salinas River is three miles from Salinas. We could walk to it or ride bicycles to it. Mary and I rode Jill. We strung ropes to the saddle horn and the pony pulled lines of bicycles to the river. Then, of course, we went swimming."

bed-and-breakfast or two, wineries, and fields.

In March each year, field-workers return to the Salinas Valley after a four-month hiatus to place little lettuce plants in the ground by machine, with six to eight workers sitting on the wings, filling rotating cones with plants. Crews hoe the fields as the plants take root. By late April, workers slice romaine or head lettuce at the base, rapidly and carefully pick strawberries, or cut small boutique lettuce plants and place them in plastic containers right in the field. In October, grapes are hand harvested; fine wines are made along the "Monterey County wine trail."

Because of the scarcity of labor, the region is rapidly developing sophisticated machinery for use in the fields. Ag-tech initiatives are transforming the valley, and more and more crops are being harvested by machines.

Mission Soledad: The Lonely Mission

❻ Mission Soledad, founded in 1791, is now reduced to a few adobe walls, but the rebuilt church provides a cool respite from the burning summer sun, and the little

The remains of Mission Soledad.

museum features Indian grinding stones, an original mission bell, and a nice walk through the garden. This was never a prosperous mission: summer is scorching, winter is damp, the wind often unrelenting, and the soil poor. Few Indians, who theoretically could have helped sustain the mission with their labor, lived in the region.

San Antonio Valley: *To a God Unknown* Country

Gateway to this remote, lovely, and relatively untouched valley is the nearly deserted town of ❼ Jolon, where fifteen-year-old Steinbeck spent several weeks at a friend's ranch. Established in 1860, Jolon once

The general store in Jolon is slated to become a museum.

boasted eight hundred inhabitants and hosted a fiesta much like the one in *To a God Unknown*. It is now reduced to an adobe ruin, an abandoned hotel, and an active Episcopal church. On his trip with poodle Charley, stopping in Monterey to have a drink at Johnny Garcia's bar, Steinbeck spoke the

poco *Spanish of my youth. There were Jolón Indians I remembered as shirttail chamacos. The years rolled away. We danced formally, hands locked behind us. And we sang the southern country anthem, "There wass a jung guy from Jolón—got seek from leeving halone. He wan to Keeng Ceety to gat sometheeng pretty—Puta chingada cabrón."*

Since 1940, the U.S. military has held this valley. (Visitors to Fort Hunter Liggett should be sure to bring a driver's license, vehicle registration, and proof of insurance to pass through checkpoints at the gates.)

Cut by streams and protected by the high coastal range, the San Antonio Valley looks much as it did when early European explorers camped near the Nacimiento and San Antonio rivers. The 1769 Spanish expedition led by Portolá was the first—traveling by land from San Diego in an attempt to find legendary Monterey Bay. Two years later, the Mission San Antonio was established a few miles further into the valley. *To a God Unknown* is set here. In Steinbeck's hands, this is contested land emblematic of California's early history. A mission priest, Mexican workers, native people, and white homesteaders inhabit the valley, and the book's central thrust is land use—be it for profit, consecration, mystery, or enjoyment.

Steinbeck's hero in *To a God Unknown* rides into the valley on nearly the same route used today.

Nuestra Señora, the long valley of Our Lady in central California, was green and gold and yellow and blue when Joseph came into it. The level floor was deep in wild oats and canary mustard flowers. The river San Francisquito flowed noisily in its bouldered bed through a cave made by its little narrow forest. Two flanks of the coast range held the valley of Nuestra Señora close, on one side guarding it against the sea, and on the other against the blasting winds of the great Salinas Valley.

To a God Unknown explores the untamed in man and nature: "The endless green halls and aisles and alcoves seemed to have meanings as obscure and promising as the symbols of an ancient religion." Madrone trees "resembled meat and muscles. They thrust up muscular limbs as red as flayed flesh and twisted like bodies on the rack. . . . Pitiless and terrible trees, the madrones.

They cried with pain when burned." The novel resonates with the mystery of place.

Mount Toro

In 1776, on the way to establish a mission in San Francisco, Juan Bautista de Anza's expedition passed through the area, camping at Mission San Antonio, King City (visit San Lorenzo County Park), Monterey, and Natividad. The expedition passed by and possibly named ❽ Mount Toro—"the bull." Steinbeck loved this "rounded benign mountain." In *East of Eden*, Abra sees snow on Mount Toro on Thanksgiving Day, and Adam responds, "that means a good year to come." And in *Sweet Thursday*, snow on Mount Toro "as far as Pine Canyon on one side and Jamesburg on the other" is a portent of a new era.

Mission San Antonio de Padua: Mission in the Wilderness

❾ Mission San Antonio, called by early padres the "mission in the wilderness," was founded in 1771 and remains one of the most remote and untouched missions in California. It was also one of the most successful. Franciscan fathers adopted European

Mission San Antonio.

The Steinbeck Family and Freemasonry

A secret society that took root in California with statehood, the Masons were respectable, industrious, civic-minded men, mainly Protestants. In Steinbeck's fiction, references to masonry signify middle-class rectitude.

When the author's paternal grandfather arrived in California in 1873, John Adolph Steinbeck joined the Hollister Masonic Lodge; later, Steinbeck's father was inducted, and he remained a loyal Mason for fifty-two years. In his mid-twenties, Mr. Steinbeck was the Senior Deacon of King City's Santa Lucia Masonic Lodge #302—where his brother-in-law, businessman Will Hamilton, was a Master Mason (Will is mentioned in *East of Eden*).

In 1892, the young Steinbeck family—John, Olive, and Esther—moved south to Paso Robles, where Mr. Steinbeck would manage another flour mill owned by Sperry Milling Company and join Lodge #286, where he was Worshipful Master from 1897 to 1899. When the family moved to Salinas in 1900, Mr. Steinbeck joined Lodge #204. Young John participated in Masonic youth organizations. On March 1, 1929, he joined his father's lodge, was raised to a third-degree member by May, and resigned immediately thereafter. He held on to his certificate of initiation, however, perhaps honoring his father's loyalty to masonry. Or perhaps as a reminder of regal Louis

Schneider, who plays a cameo role in *East of Eden*:

> My father was a medium Mason, not as high a degree as some and higher than many. There must have been some ceremonies that were semi-public because I can remember clearly Louis Schneider, the local butcher, red-faced and short and fat and with a handlebar mustache. I can see him now sitting on a throne; I think it must have been of the Order of the Royal Arch. He wore a royal robe with an artificial ermine collar and on his head was a golden crown studded with gems about the size of half chicken eggs. Louis' blue serge trouser cuffs and box-toed shoes were the only unregal things about him.

In chapter 15 of *The Grapes of Wrath*, Steinbeck lashes out at the comfortable elite who join lodges:

> little pot-bellied men in light suits and panama hats; clean, pink men with puzzled, worried eyes, with restless eyes. Worried because formulas do not work out; hungry for security and yet sensing its disappearance from the earth. In their lapels the insignia of lodges and service clubs, places where they can go and, by a weight of numbers of little worried men, reassure themselves that business is noble and not the curious ritualized thievery they know it is.

agricultural methods, planting olive trees and grape vines, designing aqueducts, and turning fields for grain. Indeed, mission flour was celebrated in the region. Traces of aqueducts and fields remain. Today's visitors can stay near the mission at the Hacienda Lodge, William Randolph Hearst's former hunting lodge designed by architect Julia Morgan, who also designed Hearst Castle. Or, by calling ahead, individuals, families or groups can book retreat accommodations at

the mission itself (missionsanantonio.net). Narrow but drivable Naciamento–Fergusson Road winds through the mountains to Big Sur and Highway 1.

King City

South on Highway 101 is ❿ King City, where, in 1887 at age twenty-five, Steinbeck's father became manager of the Central Milling Company. In December 1890, he married Olive Hamilton in a San Francisco ceremony, and the couple resided in King City for two years; Steinbeck's sister Esther was born there.

East of King City, Steinbeck's maternal grandparents, the Hamiltons, ran cattle on bone-dry land, an "old starvation ranch" Steinbeck called it. Although Sam Hamilton died in 1904, when John was two, John's favorite uncle, Tom, lived on the ranch when John was a boy, and his grandmother continued to spend time there until 1912. Tom's gentle spirit is captured in what is, in fact, his eulogy in the pages of *East of Eden*, including this marvelous notion: "He needed not to triumph over animals." It was Tom who taught John to fish, Tom who left gum under young John's pillow, guilty Tom who is Uncle John in *The Grapes of Wrath*. In 1912, at age fifty-two, he shot himself on a remote road near the ranch—a story also told in *East of Eden*. (His sister, Dessie Hamilton, died at the ranch a few years earlier, age fifty-eight, of Bright's disease. In *East of Eden*, Steinbeck collapses the time span between these two deaths.)

In 1948, Steinbeck briefly considered buying the ranch:

> *I would love to have the old place to go to for a few months of the year and let the boys find out about animals and horses and grass and smells besides carbon monoxide. . . . I do not want to run it as a ranch. Just to go to live in the old house and to walk in the night and hear the coyotes howl and the roosters and to see the rabbits sitting along the brush line in the morning sun.*

Steinbeck never did buy that ranch, and he never again lived in the Salinas Valley after he left home at age seventeen. But the smells and sounds and sights of his home valley never left him.

Hamilton Ranch.

Elizabeth Hamilton.

Samuel Hamilton arrived in California in 1851.

Chapter 4
Moving Around
A Restless Decade

John Steinbeck, age 18.

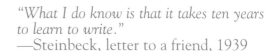

Memorial Court, Stanford University, circa 1900.

John Steinbeck spent an unsettled decade on the move with one steady goal: to master the craft of writing. Storytelling was his passion. As a boy he told ghost stories to awed friends: the human skull he kept in his bedroom, backlit in blue, undoubtedly added to the effect. That blue light also suggests Steinbeck's dramatic flair as he worked to hone his artistic stance—sometimes boldly confident in his ultimate success, just as often plagued by self-doubt.

At seventeen, liberated from Salinas and his mother's stern eye, he went off to attend Stanford University. In 1919, the school was free to deserving young men and women. Never keen on a earning a degree, Steinbeck attended sporadically for six years, taking courses that piqued his interest, then dropping out for months: once when he fell ill, another time to sell radios door to door, and for several quarters to roam from one Spreckels ranch to another, working in the fields. Even then, Steinbeck knew a writer must explore life beyond insular Salinas and sleepy Monterey Peninsula. He spent his twenties living on little money, taking jobs in New York City, Lake Tahoe, and San Francisco; swinging from experience to experience; testing out urban life; and absorbing what he might need in order to become the man he envisioned: a published, successful writer. His internal compass—a steely determination to write, formed when he was barely in high school—kept him on course.

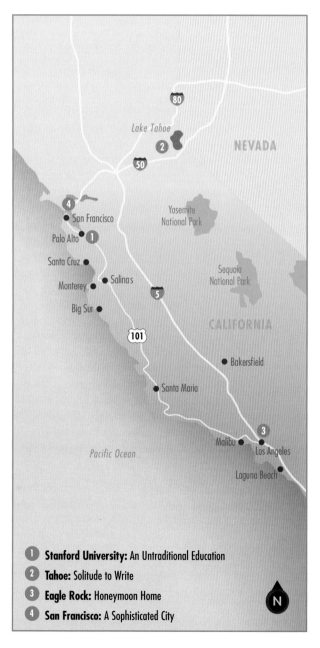

Stanford University: 1919–25

When John Steinbeck showed up for classes in October 1919, **1** Leland Stanford Junior University had been open for nearly thirty years, growing from 555 students in 1891 to 2,882 in 1919. From its inception, the university had been coeducational. Founders Jane and Leland Stanford believed that women should be offered the same academic program as men. (When women threatened to overwhelm the male population in 1899, however, Mrs. Stanford capped female enrollment at 500, in force until 1933.) Located a mere forty miles from the state's academic jewel, the University of California at Berkeley, Stanford readily proved early skeptics wrong: an eastern newspaper had quipped on Founders' Day that another institution of higher education in California was about as necessary as "an institution for the relief of destitute ship captains in the mountains of Switzerland."

Under the genial, twenty-two-year leadership of President David Starr Jordan ("Naturalist, Teacher and a Minor Prophet of Democracy," his autobiography is

Memorial Church today.

subtitled), the university developed an expansive and liberal mission. Rather than the traditional classical training so popular in the nineteenth century, Stanford offered a practical education in science and the humanities, a career-oriented course of study that was utilitarian, nonsectarian, and egalitarian. Students were to be scholars and to "have a sound practical idea of commonplace, everyday matters," said Jordan on opening day, "a self-reliance that will fit them, in case of emergency, to earn their own livelihood in a humble as well as an exalted sphere." Admission standards to this pastoral haven were liberal—only high school English composition was required—and older, working-class students without a secondary education were admitted provisionally as "specials." Through hard work, Jordan believed, specials could catch up and earn a place. About a third did. One was a close friend of Steinbeck's, Carl Wilhelmson, a former sailor from Finland with a third-grade education and a zeal for writing.

The Big Game

U.C. Berkeley and Stanford have always been fierce football rivals—although fans suffered through a five-year hiatus from 1914 to 1919 as the schools quibbled over whether football or rugby should be the official field sport. In 1919, the annual "Big Game" was back with attendant antics. Stanford students painted Cal's "C" red during Steinbeck's years. Under-graduate humor ran high: "Between halves a special engagement has been secured," announced the 1919 program. "The Alcatraz prison school will tackle the Milpitas night school in a game of American football." When he could, Steinbeck attended these rousing standoffs: In 1922, he showed up in a large overcoat outfitted with vials of grain alcohol pinned to the lining (compliments of the Spreckels chemistry lab, where he was working at the time). Writing home from Lake Tahoe a few years later, he reported listening to the game on the radio, "thinking of the great crowds" and of his sister's passion for the game: "Mary says her greatest thrill in life comes from football."

Even a recalcitrant student such as Steinbeck would have found it hard to dislike Stanford, a bucolic campus constructed on acres of grassy fields between San Jose and San Francisco, between the lifestyles of "polite" Menlo Park society and immigrant farmers of the Santa Clara Valley. The university would come to be called "the Farm," its motto "the wind of freedom is blowing" (written in German on the campus seal). Then, as now, natural landscapes surround formal monumental quads graced with the non-denominational Memorial Church, built in 1903 and restored to its early glory after the Loma Prieta earthquake in 1989. The formal inner and outer quads were built with native sandstone blocks and incorporate graceful yet solid archways in the Mission style. Trees flourish: native oaks and the ancient redwood that gave Palo Alto its name and Stanford its logo were joined by an avenue of imported palms planted along the entrance drive from El Camino Real. When Steinbeck enrolled in Professor William Herbert Carruth's class on verse writing and prosody, he was assigned verses on "The Coast Range, as Seen from Stanford"; "a Petrarchan Sonnet on the Memorial Church"; and couplets on "The Trees of the Santa Clara Valley." A confident, optimistic atmosphere was cultivated from the beginning, "something in the pioneer tradition," remarked a 1911 graduate, with "an emphasis on individual effort and the individual's right to succeed on his own terms."

Steinbeck's freshman roommate in 111 Encina Hall was a steady student from nearby Los Gatos, George Mors, a man with whom Steinbeck would stay in touch all his

The Stanford logo, a centuries-old redwood near campus.

William Herbert Carruth, one of Steinbeck's Stanford professors.

Encina Hall, circa 1890s, where Steinbeck lived when he first came to Stanford.

Stanford Friends

At Stanford, Steinbeck came to know the value of friendship, the relationship he would explore again and again in his fiction. His closest friends included Toby Street, who was also an English major with a keen interest in drama—he passed on to Steinbeck his attempt to write a play, and in Steinbeck's hands the work became *To a God Unknown*. Street later became a lawyer in Monterey, handling Steinbeck's divorce from Carol. After reading one of Steinbeck's least successful novels, *The Short Reign of Pippin IV: A Fabrication* in 1957, he wrote bluntly to John in New York City, "You'll never find any stories at the Stork Club and 21. Why don't you come home?" It was a feeling many Western friends shared. Another Stanford friend, Ted Miller, spent long hours in New York City as Steinbeck's unofficial agent in 1930, hawking Steinbeck's stories from publisher to publisher.

Carlton Sheffield, roommate during Steinbeck's second stint at Stanford, was a fellow English major with a wry sense of humor and broad tolerance: "Neither this person nor myself had a brother," wrote Steinbeck in 1926 to "Sheff's" new wife. "Because of these things, we went through our very young years lonely and seeking. We had no intimates, practically no friends. We made enemies readily because we were far above our immediate associates. In college we met, and at every point the one seemed to supplement and strengthen the other." Steinbeck corresponded with Sheffield all his life.

Carl Wilhelmson, older than Steinbeck, worked on his own novel (eventually published as *Midsummernight*) when he was Steinbeck's companion at Tahoe for weeks at a time. He was also Steinbeck's toughest critic in those days, pointing out "innumerable foolishnesses in my work," Steinbeck reported to his parents. Wilhelmson later suggested that Steinbeck contact literary agents McIntosh & Otis in New York City, who eventually became Steinbeck's agents for life.

Steinbeck's first muse was probably Katherine Beswick, an early love from Stanford. He wrote her regular and heartfelt letters from Lake Tahoe and for years after, well after his first marriage. When she recommended wine as inspiration, however, he rejected her advice: "When drinking," he wrote her, "my writing is invariably in bad taste, over-emotional and somewhat pornographic."

life. A 1964 letter to Mors captures the joie de vivre of those first months at Stanford:

> My tattoo stands up pretty well. At full moon it stands out right sharp. Maybe it's because we didn't sterilize the razor blade and I had a fine secondary infection. But it's remarkably clear for such a bungling job. . . . I was remembering how I jumped school and hid out at your mother's grocery. She must have hated it. And I remembered all the foolish lies I told . . . I don't remember your telling things like that.

John Steinbeck shortly before leaving for Stanford University, his eyes bandaged after an accident at Spreckels.

Mors probably didn't need to tell lies. He was busy attending classes. Steinbeck was sometimes doing so. He was a shy, awkward, uncertain student who avoided fraternal life, perhaps fearing rejection. Illness and scant interest kept him from full participation in sports, and he didn't make the freshman football team. His first year was hardly remarkable: fall quarter he completed only two courses, earning a B in history, a C in English composition, and an incomplete in French. Winter quarter he completed only one course, English 2, earning a C minus. Spring quarter he took a leave. Although he returned in the fall of 1920, he was officially "disqualified" by December, having received a D in news writing, a C in philosophy, and a B in short-story writing. Years later, Steinbeck would write his son Thom that his first stint at university was dismal—he worked at school and at jobs, he had no suitable clothes for dating, he had no money to take girls out. Steinbeck did not adapt well to academic discipline and to the embarrassment of being an outsider—poor and ill at ease.

From November 1920 to January 1923, he roamed, working most of the time at various ranches owned by the Spreckels Sugar Company. But he returned to Stanford in the winter quarter of 1923 and found his stride, at least for a couple of years. This time he focused on the things he loved, world history and English, or what might help him in the future—enrolling in a debate class in 1923 "to develop some confidence when I stand on my feet before people." He changed his major to journalism. He joined the English Club, where students met to read and discuss literature, and he often read his own stories aloud to the assembled group. He published his first work outside his high school yearbook: a satiric poem, "Atropos," and two stories in 1924 issues of the *Stanford Spectator*, "Fingers of Cloud: A Satire on College Protervity" and "Adventures in Arcademy: A Journey into the Ridiculous."

Edith Mirrielees's short-story classes would come to be Steinbeck's favorites during his spotty years at Stanford. In 1919, she was newly returned to campus after a brave stint overseas as leader of the Stanford Women's Unit for Relief Work in France, eighteen young women who served with the Red Cross. That gesture suggests both her passion for new experiences and the boundless

energy that served her in thirty-five years teaching at Stanford. ("One should never miss a new experience," she wrote, "even though tiresome in doing.") Steinbeck counted her as one of three "real" teachers in his life (the others being his friend Ed Ricketts and a high school math teacher, Miss Cupp).

The kindly Miss Mirrielees continued to read Steinbeck's work even after he left Stanford; he sent her drafts of his first novel, *Cup of Gold* (1929), from wintry Lake Tahoe. Steinbeck duly reported her assessment of his first fifty pages to his parents: "She says in part: 'This is

Miss Mirrielees was the "best teacher of writing I have known," Steinbeck observed, and she had "only two rules—know what you want to say . . . say it. Her only criticisms were in effectiveness . . . never in manner, style, subject, etc. But the others all tried in the name of literature to make us little counterparts of themselves."

beautifully done. I read with increasing interest and increasing wonder at the way you have steadied and strengthened your writing, so that the beautiful pieces no longer stand out separate from the rest.' And that from Miss Mirrielees is a bombshell of praise."

Steinbeck got what he wanted out of Stanford: writing instruction, greater knowledge of literature, and encouragement from teachers, particularly Mirrielees in writing, Margery Bailey—a specialist in Shakespeare and Dickens—in literature, William Herbert Carruth in verse writing, and Harold Chapman Brown in history. Steinbeck audited Brown's world civilization class quarter after quarter and went to his house for further discussion—when his interest was sparked, he was hardly a retiring student. Undoubtedly Brown helped ignite Steinbeck's keen interest in European and ancient history.

Close friendships marked Steinbeck's life, and many of these were with Stanford classmates who shared his passion for language and his off-kilter sensibilities. In the 1920s, most were trying to do pretty much the same thing he was—write and publish. The quirky, eccentric, but loyal and clearly gifted young writer drew equally independent souls to his side. This would be his gift throughout a life defined in good part by friendships made and kept.

Steinbeck's tribute to his Stanford education was to request in his will that his Nobel Prize be placed at the university after the death of his third wife, Elaine. His friends and family honored him by depositing their Steinbeck letters in the Stanford Special Collections and University Archives. The extensive Steinbeck archive—including letters written to his agent Elizabeth Otis, his friend Carlton Sheffield, his wife Elaine, and his family—is one of the richest in the world. The collection is open to researchers.

A Sojourn Outside California:
New York City in 1925

During his college years, Steinbeck concocted plans to kick loose his California moorings. He considered a merchant ship to China, a trek to Mexico City with Carlton Sheffield, a foray to Nicaragua. He craved a horizon beyond the Pacific coast. A November 1925 steamer to New York City fit the bill. For a would-be writer, New York City was an essential destination.

Steinbeck's time in New York was brief, a mere six months, but it was vital to his education. For one, he came to know the sea. He sailed to and from New York, passing through the Panama Canal, and that experience gave him material for his first novel, *Cup of Gold*, the story of pirate Henry Morgan's search for his ideal love.

The city tested his mettle. While in New York, Steinbeck played out his scrappy gift for adaptability. In a marvelous little essay he wrote in 1953—"Autobiography: Making of a New Yorker"—he says that during his first visit, "monstrous" New York City "had beat the pants off me." In the end, without steady employment and still unpublished, he was certainly disillusioned. Often he went hungry. No doubt he was lonely. And, as he admitted in 1935, "I was scared thoroughly. And I can't forget the scare." But however tough, these were invigorating months. He briefly worked construction at Madison Square Garden. A more important position—also brief—was a three-month stint as a journalist for the *American,* a Hearst newspaper, at what he called a "lilliputian" salary. But the exposure to newspaper work was invaluable. "Yesterday it was a story about the push cart peddlers in Orchard St. and the Ghetto," he wrote home,

and today it is Lord Rothmere the "Dictator of the British Press." Tomorrow it may be a murder and the next day a divorce. . . . Believe me, if I ever had a fear of meeting people of all classes, it will be banished after a month or so of this.

Lower East Side tenements.

Also there is probably no job in the city whereby I could see more of all parts of New York, than this.

Although he was soon laid off, "amputated" by budget cuts, the few months as a reporter toughened Steinbeck's prose and his outlook.

In New York, he witnessed the sharp distinction between rich and poor, images that reinforced his ingrained sympathies for those on the margins: "This place is swarming with the very poor," he wrote his parents. "Then in my position at the Federal Courts [assigned by the *American*] there is a constant stream of people who have gotten into trouble, many through ignorance and many through plain poverty." He wrote sketches about the things he saw. Like Theodore Dreiser and Stephen Crane before him, he came away with the sense that the city was an impersonal force, shaping people's destinies, drumming down those without the resources to fight back: "I find the city so absorbing, so fearsome, so dangerous and yet so blundering. If it hurts any person it is just because that person got in the way and was not noticed. It is like a great dragon with poor eyesight, trampling about. I am filled, not with the seriousness of my own and other

people's existence, but with the utter lack of seriousness of anything." He would keep the detachment that he cultivated and utilize it in his 1930s prose.

In the early summer of 1926, having lost both his job and his exotic girlfriend of a few weeks—a dancer with a good salary—twenty-four-year-old Steinbeck returned home. "I have learned a couple of things about myself," he wrote after he left New York City. "I cannot take care of myself. I need a mentor." He could indeed take care of himself—but to be a writer, he needed a buffer to keep the wider world at bay.

Tahoe

If New York City had indeed "beat the pants off" him, Steinbeck might have abandoned his dream of being a writer. Instead, his instincts led him home to California, back to his roots. He traded a perilous existence in New York for the safety of a writerly retreat: a 1926 summer job at Stanford University's Fallen Leaf Lake community near ❷ Lake Tahoe followed by two years along the south shore of pristine Lake Tahoe as a winter caretaker and the summer companion of children at the lakeshore Brigham estate. Steinbeck's Tahoe winters were particularly valuable: he hibernated, crafting sentences, writing and rewriting what would become his first novel. "I drive people crazy with singing my sentences, but I find it necessary for the sake of rhythm," he wrote to Katherine Beswick. It was best to be alone in a small cabin.

The Sierra Nevadas are forbidding mountains from October until May. Blizzards hit. Visibility is cut to a few feet. In the 1920s, life ground to a halt. The area was relatively isolated, connected to the Bay Area not by smooth Interstate 80 but by tortuous Highway 40 over Donner Pass. Another option was the Southern Pacific rail line that stopped in Truckee, a raucous little town about twenty miles from the lake—and where, in the summer months, Steinbeck sometimes took dates to drink and dance. From there, a narrow-gauge spur ran to North Lake Tahoe, where the rustic elegance of the Tahoe Tavern attracted tourists and residents alike: "Things happen there," Steinbeck wrote home in February 1928, "and there are electric lights and things." Intrepid guests came for "winter sports." A community store, Richardson's, remained open until mid-November. "I do not patronize them," Steinbeck wrote. "They take too much of advantage of us in their prices. We can do better sending out." "Sending out" meant relying on the narrow-gauge train that ran only twice a week from October to May and brought supplies to the caretakers and settlers braving the Lake Tahoe winter. During Steinbeck's two winters as a caretaker on the sparsely populated south shore, a highlight of his week was the mail delivery at Camp Richardson, a two-mile walk from his cabin. Snowstorms were frequent, and the winter of 1926–7 was the worst in twenty years.

After throwing himself into the jazzy turbulence of 1920s New York City, Steinbeck put himself to other tests at Tahoe: to "break . . . in the middle" his fear of being alone, for one, and to test the intensity of his commitment to writing. In frequent letters home—writing twice weekly most months—he reported on routines that must have helped shape his world. He scrupulously noted that he would repay his parents for hams and bacon they sometimes sent, for yellow writing

paper, for eggs lovingly packed in handmade crates for the long train trips from Salinas to Tahoe City. His anxious mother sent him gifts of warm socks and sweaters. Although he accepted food, he vigorously resisted other gifts from Olive: his need for clear boundaries was strong. He set writing goals, reporting fifty pages written, seventy-five, one hundred. "I have my supper at five in the afternoon and get all done with it by six," he wrote home in the fall of 1927:

From six to eleven I work constantly. At eleven I make some chocolate or some coffee and toast and have a little après-mint and then to bed and read

Fallen Leaf Lake today.

for half an hour and to sleep. I sleep unusually well when I have worked about six hours with my hands and then about six with my head. In fact it gives me a sense of well being not often felt.

After being bruised by New York, such a routine must have soothed the young writer. Solitude allowed him to write and rewrite the novel he so hoped would find a publisher.

The lodge at Fallen Leaf Lake.

During his two winters at Tahoe, Steinbeck disciplined himself with the same will that he would call forth when writing *The Grapes of Wrath*—hunkering down to push through to a goal. By April 1927, his novel, "written twice, once by hand and once with the typewriter," was proceeding very well. "I have never been able to work so steadily nor so successfully before," he wrote to his parents—surely craving their continued support for his choice of career. To others he admitted that he was less certain of his progress. He confided to Carlton Sheffield in February 1928 that *Cup of Gold* is, "as a whole, utterly worthless." Steinbeck's self-doubts were, for much of his early career, as relentless as was his will to produce fine work.

Mainly, however, the Lake Tahoe years matured Steinbeck—they wore down his raw edges. He completed a novel that would be published. During the summer months, he cared for the children of the estate with cultivated enthusiasm. Both summer and winter, he worked hard outdoors, confronting is own tendencies toward indolence—chopping wood, for example, and one December cutting four hundred cakes of ice off the lake. These were invigorating years. He regularly plunged into the icy waters of Lake Tahoe with his dog Jerry, who loved an arctic swim. He skied at Emerald Bay; sketched a little play about a pleasant Christmas dinner; planted a garden that would be "eaten by vermin"; and tried to keep his two dogs, Omar and Jerry, from fighting constantly. His father visited in the fall and winter, cooking and cleaning for his son. Throughout the year,

Steinbeck fished and hunted, pleased that he could eat what he gathered (duly reported to concerned parents, who wondered if he ate enough). And during the summer of 1928, he worked at a fish hatchery: "we are overcrowded with fishes and undercrowded with help," he told Katherine Beswick, "so that some times we work far into the night." But such things make adults of unsettled young writers.

Lake Tahoe meant one more thing to Steinbeck—it was here that he found his "mentor," his essential buffer to the world. In midsummer 1928, the woman who would become his first wife walked into the Lake Tahoe fish hatchery in Tahoe City. A sign over his door read "Piscatorial Obstetrician," and perhaps Steinbeck's wit appealed to her, a woman with the same offbeat sense of humor. It was love at first sight, reported Carol Henning's sister Idell. During their first five days together, Carol typed Steinbeck's manuscript of *Cup of Gold* (then titled "The Cup of Gold: Being the Life of a Pirate, with Occasional Historic Accuracies"). That exercise must have given her an idea of what she was getting into when she married John Steinbeck eighteen months later. "You are not as important as his work," Toby Street would warn her. Carol already understood that. She willingly signed on to be muse, patron, critic, and editor during these early years— in short, his indispensable companion in his quest for writerly acclaim.

Down South: Eagle Rock

"It will be a long time until I go" to Los Angeles, Steinbeck wrote his mother in September 1927. "I dislike it very much." But when he and Carol wanted to put distance between

themselves and their parents, Southern California, in particular ❸ Eagle Rock, seemed an appealing place. College roommate Carlton Sheffield was living there with his wife, Maryon, and teaching English at Occidental College. Shortly after settling in with the Sheffields, in January 1930, John and Carol married.

Life at Carlton Sheffield's house in Eagle Rock was bohemian, raucous, and fun—a few months of revelry, an extended honeymoon, Steinbeck's last hurrah before settling in to write full-time for the next decade. Others shared in the fun: Ritch and Tal Lovejoy (he was an artist and writer, she a blithe spirit and model for Mary Talbot in *Cannery Row*) and Tal's sister Nadja were also living with the Sheffields. "In this community we make beer, much beer," wrote Steinbeck (eighteen gallons every five days, reported Sheffield), "and it is both cheap and pleasant to induce a state of lassitude intershot with moments of unreal romance. I have only in the last two weeks been wooing that state. Before that some foolish asceticism kept me at the pad and pen."

The seven concocted a zany venture. Ritch and Tal introduced the others to a Swiss product called

Carol Henning, circa 1924.

Drawings made by Carol when she and John lived in Eagle Rock.

Steinbeck's San Francisco

For Steinbeck, ❹ San Francisco was always "the City." From the gold rush through the mid-1960s, San Francisco meant sophisticated living in the West, the ladies always in gloves and hats, the restaurants serving exotic fare, the lovely skyline delicate and unearthly in the fog. When he did his "tour of duty as an intellectual bohemian" in late 1928 through 1929, San Francisco made a lasting impression—"How beautiful it was and I knew then how beautiful," he wrote in a 1958 essay, "The Golden Handcuff," written for the *San Francisco Examiner*. Both he and Carol were poor and meals were cheap; life was good, golden like the bridge built a few years later.

Steinbeck moved from Tahoe to San Francisco to be with Carol, who worked for Schilling Spice and later in advertising and circulation for the *San Francisco Chronicle*. He took a job at Bemis Brothers Bag Company, where his future brother-in-law, Bill Dekker, and family worked. During his year in the city, Steinbeck lived in tight rooms at 1901 Vallejo Street, 2853 Jackson Street, and 2441 Fillmore Street. "I am so much enjoying living here in the city," he wrote Katherine Beswick. "I have practically nothing to live on but that doesn't seem to make any difference."

He and Carol gloried in city life. He courted her, read to her, and once, with his friend Carl Wilhelmson, stuck a herring on each spike of the fence around the apartment she shared with Idell. Living far from the East Coast cities that nurtured modernism and antic sensibilities, John and Carol sported a raw, western brand of rebellion. Young, hungry to succeed, unconventional,

and restless, the two spent their months in the city exhibiting the Lost Generation's determination to experiment and "make it new."

Before and after his 1928–29 sojourn in the city, Steinbeck visited San Francisco several times. He probably attended the 1915 Panama-Pacific International Exposition and definitely visited the 1939 Golden Gate International Exposition to hear his soon-to-be second wife, Gwyn Conger, sing. In the 1940s he sometimes was incognito, avoiding the likes of Herb Caen, who took San Francisco's pulse in a daily column for half a century. In the 1950s Steinbeck hosted his sisters at the Clift Hotel, his mother's favorite.

Herb Caen came to best represent Steinbeck's San Francisco. Steinbeck wrote to a Salinas friend years later,

California Street in San Francisco, circa 1925.

The Caen type of gossip column, and you could with accuracy call it the Pepys type or the Defoe type or the Addison type, has a long and sometimes honorable history. . . . There is no question of the value of this form historically. Without Pepys and Evelyn we would know what happened in the 17th century but not what people thought about it. Herb has done a remarkable job. He has made a many faceted character of the city of San Francisco. It is very probable that Herb's city will be the one that is remembered. It is interesting to me that he has been able to do this without anger and without venom, and without being soft.

Caen felt equal warmth for Steinbeck, devoting a "Crock of Chrysanthemums" to Steinbeck when he died.

A Letter Writer

Throughout his life, when at some distance from home, Steinbeck kept in regular contact with his family. In the 1920s he wrote "the regular Sunday letter"—addressed "Dear Folks" and intended for the family to share. This habit of contact as well as his steady friendships are qualities to bear in mind when considering Steinbeck's early years. However much he was driven to roam, he always kept open lines of communication with family and close friends. Letter writing would be a lifelong practice, and Steinbeck's letters are affectionate, witty, and often revealing epistles. Words were the stuff of his life.

March 1926, New York City

And do not be in the least doubt about my ultimate success. I am not. I am more convinced of it every day I spend here. I am brighter than most people and I can write better than most people and it is only a question of time until I can convince somebody of it and then I will go like wild fire. This may sound like the crackling of twigs under a kettle, but it is not enthusiasm. It is the result of my analysis of the conditions of this city. The first fetish is advertising. I will get it. The second is eccentricity, I can simulate it, and the third is delivery (this you notice is the least important) and I am fully capable of it.

May 3, 1927, Camp Richardson on Lake Tahoe

I have been able to jump in the lake every day. Wonderful what it does for your self-respect. Bathing in a bucket ain't all it might be.

August 24, 1927, Camp Richardson on Lake Tahoe

I think I am going to have a launch this winter and that will cut out all that walking to the post office thank heaven. Then I can get the supplies I want without having to carry them home on my back, and then I could get to the Tavern and get a train if I wanted to. And then I could convey Dad to the cabin with ease and even with luxury: I am rooting for the launch.

Thanksgiving 1927

I have taken to writing with a steel pen. I do my first draft with a pen you know. It is the first time I have used a dip pen since I was in grammar school. And I like it. You can throw away the point if it doesn't suit you and put in a new one.

Negacol, a plastic that could be used to make highly detailed casts from almost any surface. The plan was to experiment with Negacol's amazing properties, a "vague but optimistic" agenda, Sheffield noted years later in his autobiography:

We thought there should be a good market for personalized masks of individuals, made and finished to order like portraits or photographs, to hang on walls, to be mounted into bookends or plaques, to be poised on pedestals or to serve as paperweights. We could produce perfect casts of hands, arms, feet, or valued personal possessions. . . . John bubbled with ideas. There should be a fertile field in young movie stars—or would be stars—and perhaps we could work out a publicity tie-in by which heads of such hopefuls might be used in display windows to enhance the attractiveness of merchandise . . . And there was a tremendous potential field in supplying schools, museums, laboratories, and novelty shops with perfect reproductions of flowers, fruits, insects (large), animals (small), and marine specimens. The possibilities were limitless. We were very naïve.

Carol in particular must have delighted in the possibilities, for she had an artistic bent and loved drawing and creating small figures out of clay. At first, enthusiasm for the project ran high, and they made casts of all seven of the faces in the household, but each cast demonstrated the unreliability of their artistic endeavors. Some facial types looked ghastly when duplicated with exacting fidelity. The business venture collapsed.

John and Carol eventually settled nearby in Eagle Rock, in a run-down house they repaired at 2741 El Roble Drive, but the Sheffield house remained a lively hub. Beautiful and offbeat Tal and Nadja, daughters of an Alaskan Russian Orthodox priest, retold childhood ghost stories. With Maryon Sheffield, perhaps the least bookish of the crowd, the women formed the Eagle Rock Self-Expression Society. They went roller-skating for groceries. Carol and Maryon wrestled. They "initiated" the Sheffields' new furniture by doing cart-wheels over the divan and pouncing on chairs. At the "first annual cross-country hurdle race," the women leap-frogged bushes and squeezed through hedges. Quieter hours were spent at the "sunbath," a partially concealed and popular backyard retreat where the ladies and visitors of any gender lounged nude and consumed vast quantities of Carlton's home brew. Nearly every one of Carol's drawings of the group shows them clutching beers.

Although John always relished inventions and projects, he soon tired of the antics that distracted him from writing. And Carol needed a paying job. "John and Carol," reported Sheffield, "enjoyed participating when the party spirit was high, but were less inclined to make life a continuous fiesta." In the fall of 1930, they retreated to the Monterey Peninsula. Married, age twenty-eight, and supported in part by loyal parents, Steinbeck knew that, to become not just a published writer—which he was—but a writer of great import, he had to write with serious intention.

The Negacol masks made by Steinbeck and friends in their failed business venture.

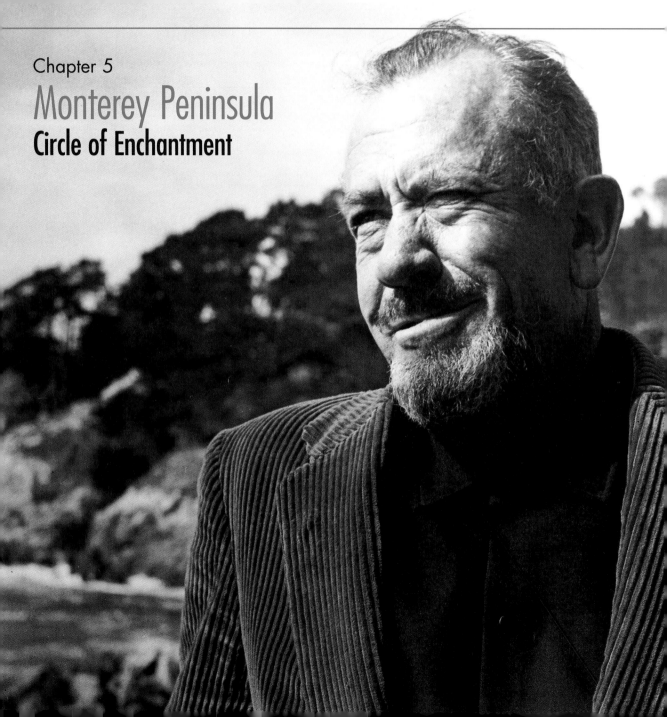

Chapter 5

Monterey Peninsula
Circle of Enchantment

THE CIRCLE OF ENCHANTMENT

Pebble Beach promotional brochure.

John Steinbeck on 17-Mile Drive, 1960.

John Steinbeck is as intimately associated with the Monterey Peninsula as he is with the Salinas Valley. A gentle rivalry between Salinas and the peninsula erupts at times. Is he a valley man or a coast man? After all, a street in New Monterey was renamed Cannery Row in 1957 because Steinbeck wrote a book about it. His best friend, Edward Flanders Ricketts, had a lab on Cannery Row, a weathered, beloved building that still stands. In Monterey, the paisanos described in *Tortilla Flat* lived hand to mouth in forests and shacks. In Pacific Grove, his family had a summer home, a tiny board-and-batten cottage where he and Carol lived in the 1930s. And, in Carmel, Steinbeck's politics were forged. Each peninsula community shaped this writer's psyche during the 1930s, the decade when he wrote some of his best fiction.

The Monterey Peninsula exudes a more freewheeling air than inland Salinas, a town that is surely a part of the more conventional West, with its rodeo and hillside cattle ranches, its growers and crop rotation. Prosperous Salinas Valley farms have long depended on a stable workforce of farm laborers; the peninsula has drawn a more diverse populace—fishermen, artists and artisans, tourists, military personnel, international language learners. During Steinbeck's formative years, there were few radical changes in the Salinas status quo. The same was not true on the Monterey Peninsula. The peninsula is a dynamic place, perhaps best defined by the ecological notions of diversity, adaptation, and evolution.

To appreciate fully John Steinbeck's California fiction, one must recognize that the two ecosystems he knew best growing up, the fertile Salinas Valley and the Monterey Peninsula, generated very different stories based on different histories. Anglo-Saxon, westering pioneers are the major players in Steinbeck's valley fiction—Joseph Wayne in *To a God Unknown*, Jody's grandfather in *The Red Pony*, the Joads, Adam Trask, and Sam Hamilton in *East of Eden*. These Anglo pioneers are empire builders—dreamers on the move. Historically, as in Steinbeck's fiction, most mid-nineteenth-century farmers and ranchers came from the East to till soil and graze cattle in the inland valleys of California.

Settlement on the Monterey Peninsula, however, was multidirectional and multiethnic, the land more accessible to ownership on small tracts. "Mongrel" Monterey, an 1887 article in *Harper's* magazine quipped. It's a fitting term. The peninsula's layered settlement history drew a diverse and yeasty mix of peoples: Spanish padres and soldiers in the eighteenth century, followed by Mexican settlers; Chinese and Japanese fishermen and Portuguese whalers in the mid-nineteenth century; Italian and Sicilian fishermen in the early twentieth century. Powerful Anglo railroad owners fueled a development boom in the 1880s, and Scandinavians and Italians built canneries before and after World War I. The peninsula's human population, even today, is as diverse as the marine life in the two-mile deep canyon that bisects Monterey Bay, a canyon twice the depth of the Grand Canyon.

Steinbeck captures the peninsula's mix. What fascinated him was hardly noted in the clamor for the development of Pebble Beach properties, for ever-larger fishing boats and greater sardine catches, or for

Highway 1: A Gateway to the Peninsula

Approaching the Monterey Peninsula from the north on Highway 1, as many visitors do, is to first glimpse the bay as "a blue platter," to feel the same thrill that overcomes Nick Carraway in *The Great Gatsby* when he sees New York City from the Queensboro Bridge: "always the city seen for the first time, in its first wild promise of all the mystery and the beauty in the world." From Highway 1, Monterey Bay, whether sparkling blue in sunshine or gray with fog, beckons with similar allure. "Some time or other," declared a 1928 pamphlet on the "Circle of Enchantment," "someone, a pioneer ancestor of yours perhaps, looked upward and dreamed of this Peninsula." One late-nineteenth-century brochure is named, succinctly and aptly, "Fulfillment."

View from railroad yard to wharf, circa 1908.

Monterey Ba

In his fiction, Steinbeck mentions the little towns and attractions along Highway 1: the amusement park in Santa Cruz; Watsonville, where his sister Esther lived; the inland Pajaro Valley (site of *In Dubious Battle*), where apples grew "crisp and full juiced"; Moss Landing, where the Pacific Gas and Electric Company (PG&E) constructed the largest steam-generated plant in the West—and where a whaling station once stood. "Johnny Bear," one of Steinbeck's best stories, is set in the gritty little town of ❶ Castroville, now the Artichoke Capital of the World.

One evening Steinbeck and a Stanford friend, Toby Street, "were coming back from Palo Alto on the way to Salinas and we stopped for a beer at a bar just outside Castroville," reported Street in an interview.

"We were sitting there talking, and suddenly we heard the bartender

speaking to somebody wearing bib overalls"—a large, clumsy man, a mute, telling stories with his fingers. Steinbeck drew from that experience in writing "Johnny Bear."

Past Castroville, Highway 1 cuts through sand dunes, once training grounds for the U.S. Army and before that for Presidio infantry, cavalry, and field artillery units. (It's now known as Ford Ord Dunes State Park.) Soldiers from the 11th Calvary Unit, stationed at the Monterey Presidio in the 1930s, make cameo appearances in *Cannery Row*. In 1939, the lovely bay seemed vulnerable to enemy attack, and the U.S. government carved out additional acres of land for ❷ Fort Ord, a major army installation from 1940 to 1994. Fort Ord is now home to California State University, Monterey Bay. A bicycle/walking trail that starts in Castroville loops through the dunes and Seaside and hugs the bay into New Monterey, Cannery Row, and Pacific Grove.

Now booming with new homes and artists' studios, dotted with fine little Mexican cafés and Japanese sushi restaurants, ❸ Seaside was, in Steinbeck's time, the underside of the bay, home to a post office, a dump, and a Southern Pacific Railroad depot. When Monterey houses of prostitution closed during World War II, a few moved to Seaside. Seaside was also where, in *Cannery Row*, excellent bargains could be struck. Mack and the boys were "some time acquiring a stove" in Seaside for the Palace flophouse. After World War II and President Truman's order to integrate the armed services, Seaside and Fort Ord attracted a number of African American military personnel; by 1980, this area had the most concentrated black population between Los Angeles and Oakland.

Marilyn Monroe as Castroville's 1948 artichoke queen.

additional reduction plants to process sardines into highly profitable fish meal and fish oil. In a place where, by 1900, most land had been claimed by the church, the military, and the Pacific Improvement Company (later the Pebble Beach Company, which opened the famed golf course in 1919), ordinary folk inhabited the margins. Three of Steinbeck's most endearing books, his Monterey trilogy, are about adapting to life on the edge: *Tortilla Flat*, *Cannery Row*, and *Sweet Thursday*.

Steinbeck's View of a Simpler Time

In July 1946, the *Monterey Peninsula Herald* asked John Steinbeck to write a piece on Monterey. The annual Feast of Lanterns, held in Pacific Grove each July, is his metaphor for the peninsula's freewheeling spirit.

The festival officially began in 1905 as a pageant reenacting an old Chinese legend about villagers searching in lighted boats for separated lovers. Some say that the festival grew out of citizens' desire to replicate the lighted Chinese squid boats—squid drying having been banned on Point Alones in 1905. For the first Feast of Lanterns, the town rented several Chinese and Japanese fishing boats. Chinese lanterns and lights were—and still are—placed in windows and porches around town. Steinbeck wrote,

There was the great Feast of Lanterns—a hundred decorated boats, said the posters. Actually seven boats turned up and four of them forgot to light their lanterns. On the first turn three of the boats wandered away; on the second three more got lost, but the remaining boat went around and around for two hours completely oblivious to the hysterical cheers of the spectators. It is to be hoped that this spirit will continue—that no city planning, no show business sense overturns this magnificent attitude. The pledge that it will be kept should be made on the graves of the Elks who were late for the parade and the Eagles who never got there at all, and the fishermen who went around and around.

Settlement: Spanish Monterey

Centuries before Steinbeck, sailors and explorers first saw the bay from the west, from ships. The Chinese may have been the first lured to the peninsula, a legend Steinbeck knew: "I have been planting cypress trees to fill in some of the old ones that

Monterey Harbor, circa 1925.

Visitors gather at Lovers Point in Pacific Grove to watch Feast of Lanterns festivities in 1910.

white oaks, and water in great quantity, all near the shore." He named the peninsula in honor of his sponsor, the Condé de Monterey.

have died," he wrote in 1948. "They seem to belong here. The Monterey cypress is unique in the world except for one part of China, and the myth is that Chinese explorers long centuries before Columbus planted them here. It is known that the Chinese planted trees instead of flags as a token of discovery." Later, the Spanish planted flags as symbols of possession. In 1542, Juan Rodriguez Cabrillo, who was seeking "cities rich with gold," claimed the land for Spain. Sixty years later, Sebastián Vizcaíno wrote that "we found ourselves to be in the best port that could be desired, for besides being sheltered from the winds, it has many pines for masts and yards, and live oaks and

Nearly 150 years after Vizcaíno's expedition, Father Junipero Serra said mass on the same spot on June 3, 1770. Here Serra and commander Gaspar de Portolá dedicated themselves to building a Royal Presidio of Monterey and the Mission of San Carlos Borromeo. A year later, Serra moved his mission to Carmel, wanting both better land for crops and separation from a male enclave of soldiers. Both communities prospered. The Carmel Mission sheltered some 876 Indians at its peak in 1795. The presidio, housing soldiers and their families, servants and artisans, commanded the heights of Monterey and ensured the community's stature as capital of Alta California. Today, ❹ the Presidio Museum of Monterey is located on the lovely knoll where Vizcaíno, Portolá, and Serra once claimed the land for Spain. A cross marks the spot where Father Serra said his first mass.

A view of the Pacific coast today, the Great Tide Pool.

Carmel Mission, circa 1900.

Spanish or Mexican California, with Monterey as its capital, has been highly romanticized—by generations of California fourth-graders building popsicle-stick missions; by lovers of *Ramona*, book and pageant, who read the novel as a eulogy for the elegant Spanish rancho; and by real estate developers, "minds in-flamed by moving pictures," as Steinbeck wrote about the Mission architectural style of Santa Barbara, imitating "mud houses, architecturally reminiscent of the poorer parts of Spain in the fifteenth century." For Steinbeck, Spanish California was a rough-hewn sixty-year period to which he alludes occasionally, ironically, and critically—even empathetically—but never romantically.

Lives were trampled in the land-grabbing fervor, Steinbeck suggests:

> *Hard, dry Spaniards came exploring through, greedy and realistic, and their greed was for gold or God. These tough, dried-up men moved restlessly up the coast and down. Some of them stayed on grants as large as principalities, given to them by Spanish kings who had not the faintest idea of the gift. These first owners lived in poor feudal settlements, and their cattle ranged freely.*

Steinbeck's texts are punctuated with references to a shadowed history of Spanish and Mexican acquisition, exploitation, and assimilation. (Most of the large land grants—up to sixty miles long—were made during the twenty-five years that Mexico held California, 1821–46.)

Tortilla Flat may be Steinbeck's ode to what was best in Spanish Monterey—its ephemeral beauty and stately pace and the Californios' camaraderie. That book captures the sleepy appeal of Spanish Monterey—bypassed as the capital of California in 1848 and again by the gold rush in 1849—the peninsula town that seemed caught in a time warp for the second half of the nineteenth century, perhaps until World War II. "Clocks and watches were not used by the paisanos of *Tortilla Flat*," Steinbeck writes. "For practical purposes, there was the great golden watch of the sun." And the paisanos of *Tortilla Flat*, "a mixture of Spanish, Indian, Mexican, and assorted Caucasian bloods," carefully negotiate conflicting cultural claims that were the legacy of Spanish and Mexican rule. Danny, Pilon, Pirate, and Jesus Maria—Steinbeck's paisanos, all based on real people—balance their own mongrel bloodlines, reverence for the Catholic Church, an acquisitive dominant culture (represented by an Italian merchant, Torelli), and women's claims on domesticity and historicity ("Dolores Engracia Ramirez was a member of the 'Native Daughters of the Golden West'"). Varied traditions and cultures are significant aspects of Monterey Peninsula history.

Anglo Development: Hotel Del Monte

Robert Louis Stevenson, a visitor in 1879–80, noted peninsula development and anticipated Steinbeck's fictional terrain—stories about "quaint" survivors of lavish development. "The Monterey of last year exists no longer," Stevenson wrote in 1880. "A huge hotel has sprung up in the desert by the railway. . . . Alas for the little town. It is not strong enough to resist the influence of the flaunting caravanserai, and the poor, quaint, penniless native gentlemen of Monterey must perish, like a lower race, before the millionaires of the Big Bonanza."

A bonanza it most certainly was, something akin to the overnight transformation of the Sierra Nevada foothills into gold mining camps. In 1852, a wily Scottish clerk named David Jacks bought the former Pueblo of Monterey (just under 30,000 acres) at auction for $1,002.50 and over the years snagged most of the land on the peninsula, eventually owning 90,000 acres in Monterey County. On January 1, 1880, the Southern Pacific Railroad came steaming onto the peninsula

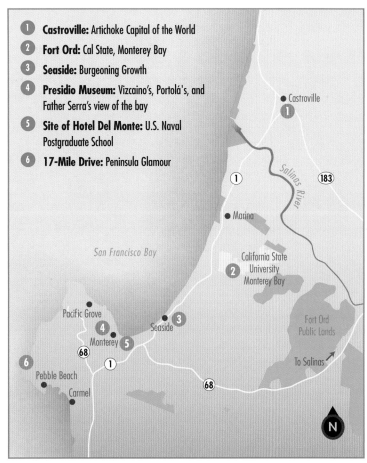

1. **Castroville:** Artichoke Capital of the World
2. **Fort Ord:** Cal State, Monterey Bay
3. **Seaside:** Burgeoning Growth
4. **Presidio Museum:** Vizcaíno's, Portolá's, and Father Serra's view of the bay
5. **Site of Hotel Del Monte:** U.S. Naval Postgraduate School
6. **17-Mile Drive:** Peninsula Glamour

1925 brochure for the Hotel Del Monte.

Who Were the Paisanos?

In the 1890s, Lucy Morse, a student at Stanford University, came to the peninsula to study its history and interview old residents. She wrote a narrative that includes this description of "native Californians of Monterey" as

> peculiar people. Good natured, happy, courteous, genial; knowing and apparently caring little for the outside world, and totally oblivious of the wealth of their historic surroundings. However there is something of delight as well as a touch of pity, in meeting people who do not put commercial value upon a sight of their ancestral homes nor try to live off the tourist. Though Spanish by descent, many of them knowing no other language, few of them without a trace of Indian blood, they are patriotic American citizens. Pictures of Dewey and Sampson are hung on many an adobe wall.

Steinbeck writes in a similar vein about "good people of laughter and kindness" who are "clean of commercialism, free of the complicated system of American business, and having nothing that can be stolen, exploited or mortgaged that system has not attacked them very vigorously."

Steinbeck knew the paisanos of Monterey. Their exploits were the stuff of news stories. Pilon of *Tortilla Flat* was in life Eduardo Romero (called Pilon by friends), "a chronic thorn in the side of Monterey police . . . [who] inspired many of Steinbeck's yarns," reported the *Monterey Peninsula Herald* in 1957, the year Pilon died. He was "truly an institution in this community," added Municipal Judge Ray Baugh, the man who was called to sentence him from time to time. Pilon and Eduardo Martin lived in Iris Canyon in Monterey, rows of wine bottles lined up outside their camp: "Absolutely, Pilon and me, we was just like brothers," Martin said in 1957 at his proclaimed age of ninety-seven. "We were always together. When you see one, you wait a few seconds, and then you see the other one." When Pilon got drunk with Eduardo one day in 1953, he stabbed his friend and was charged for the crime. Steinbeck wired a telegram to Judge Baugh: "I protest Pilon's arrest. Are the times so degenerate? Since when is it a crime to knife your friend? Pilon's motive was certainly pure, probably philanthropic and possibly noble. Judge Baugh, who is paisano himself, will surely gild justice with understanding." And Baugh did.

Sal Colleto, a Monterey fisherman, said in his memoir that Pilon helped his father cut down the pine trees in back of the American Legion Hall:

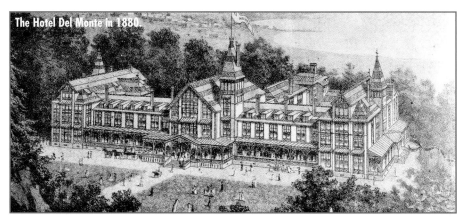

The Hotel Del Monte in 1880.

There was always available Pilon, and some of his Mexican and California Indian friends. They were always around because that's where the center of activity was, and they liked my Dad's wine, which was used customarily with the meals. The California Indians did not want money for their services. They wanted food and wine.

Steinbeck's intention was not to stereotype. When *Tortilla Flat* was being turned into a Broadway play by Jack Kirkland in 1937, Steinbeck wanted an all-Mexican cast, as he told a local reporter. When he saw the script, he didn't like it:

There are so many little undertones that he has got wrong. I don't want to maintain my book but I would like to maintain the people as I know them. Let me give you an example. Jack makes them want wine and need wine and suffer for wine whereas they want the thing wine does. They are not drunkards at all. They like the love and fights that come with wine rather than the wine itself.

Eduardo "Pilon" Romero, Eduardo Martin, and Tomas Romero.

from San Francisco. Three of the railroad's "Big Four," who earlier drove the Golden Spike on their way to fabulous wealth, bought land for a hotel and, later, acres of Jacks's empire. The four men—Collis P. Huntington (railroad magnate, lobbyist in Washington, D.C.), Leland Stanford (governor of California, U.S. senator, founder of Stanford University), Charles Crocker (merchant and railroad builder), and Mark Hopkins (Crocker's partner)—created the Pacific Improvement Company and set about to "improve" the peninsula. Competitive Crocker conceived of a resort to rival those on the French Riviera and had his vision constructed in 100 days. Beginning in June 1880, trains brought well-heeled tourists from San Francisco to what quickly became the premier resort on the Pacific Coast, ❺ the Hotel Del Monte.

From 1880 until its closing in 1943, the "Queen of American Watering Places" promised peninsula living at its best—and came to be the face that Monterey showed the world. In its first six weeks of operation, the hotel turned down three thousand requests for accommodation. Located near what advertisements bragged was the "Riviera of America," the Del Monte was a place "where every day is a perfect day." A 126-acre garden, "the most varied in the world," was graced

Spreckels family at the Hotel Del Monte, 1905.

drive from the hotel by auto. In 1881, a scenic drive for guests was opened, renowned 17-Mile Drive. And, in the 1890s, the hotel announced a new golf course, which came to be known as the "oldest course west of the Mississippi," other smaller, earlier courses having closed. The famed Pebble Beach golf course (originally Del Monte's second course at Pebble Beach), carved out of Pacific Improvement Company lands, opened officially for play on February 22, 1919. An art gallery devoted exclusively to California art opened in 1907—a year after the San Francisco earthquake destroyed many artists' studios and livelihoods. Hotel Del Monte offered luxury piled on top of luxury.

For thirty-five years, the Hotel Del Monte's lavish accommodations signified West Coast style and celebrated the region's incomparable beauty. When the hotel's fortunes drooped prior to World War I, Samuel F. B. Morse—hired in 1915 to liquidate holdings of the Pacific Improvement Company—ended up revitalizing the hotel and, in fact, preserving the region's appeal through expanded golf facilities, controlled housing development, and acres left for open land. Reorganizing the old Pacific Improvement Company as Del Monte Properties Company, he sold lots in Pebble Beach and Del Monte Forest. Sport, health, and beauty made an irresistible package. Peninsula developers marketed the perfectibility of life. In 1943, the hotel was leased to the U.S. Navy, which eventually purchased the hotel and 603 acres of surrounding land. In 1951, the U.S. Naval Postgraduate School moved in, where it still resides today.

with plants from six continents and featured a multi-acre maze and an "Arizona garden" filled with cacti brought from the desert. The hotel housed four hundred guests in Victorian splendor. Each room had a telephone, an uncommon luxury in 1880; hot and cold running water, also innovative; and lovely fireplaces, many with ornamental tiling—"those in the office representing scenes portrayed by Scott in his Waverly novels," reported one journalist. In addition to the hotel grounds, the operation at Del Monte included seven thousand acres of forest. In 1883, the Pacific Improvement Company purchased another eleven thousand acres in Carmel Valley, from which it created a water system.

Choices of diversion for guests were many. On the bay, the hotel built the first glass-enclosed swimming pool in the nation, pumping seawater into large swimming tanks that were surrounded by a "wilderness of tropical plants." Eventually, the hotel had five polo fields, a one-mile racetrack, tennis courts, a game preserve, and a guest ranch at the headwaters of the Carmel River, an hour's

Where Is Tortilla Flat?

Steinbeck claimed that many of his settings were composites. That is true of *Tortilla Flat*. In California, the term "tortilla flats" described Mexican enclaves. Steinbeck's *Tortilla Flat* might have been near Johnson Avenue in Monterey (up Madison to Monroe) by the American Legion Hall—the region photographed by Nelson Valjean, an early biographer who knew Steinbeck. A ravine runs behind, like the gulch described in the novel. Monterey high school Spanish teacher Sue Gregory lived in this area, at 889 Johnson Avenue. Her grandfather was William Hartnell, the patrón, and old paisanos came to her with problems as they had come to her grandfather. She advised the high school Spanish club at her house and told Steinbeck stories about paisano life. In a December 1936 article in the *Monterey Peninsula Herald*, Police Chief Monte Hallum said, "These were pretty good people. They were friendly and helped within their means. . . . Some of *Tortilla Flat* is fiction but a lot is true."

Some say Tortilla Flat was in New Monterey, up from the bay on Huckleberry Hill. A man named Pirate with scores of dogs lived there. Others claim it was west of Monterey Peninsula College (Jack Rabbit Hill), on the corner of Fremont and Abrego. Pilon and his friend Eduardo Martin lived there and often slept in an old bathtub.

> We had a whole lot of fun. We pretty well drinking wine. In Iris Canyon, across the highway from the cemetery. We lived in a box in Iris Canyon behind the willows. A big box. Like a coffin. Make out of tin. We used to get in there to drink wine. Especially when raining.

In 1940, *Fortune* magazine located "John Steinbeck's Tortilla Flat" off Highway 1 on a hillside near the Carpenter Street exit. That Carmel location is roughly verified by Emil White in *Circle of Enchantment:* a broad field "bounded by First and Third Avenue, Carpenter Street and the boundary of the Hatton Ranch had been named *Tortilla Flat* by the mail stage drivers. The Gomez house, at Santa Rita and First, which stood until September 1941, is reported to have provided the setting for Steinbeck in *Tortilla Flat*." And Bruce Ariss, friend of John Steinbeck, concurs in his book *Inside Cannery Row*.

It is likely that they are all right. Steinbeck loved composite locales—and to keep people guessing.

In 1936, the Del Monte Hotel published *Famous Recipes by Famous People*, and Steinbeck contributed a recipe, "Tortilla Flat." "Soak beef four hours in vinegar and drain. Cook in one can of tomato sauce and mushrooms in a good-sized casserole. Remove from fire and add a cup of rich cream."

House on Tortilla Flat, circa 1939.

Parties at the Del Monte Were Legendary

On December 9, 1933, "Repeal Night" was held in the hotel's Bali Room, a room painted with Balinese dancers. Samuel Morse was no teetotaler. "Baccus, the god of wine, will preside at Court in all his pomp and glory . . . after a drought of 15 years." The $2.50 cost included dinner and a dance. The Carmel Art Association's Bal Masques were held in 1934, 1935, and 1936, the first invitation graced with a flying pig, later Steinbeck's personal symbol ("To the stars on the wings of a pig" he inscribed under a stamp he had made). On July 7, 1939, a *Tortilla Flat* theme dance was held at the Del Monte.

But all other parties were eclipsed by Salvador Dali's "party of the century" on September 2, 1941—a party, Samuel Morse told Dali when the idea was hatched, "such as has never been given on the Monterey Peninsula." "Surrealistic Night in an Enchanted Forest" was a benefit, proceeds going to European refugee artists. On paper, all seemed promising: the cost was $4.00 with dinner, $2.50 without. "It is requested that you come in costume, preferably in a costume copied after your dream, or in a costume of a primitive animal or of the people of the forest," read the invitation.

To create the effect of a grotto (and "depress the guests," reported the newspaper the next morning), four thousand gunnysacks filled with two tons of paper were suspended from the ceiling. Two thousand pine trees were brought in, twenty-four animal heads, twenty-four store window mannequins, and dozens of animals from the zoo in San Francisco—monkeys, a lion cub, and a giraffe. A wrecked car sat in one corner, and beside it, a nude model who had been drugged for the evening (to keep her immobile). Dali's wife, Gala, "Princess of the Forest," sported a unicorn's head and reclined on a huge bed throughout dinner, cavorting with a tiger cub. A long table extending from the bed was decorated with squash, pumpkins, dried corn,

Bob Hope and Jackie Coogan at Dali's Surrealistic Night Party.

Drugged model near wrecked car.

melons, and fruit; along it strolled "an impassive porcupine." The planners wanted diners to feel like they were feasting in bed with Gala. "We will startle everybody," said the planners. They undoubtedly did. Bob Hope attended, as did Robinson Jeffers, Ginger Rogers, Bing Crosby, Clark Gable, Alfred Hitchcock, and the Vanderbilts.

The headline in the *Monterey Peninsula Herald* the next day read, "Dali Baffles Best People." Alas, since excessive funds were spent on decorations and preparations, little money was raised for refugees. As history would have it, that was the Del Monte's last gala. The war forced it to close its doors.

Although the Hotel Del Monte is hardly mentioned in Steinbeck's books, save through parody or in an ironic, irreverent aside, each reference reminds readers of the cultural gaps in Monterey: "Through the streets of the town, fat ladies, in whose eyes lay the weariness and the wisdom one sees so often in the eyes of pigs, were trundled in overpowered motorcars toward tea and gin fizzes at the Hotel Del Monte," he writes in *Tortilla Flat*. The paisanos steal vegetables from Del Monte gardens to feed the hungry children of Teresina Cortez. In *Cannery Row*, the famous humorist Josh Billings dies in the Hotel Del Monte.

Steinbeck has fun with these cultural gaps. Mack and the boys model their first party for Doc on Del Monte glitz. In their preparty imaginations "the place has got the hell decorated out of it. There's crepe paper and

there's favors and a big cake . . . and it wouldn't be no little mouse fart party neither." Indeed, "In their minds the decorated laboratory looked like the conservatory at the Hotel Del Monte." The wild masquerade in *Sweet Thursday* was probably modeled on Salvador Dali's equally fantastic gala in 1941.

Steinbeck's Peninsula: Change and Adaptation

Steinbeck's peninsula fiction is about those who make do, those who could not pay the toll on 17-Mile Drive, those who could not afford a room at the Hotel Del Monte. To read his Monterey fiction in order—from 1935's *Tortilla Flat* to 1945's *Cannery Row* to 1954's *Sweet Thursday*—is to trace a rough arc of the peninsula's economic and social transformation as told

Fisherman's Wharf, circa 1930.

Driving the Peninsula: 17-Mile Drive

The Monterey Peninsula's famed beauty is on full display along **6** **17-Mile Drive,** accessed from five gates, one off Highway 1 via the Highway 68 West exit and roundabout.

In 1903, Teddy Roosevelt rode a horse along roughly the same terrain: "splendid gallops," he wrote to his daughter. Most nineteenth-century guests at the Hotel Del Monte, however, left in a "tally ho," a carriage seating six to eight people pulled by four to six horses. At one point, the hotel owned fifty of these carriages, each of which made the trip along one of the state's first paved roads up to three times a day. Clearly 17-Mile Drive was one of the peninsula's top attractions. Since 1901 it has been a toll road, costing twenty-five cents per person originally (free to hotel guests) and twenty-five cents for a two- to three-seat car in 1913. Costs remain modest, a little over $10 for entrance, the fee reimbursed if you dine at one of the Pebble Beach Resort's gracious restaurants. Or enjoy cocktails and bagpipes at Spanish Bay, overlooking the dunes where the seer lives in *Sweet Thursday*.

The "grandest drive on the continent," an 1892 flyer boasted. The original drive left the hotel and went to Monterey adobes, to the Chinese fishing village (now Hopkins Marine Station), through Pacific Grove, along sand dunes near what is now Spanish Bay, and then along coastal land of disputed title—"Pescadero Beach,

The Crocker House on 17-Mile Drive.

long and sandy; then Chinese Cove, small cozy and sheltered; then Pebble Beach," originally covered with pebbles. At Carmel Bay, the road looped back.

Sentinel Point (then Midway Point, now the Lone Cypress) became the most celebrated spot on the drive. For author Mary Austin, writing about the peninsula in 1914, the cypress trees "might have grown in Dante's Purgatorio, or in the imagined forests where walked the rapt, tormented soul of Blake."

Where the beach and tennis club is now located—Stillwater Cove—was once a Chinese fishing village where children sold abalone shells—the first souvenir stalls on the peninsula.

The Crocker Irwin House, perhaps the most elegant house on the peninsula, is just north of Pescadero Point. In 1952, the sale price was $350,000; in 1999, it sold for $13.2 million. Originally built for Mrs. Templeton Crocker, the house, called the "Crocker Marble Palace," cost more than $2 million to build and decorate between 1926 and 1931. The cost was inflated by gold bathroom fixtures, black marble bathtubs, and travertine walls. The stone is reputedly from Mt. Vesuvius. In 1947, the Byzantine-style mansion was featured in *My Favorite Brunette*, starring Bob Hope and Dorothy Lamour; it was also featured in the 1975 movie *Escape from Witch Mountain*.

Any 17-Mile Drive excursion should end in fine dining, perhaps at The Lodge at Pebble Beach or Roy's at Spanish Bay. Elaine Scott stayed at The Lodge in 1949, when she was dating Steinbeck (she became his third wife). Joan Crawford accompanied her, providing cover for John and Elaine's rather scandalous relationship—Elaine was a married woman.

Steinbeck, on the path to the Lone Cypress on 17-Mile Drive in 1960. He was filming an introduction to Barnaby Conrad's film *Flight*, based on Steinbeck's short story of the same name.

The Lone Cypress.

in tall tales of barter and exploitation, of destruction and gritty survival. Each is a parable of adaptation, initiated by the upheaval of war. If Anglo development is about creating wealth, owning land, and controlling resources, Steinbeck's ne'er-do-wells survive by another pattern—adaptation, niche survival, and tribal bonding.

In *Tortilla Flat*, the region's sustainable economies are contained in the paisanos' ongoing efforts to finagle wine from the Italians or "in desperation," working "a whole day cleaning squids for Chin Kee" to make two dollars. Land use is a leitmotif in all three peninsula books. The paisanos of *Tortilla Flat* inherit houses. One burns down, and who then owns that land? (Mexican land rights were, in fact, contested by Anglos well into the twentieth century.) In *Cannery Row*, the wily Mack cuts a real estate deal at the beginning of the book—"renting" the Palace Flophouse from Lee Chong and then creating a decent life by nibbling on the peninsula's economic and ecological bounties. In the same novel, the Malloys stake out a vacant lot as their own, renting abandoned cannery pipes to the less fortunate and complaining as upward mobility bruises their contentment. In *Sweet Thursday*, the new owner of Lee Chong's Market, a streetwise Mexican from Los Angeles, moves to the peninsula for money and then is duped out of Palace House ownership by the equally manipulative Mack. The books can be read as ironic commentaries on documented histories of peninsula land use.

Tortilla Flat concludes with Danny's house burning: "Better that this symbol of holy friendship, this good house of parties and fights, of love and comfort, should die as Danny died, in one last

Hotel Del Monte burns in 1924.

"In 1936, Ed Ricketts's lab burned, and he escaped with only clothes and typewriter."

glorious, hopeless assault on the gods." Steinbeck's fictional fire mimics scores of peninsula conflagrations, many with special significance. In 1906, the Alones Point Chinese settlement burned down. In 1909, the Mammoth Stables in Pacific Grove, reputed to be the largest in the west, burned to the ground—as did the Hotel Del Monte in 1887 and the hotel's reconstructed main building in 1924. The original Pebble Beach Lodge burned in 1917. The Del Monte Bathhouse went up in flames in 1930. Ed Ricketts's lab was destroyed in 1936, one of many fires on Cannery Row. Fires suggest something about the peninsula's dynamism: Change is endemic here.

In 1930, Steinbeck and his wife Carol, newly arrived on the peninsula, watched the Del Monte Bathhouse burn:

> *There was a great fire last night. The Del Monte bathhouse burned to the ground. We got up and went to it and stood in the light and heat and gloried in the destruction. When Cato was shouting in the Roman Senate "Carthago delenda est," I wondered whether in his mind there was not a vision of the glorious fire it would make. Precious things make beautiful flames.*

In 1906, four-year-old John Steinbeck probably did not witness the conflagration that destroyed the Chinese settlement on Point Alones. Nor would he have understood the consequences of this fire for the Chinese in the area, dispersed or relocated to Monterey's McAbee Beach. But he probably saw the ashes, only a few blocks from his family's summer home. And he recognized the loss.

These fires are emblematic of something deep in Steinbeck's psyche— awareness of devastation and the need for adaptation. Many plant species depend on fire for their propagation. Fires favor the fringe dwellers, giving them a new foothold while in the same stroke making way for new development that will repeat the displacement cycle. Steinbeck located his peninsula novels within the flux of experience that fires represent.

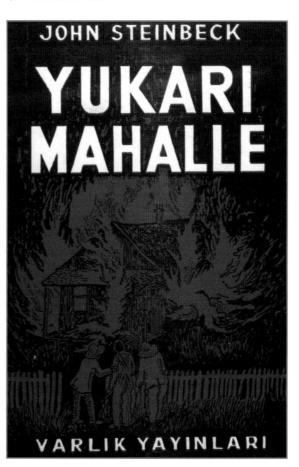

A 1951 Turkish edition of *Tortilla Flat*.

Chapter 6
Pacific Grove
The Writer's Retreat

Lighthouse Avenue, Pacific Grove, circa 1910–15.

Carol and John in the 1930s.

After months of living hand-to-mouth as newlyweds in Eagle Rock, John and Carol headed north to familiar Pacific Grove, where they would live from 1930 to 1936. Steinbeck's parents gave them twenty-five dollars a month and the family's three-room summer cottage that his father had built early in the century.

While Carol combed the peninsula for jobs, John wrote daily—determined, as he had been since he was a teenager, to find an audience for his prose. "I expect to give myself until I'm forty," he wrote a friend. "That will be twenty-five years of trying." In Carol, he found a woman who endorsed his steely determination. Throughout the Pacific Grove years, she was his ready companion, muse, editor, and typist. Theirs was a collaborative marriage, happy, stormy, and committed.

During the Great Depression, Pacific Grove was an ideal spot for an artist or a visionary. Founded as a Methodist retreat in 1875, the town was quiet, affordable, often surprisingly progressive, and dry—alcohol consumption was banned until 1969. Steinbeck needed solitude; he needed Carol to buffer him from the world; he needed a familiar setting, a tiny workroom, friends and family close by, a garden, and a dog. During the six years in Pacific Grove, Steinbeck went from being an unknown writer with one book to his name—*Cup of Gold*, which appeared in 1929 to scant reviews—to an accomplished author with five published works of fiction.

In Pacific Grove, John Steinbeck found his authorial voice. "I must have at least one book a year from now on if I can manage it," he wrote in 1930, shortly before moving to the family cottage. During the 1930s, he almost reached his target.

Pacific Grove Cottage, circa 1908.

"Such a nice little place. And once there were good times there."

The Writing Life

In their tiny house two blocks from Monterey Bay, John and Carol Steinbeck were as financially and ideologically detached from the Pacific Improvement Company and Hotel Del Monte revelers as Steinbeck had been from the growers of the Salinas Valley. During their Pacific Grove years, John and Carol were comrades, a team, themselves against the world. They were unconventional, plucky, and resolute. Both delighted in the unexpected: Once they took friend Ed Ricketts's iguana, strapped it to a roller skate, hooked a leash to the skate, and walked nonchalantly down Cannery Row. Like Ernest and Hadley Hemingway in 1920s Paris, John and Carol dressed alike, both in rough garb, pants, and slouchy jackets.

The two scraped by financially: "Sometimes I catch eels and sea trout and the Italian fishermen take us fishing in their boats," he wrote a friend. Sometimes, they launched their own skiff, *Yancy*, from Hopkins Marine Station beach, reeling in rockfish and salmon. And occasionally they got food from the welfare office—two cans of peaches, one pound of cheese, a can of corned beef—according to Carol.

Both loved their spacious backyard garden. With his father's help, John built a barbeque soon after the couple moved in. At a low point in 1931, starved for

Two Iconoclasts

Carol Henning Steinbeck shared her husband's bohemian tastes. Like Grampa and Granma Joad, John and Carol "fought over everything, and loved and needed the fighting." Carol was Steinbeck's unflinching lliterary critic—urging him to write about California, to write lucid prose (like that of Willa Cather, her favorite author), and later to become more politically engaged. She was creative—sketching a series of pink nude sportswomen and writing "feelty verse," as she told a reporter. She gave her self-published 1933, *A Slim Volume to End Slim Volumes*, to John for Christmas. Here is part of one of her caustic poems, modeled on Dorothy Parker's verse:

I Don't Like Mr. Hearst

Mr. Hearst has no soul
I hope he falls down into a hole
I wouldn't touch Mr. Hearst with a ten-foot pole.
He makes me sick. . . .

I've got no use for this cheap skater
I hope he breaks his neck on a potater,
And nobody finds it out until nine months later,
Or never.

From Carol's series on nude sportswomen.

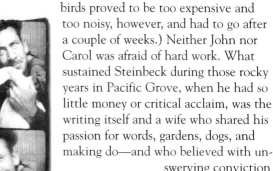

John and Carol with duck in photo booth.

Steinbeck in the 1930s.

amusement, John and Carol bought two ducks for the garden pond and named them Aqua and Vita. (The birds proved to be too expensive and too noisy, however, and had to go after a couple of weeks.) Neither John nor Carol was afraid of hard work. What sustained Steinbeck during those rocky years in Pacific Grove, when he had so little money or critical acclaim, was the writing itself and a wife who shared his passion for words, gardens, dogs, and making do—and who believed with un-swerving conviction in her husband's ultimate success.

Mythologist Joseph Campbell, who lived briefly on the peninsula in 1932 (and carried on an equally brief flirta-tion with Carol), thought Carol got a raw deal in this marriage contract: no children, a pre-occupied husband. But Carol was com-mitted to John. "Nothing mattered but John," she would say later, "I put all there was of me into his life."

Carol worked at odd jobs. In 1931, she and a friend researched, designed, and had printed the first directory of Carmel residents; in 1932, she worked as Ricketts's secretary; and later she worked at the Pacific Grove

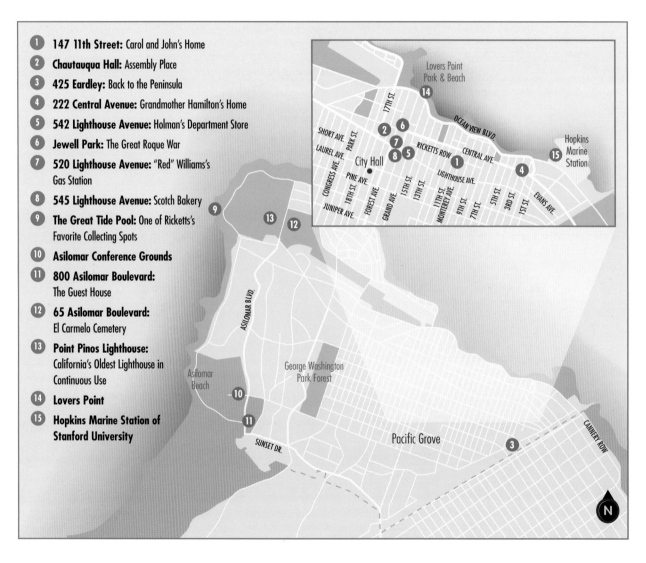

1. **147 11th Street:** Carol and John's Home
2. **Chautauqua Hall:** Assembly Place
3. **425 Eardley:** Back to the Peninsula
4. **222 Central Avenue:** Grandmother Hamilton's Home
5. **542 Lighthouse Avenue:** Holman's Department Store
6. **Jewell Park:** The Great Roque War
7. **520 Lighthouse Avenue:** "Red" Williams's Gas Station
8. **545 Lighthouse Avenue:** Scotch Bakery
9. **The Great Tide Pool:** One of Ricketts's Favorite Collecting Spots
10. **Asilomar Conference Grounds**
11. **800 Asilomar Boulevard:** The Guest House
12. **65 Asilomar Boulevard:** El Carmelo Cemetery
13. **Point Pinos Lighthouse:** California's Oldest Lighthouse in Continuous Use
14. **Lovers Point**
15. **Hopkins Marine Station of Stanford University**

Library and for State Employment Relief. For his part, Steinbeck wrote daily, usually until late afternoon. He mentally composed stories and wrote out clean copies rapidly, often in his father's used ledger books in order to save money on paper. The act of writing obsessed and haunted him, consumed and transformed him. As completely as was possible, he merged self with work. To write, he went into a trance of sorts—a "work dream" he called it in a 1948 ledger: "almost an unconscious state when one feels the story all over one's body and the details come flooding in like water and the story trudges by like many children." There is a physicality to his discussions of work that testify to its hold on him: "when there is no writing in progress, I feel like an uninhabited body," he wrote to one friend. Creative products became offspring. He described one work as a "literary foetus." Characters, he said, "are my own children." Writing books gave him "satisfaction . . . much like that of a father who sees his son succeed where he has failed." Letters repeat this refrain—books, not children, were his progeny, his destiny. Carol may well have wanted children—she probably was pregnant and had an abortion at some point in the 1930s—but she knew that he didn't and wouldn't.

Steinbeck's moods often blended with the foggy coastal weather, as he wrote a friend: "It is a gloomy day; low gray fog and a wet wind contribute to my own gloominess. Whether the fog has escaped from my soul like ectoplasm to envelop the peninsula, or whether it has seeped in through my nose and eyes to create the gloom, I don't know." Many of the stories he wrote during those first raw years in Pacific Grove (published in 1938 in *The Long Valley*) are about people living sheltered, often desperate, and lonely lives. Steinbeck, unhappy in his own fictional progress, struck tones of defeat and ostracism and rejection, emotions he knew so intimately. In Pacific Grove, this intensely private, unsettled young man, familiar with the demons of loneliness and despair, created fictions that reflect his own psychic complexity.

The loneliness of unsheathed self is one fictional chord struck by this burgeoning writer in his beloved Pacific Grove retreat. Home as a haven is another.

"I think flowers' colors are brighter here than any place on earth and I don't know whether it is the light that makes them seem so or whether they really are."

Inside 147 11th Street, where Steinbeck's sister Beth lived until the mid-1990s.

"The little Pacific Grove house is many things to me"

The unassuming red cottage at ❶ 147 11th Street, where John and Carol came to live in the fall of 1930, represents something at the core of Steinbeck's fictional vision. Simple living is part of his personal and fictional terrain. Throughout his life, he wrote about ordinary

John built the fireplace at the 11th Street house in 1930; the turtle is probably from the *Sea of Cortez* trip.

people; he, for the most part, had Spartan tastes. Even when fame came to him in the 1940s and 1950s and he moved east, he never purchased houses that flaunted wealth. His Sag Harbor, New York, summer home was an East Coast version of the 11th Street home, a tiny cottage surrounded by water. *Travels with Charley* is a narrative about his own traveling house—a compact and simple camper on top of a pickup truck that protected his anonymity as he drove across America. He wanted the same in 1930s Pacific Grove: "Must have anonymity. . . . Unless I can stand in a crowd without any self-consciousness and watch things from an uneditorialized point of view, I'm going to have a hell of a hard time," he wrote his agents in 1937. The Pacific Grove cottage sheltered his identity and his spirit.

"We went to PG and closed the little house for the duration of the war. Wish we could have stayed. It was so pleasant and quiet. I would have liked to just sink into it. The garden was so quiet and nice and the ocean just the same as always."

"The White Quail," a 1933 story, begins with a description of a view similar to that out of Steinbeck's Pacific Grove window: "small diamond panes set in lead. From the window . . . you could see across the garden." When the house was refurbished in 2017, the windows were replicated, and the structure is essentially the same as it was in the 1930s.

Steinbeck's Gardens

Steinbeck's lineage was in the soil. Grandfather Sam Hamilton, an inventor and blacksmith, became a rancher. Grandfather Steinbeck dried and shipped apricots and plums from his Hollister orchard. At age ninety, Grandmother Steinbeck was still making jams and jellies from their fruit. At the Pacific Grove cottage, Mr. Steinbeck cultivated vines and flowers in the yard as early as 1905 and worried often about the upkeep of the flowers in later years.

John Steinbeck carried the hoe, so to speak. At age three, he made a garden for Grandmother Steinbeck, "and planted me radishes and lettuce," wrote a delighted grandmother. He dug in the wet soil at Lake Tahoe in the mid-1920s and mailed his parents a box of scarlet snowflower sprouts, with detailed instructions for their propagation. His parents, in turn, sent him nasturtium seeds. And he shared with his father a warm connection to the Pacific Grove lot, the "wonderful" garden, "very wild and full of weeds and the flowers bloom among the weeds. I detest formal gardens." He would write about that garden often: "My garden is so lovely that I shall hate ever to leave it," he

Barbecue built by John and his father, now a planter. In the cement, John scrawled in Latin: "Johns, father and son, made this for the glory of the stomach."

wrote a friend in 1931. "I have turtles in the pond now and water grasses. You would love the yard. We have a vine house in back with ferns and tuberous begonias. We have a large cineraria bed in bloom and the whole yard is alive with nasturtiums."

The Town of Pacific Grove

Pacific Grove and Monterey sit side by side on a hill bordering the bay. The two towns touch shoulders but they are not alike. Whereas Monterey was founded a long time ago by foreigners, Indians and Spaniards and such, and the town grew up higgledy-piggledy without plan or purpose, Pacific Grove sprang full blown from the iron heart of a psycho-ideo-legal religion.

Few places in California could have better sustained this young writer than the conservative, neatly planned enclave of Pacific Grove—quiet, orderly, a "city of homes," declared promotional brochures, with

"saloonless streets." From its inception, Pacific Grove was the most subdued of the three peninsula towns, the starchiest, a place of "deep quiet," wrote Steinbeck. The location of Pacific Grove was "so healthy that doctors scarcely make a living," promised an 1875 pamphlet. Summer fogs keep Pacific Grove cool. It is a town perfect for a writer craving solitude.

The town's moral sensibilities were set by Methodists, who in 1875 announced plans to found a seaside retreat in Pacific Grove. The Pacific Grove Retreat Association formed an agreement with wily David Jacks for the "purchase, improvement and control" of 100 acres of beachside property. Lots were drawn out— thirty-by-sixty-foot "tenting lots"—to accommodate some four hundred people, and on August 9, 1876, the first camp meeting was held at the Grand Avenue open air temple, lasting three weeks.

To attract additional visitors, an Assembly and Summer School of Science was instituted in 1879 under the umbrella of the Chautauqua Literary and Scientific Circle. Summer residents from the hot Central Valley were promised a series of edifying lectures and courses. Across America, Chautauqua Circles were popular for nearly half a century, offering adult education for the masses. By the 1890s, more than fifty such summer assemblies could be found in the United States, five on the West Coast. "It took the whole intellectual product of the period, decanted and distributed it with sincerity and skill," wrote author Mary Austin in a 1926 issue of the *Carmel Cymbal*. She added, "There can be no doubt that a vast majority of Americans, particularly American women, sincerely suppose that 'culture' is generated in 'courses,' and proceeds as by nature from the lecture platform." Indeed, Austin's curt assessment has merit. But, for nearly fifty years in Pacific Grove, many families found the sea and intellectual dabbling a fine mix. A 1,500-seat

❷ Chautauqua Hall was built in 1881 and still stands. Here, attendees listened to lectures by ministers, scholars, and scientists or attended talks on cooking, music, and art. The 1892 session promised, for example,

Cover of 1892 Chautauqua program.

Steinbeck's Dogs

All his life, Steinbeck needed a garden and a dog, sources of emotional fulfillment. After all, without ambassador Charley, what spark would his travels have ignited? A dog was family. When he lived alone at Tahoe, he shared the cabin with Airedales Omar and Jerry.

When they were first married, John and Carol rented and fixed up a house in Eagle Rock and bought their first family dog, Bruga, a "Belgian shepherd puppy, pure black, which is going to

"Joggi, 14 months."

be a monster." A few months later, in May 1930, Bruga "died in convulsions which seemed to be the result of poison." Steinbeck wrote, "Carol is well but very much broken up about Bruga. She never had a dog of her own before and she had become horribly fond of the little wretch." Dogs were emotional outlets for both of them, sources of humor and despair. In Carol's 1930s scrapbooks, photos of dogs are carefully labeled. People are rarely identified.

An Airedale named Tillie replaced Bruga in 1931, and she had puppies, "as sinful a crew as ever ruined rugs. . . . At present they are out eating each other. . . . They are eating the fence now. The appetite of a puppy ranks with the Grand Canyon for pure stupendousness." Alas, Tillie got distemper, and Steinbeck—in a fit of odd temper himself—pulled out the dog's whiskers "to strengthen their growth." Tillie, "who had the most poignant capacity for interest and enjoyment in the world," lived only eighteen months with the Steinbecks and then died, leaving Steinbeck bereft: "I need a dog pretty badly," he wrote to his publisher a few weeks later. "I dreamed of dogs last night. They sat in a circle and looked at me and I wanted all of them." In *Tortilla Flat*, Pirate's dogs also sit in a circle and gaze at him with devotion. The dog Darling in *Cannery Row* is undoubtedly as spoiled as Steinbeck's many pooches were.

"It wasn't all fun and parties," Steinbeck wrote in an essay about the 1930s. "When my Airedale got sick, the veterinary said she could be cured and it would cost twenty-five dollars. We just couldn't raise it, and Tillie took about two weeks to die. If people sitting up with her and holding her head could have saved her, she would have got well. Things like that made us feel angry and helpless." Helplessness was always, for Steinbeck, leavened by a quirky humor that never failed him: he rounds this paragraph with a characteristic grace note: "When WPA came, we were delighted because it offered work. There were even writers' projects. I couldn't get on one, but a lot of very fine people did. I was given the project of taking a census of all the dogs on the Monterey Peninsula, their breeds, weight and characters." (That was not his job but it was Frances Whitaker's, who took a census of dogs and cats in Carmel for the WPA, a short-lived position.)

Steinbeck had to rewrite *Of Mice and Men*, the last book started in the Pacific Grove house, because a ravenous young Toby, their new puppy in early 1936, ate the first part of the manuscript. "John went completely berserk and had to be locked up," said friend Marjorie Lloyd. In a more temperate mood a few days later he wrote, "Minor tragedy stalked. I don't know whether I told you. My setter pup, left alone one night, made confetti of about half my ms. book. Two months work to do over again. It sets me back. There was no other draft. I was pretty mad but the poor little fellow may have been acting critically. I didn't want to ruin a good dog for a ms."

David Starr Jordan, then president of Stanford University, lecturing on the "Passion Play at Oberammergau" with stereopticon illustrations, as well as a "charming astronomical" lecture. A season pass that year cost three dollars, and daily tickets cost fifty cents. The Chautauqua was a profoundly egalitarian movement.

In 1880, David Jacks sold his ranchos, including the retreat land, to the Pacific Improvement Company, which had a greater interest in selling lots quickly than the Methodists had. Even after the Methodists lost

Tent cabins in Pacific Grove, circa 1882.

Pacific Grove houses today.

control of land sales, the retreat association continued to guard the Pacific Grove image zealously. It was one of the first gated communities in the state; the gates closed at 9:00 every evening. The governing body, "patriarchal and unique," according to the association, kept "without the borders of the town all disreputable, unruly and boisterous characters, and all unwholesome and demoralizing sports and pastimes."

Undoubtedly it was climate, location, and moral up-lift that drew the Steinbeck family to the town in the early twentieth century. Mr. Steinbeck's deed, like all in Pacific Grove, included a clause prohibiting the sale of liquor on the premises—a fact Steinbeck notes in *Sweet Thursday*. Well into the twentieth century, moral living was Pacific Grove's iron core, and it remained a "unique resort where culture, refinement, and morality are the prevailing attributes," as a 1928 pamphlet declared.

When Steinbeck moved to Pacific Grove in 1930, the hot local topics were paving and widening the streets and opening a road between Pacific Grove and Carmel, which became the Holman Highway. After forty years of business, Holman's Department Store was adding another story. The city council was trying to condemn the popular but decrepit bathhouse at Lovers Point (the city putting a value of $30,000 on the land, the owner $175,000). The paper noted regular lapses during Prohibition: "Abbott nabs brewery at Local ranch: Sheriff Seeks Salinas' 'Al Capone' With his Gang fellows." On the first page of the paper was a little column devoted to "brief items of things that make Pacific Grove a brighter and better place in which to live." On the second page ran a "Come to Church" section. In 1932, a front-page article sternly noted a man's twin lapses: "D. A. Florey of Pacific Grove, said to be a communist organizer, is in the Monterey county jail in Salinas today pending his hearing on charges of wifely non-support." It was a very small town.

The "city of homes" has remained just that—a pleasant community. The nineteenth-century sense of purpose, orderliness, and uplift is evident in contemporary Pacific Grove—streets numbered, the town in a grid, Victorian houses tidy, many still framed by board-and-batten construction. On little lots that once sold for fifty dollars, tiny houses—some tent structures later framed—have been restored, many decorated with monarch butterflies (Pacific Grove is "Butterfly Town USA") or strung with Chinese lanterns in mid-July.

John and Mary. A neighbor recalled, "A man came every summer and rented a donkey cart for 25 cents per hour. On 17th and 18th Streets. The block was all wooded at that time. Tents went up every summer."

Monarch Butterflies in Pacific Grove

Environmental awareness came early to Pacific Grove. The yearly migration of butterflies to trees off Lighthouse Road was sharply watched, and in 1938, a fine of $500 was imposed for harm to any butterfly. Beginning in October, butterflies from northern climes fly forty to fifty miles

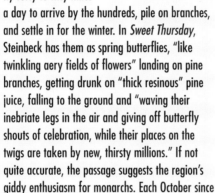

a day to arrive by the hundreds, pile on branches, and settle in for the winter. In *Sweet Thursday*, Steinbeck has them as spring butterflies, "like twinkling aery fields of flowers" landing on pine branches, getting drunk on "thick resinous" pine juice, falling to the ground and "waving their inebriate legs in the air and giving off butterfly shouts of celebration, while their places on the twigs are taken by new, thirsty millions." If not quite accurate, the passage suggests the region's giddy enthusiasm for monarchs. Each October since 1939 the town has hosted "Butterfly Days," with children parading down Lighthouse Avenue.

425 Eardley Street.

"City of Homes"

In time, Steinbeck would own two homes in Pacific Grove; Grandmother Hamilton briefly lived in another; and John stayed for a few weeks at his sister's cottage at Asilomar, writing *Sea of Cortez*. All of these homes still stand and are relatively unchanged. In a short drive around Pacific Grove, one can visit each little house—respecting, as Steinbeck fiercely guarded for himself, residents' privacy.

In 1941, shortly before their marriage ended, John and Carol purchased a small house with a large garden at ❸ 425 Eardley Street. This was an odd little house—haunted, John would claim—with a living room ceiling curved like a tent and carved birds perched around the ceiling. Rooms in the house were lined up like a freight train, his second wife Gwyn would complain. When he lived there, a Mexican bell hung at the gate. This house is the scene for what is, perhaps, Steinbeck's worst recorded moment, a man torn between two women—Carol, his wife of eleven years, and, Gwyn, whom he'd met shortly after publication of *The Grapes of Wrath*. When Gwyn came to visit in 1941, he left the two women alone in the house, saying on the way out that he couldn't decide between them, that "the one who feels she really wants me the most, gets me." Although Carol won that round—Gwyn left that day—Gwyn captured the man in the end. In April 1941, John and Carol separated.

The houses around Central and Lighthouse Avenues, the main streets in Pacific Grove, are little changed from Steinbeck's time.

Holman's Department Store, 542 Lighthouse Avenue, in 2005; the building has been transformed into luxury condominiums.

John's Grandmother Hamilton—Liza Hamilton in *East of Eden*—lived at ❹ 222 Central Avenue from 1914 to 1918. Steinbeck never lived here; however, Carol's sister and brother-in-law, Idell and Paul Budd, rented this house while Paul worked briefly at the Hopkins Marine Station. In 1936, Steinbeck and Paul built a small workroom for the house.

❺ Holman's Department Store, at 542 Lighthouse Avenue, was founded in 1891 and boasted forty-six departments when Steinbeck moved to the area: "Known far and wide as the biggest small town store in this part of the state," ads read. It had a grocerteria and a beauty shoppe and sold tires and home furnishings. Ritch Lovejoy, one of Steinbeck's friends, drew ads for Holman's. In 1932, Holman's sponsored a "sky skater," just like the one mentioned in *Cannery Row*. The sky skater is a "mysterious marvel who will thrill and entertain spectators," reported the local paper, "by gyrating on a tiny platform far above the top of Holman's department store." A Steinbeck fan wrote in the 1950s asking if his model for old Doctor Merrivale, who shoots at the skater with an air rifle in *Cannery Row*, might be a Fresno dentist who purchased an air rifle to shoot construction workers. Steinbeck answered,

No, I'm afraid it wasn't your man. The prototype of my man was Hudson Maxim, the inventor. When he grew old he took to renting rooms in London near the corner where Salvation Army bands took their station and shooting at the bass drum with a spring gun. Time after time he was apprehended and always promised to reform. But it was a vice with him and he couldn't give it up. It was a limited vice, however. He only shot at that one thing.

"The Great Roque War"—Chapter 8 of *Sweet Thursday*

Croquet courts on the grounds of the El Carmelo Hotel, 1890s.

There was no such war, with Greens squaring off against Blues, grumpy elders fiercely defending championship titles on Pacific Grove courts. "The old men got to carrying mallets tied to their wrists by thongs," writes Steinbeck, "like battle-axes." No, not quite. But as early as 1900 there were roque courts in Pacific Grove. And in 1932–33 there was a war, of sorts, called in local papers a "showdown fight" or a "battle which cheerfully blazed in the city hall." Battle lines were drawn after dedication of the splendid Pacific Grove Museum in December 1931. Donor Mrs. Lucie A. Chase, who had lived in Pacific Grove for twenty-nine years, thought it prudent to remove the unsightly roque courts in ❻ Jewell Park, across the street from the museum, when Central Avenue was being widened. The Ancient and Honorable Roque and Horseshoe Club of Pacific Grove, however, had other notions. They had long played their game in Jewell Park and they didn't opt for change. (Roque is a game much like croquet, but four balls are used, fired in succession, in a game lasting two–three hours.) "Why don't these men put their hands in their pockets and buy a cheap little lot for their court?" Mayor Platt suggested. A hostile councilman said they should stay home and play marbles. But in April 1933 the issue went up for a vote, and the town voted 1,220 to 295 to rebuild the courts in Jewell Park.

In the fall of 1927, John wrote to his family from the shores of Lake Tahoe, "Today I have been thinking constantly of Pacific Grove. The morning started it. There was a low lying mist which made the lake look just like Monterey Bay in the morning. And then I could not get away from thoughts of the cottage and the crabs caught with beef steak and of the sand pile, and how you used to drive us to the beach when we were cross and could not think of anything to do to take up our time. The thing prevailed nearly all day."

From 1934 to 1970, Everett "Red" Williams ran ❼ the Flying A service station, 520 Lighthouse Avenue, across Fountain Street from Holman's Department Store. Williams sold Steinbeck the "Hansen Sea Cow"—actually a Johnson Sea Horse—that he took with him on the 1940 *Sea of Cortez* trip.

"It was wartime and I didn't have a new motor to sell him but I had a used one that I said I'd lend him," Williams recalled. "That's the last I saw of it. It didn't run too good, and when they got down there it ran intermittently."

Steinbeck mentions ❽ the Scotch Bakery, which was at 545 Lighthouse Avenue, in *Cannery Row*, and he probably bought one of their old trucks to use when he went on research trips for *The Grapes of Wrath*. The sign "Scotch Bakery" was taken down in 2005, after a minor community struggle to keep it up failed.

The Great Tide Pool

One of Ed Ricketts's favorite collecting spots was ❾ the Great Tide Pool, located along Ocean View Avenue. In *Cannery Row*, chapter 6 begins,

Site of Red Williams's gas station, 520 Lighthouse Avenue, in 2005.

The Great Tide Pool.

Doc was collecting marine animals in the Great Tide Pool on the tip of the Peninsula. It is a fabulous place: when the tide is in, a wave-churned basin, creamy with foam, whipped by the combers that roll in from the whistling buoy on the reef. But when the tide goes out the little water world becomes quiet and lovely. The sea is very clear and the bottom becomes fantastic with hurrying, fighting, feeding, breeding animals.

In *Between Pacific Tides*, Ricketts describes hermit crabs as "pleasant and absurd" the "clowns of the tidepools"—quite similar to Steinbeck's description of his fictional ne'er-do-wells Mack and the boys, who "ooze" into the Palace Flophouse and make it their new home.

Asilomar

People stroll and dogs cavort on lovely Asilomar Beach. ❿ The Asilomar Conference Grounds, the "refuge by the sea," is across the road. Built in 1913

"Among themselves, when they are not busy scavenging or love-making," writes Ed Ricketts, "the gregarious 'hermits' fight with tireless enthusiasm tempered with caution. Despite the seeming viciousness of their battles, none, apparently, are [sic] ever injured. When the vanquished has been surprised or frightened into withdrawing his soft body from his shell, he is allowed to dart back into it, or at least to snap his hindquarters into the shell discarded by his conqueror."

as a YWCA conference center on land donated by the Pacific Improvement Company, Asilomar's stately lodge and campus were designed by Julia Morgan, acclaimed architect of Hearst Castle as well as seven hundred other buildings around California.

The state's first female architect, Morgan designed Asilomar in the Arts and Crafts style, using local materials and stressing harmony with the environment. Since 1956, Asilomar has been a state conference center, and rooms are also available to the public. Public wooden walkways wind through the dunes, which have been replanted with native grasses, "little trailing plants which slow up the pace of the walking dunes." In *Sweet Thursday*, Ed Ricketts meets the seer near Asilomar Beach (before the dunes were transformed into Spanish Bay resort): "In the dunes there are deep little creases where the wind-crouching pines have made a stand against the moving sand, and in one of these, only a hundred yards back from the beach, the seer had his home."

Set back in the woods at ⓫ 800 Asilomar Boulevard is a little house, now on Asilomar grounds, called the Guest Inn. In the spring of 1941, John Steinbeck, separated from his wife Carol, stayed at his sister Esther's "house in the woods in P.G.," as he called it. Here he wrote part of *Sea of Cortez*.

⓬ El Carmelo Cemetery, where Steinbeck's sister Esther is buried, is at 65 Asilomar Boulevard. This is the "pretty little cemetery where you can hear the waves drumming always" mentioned in *Cannery Row*. Ed Ricketts's funeral was held here in the Little Chapel

Asilomar State Beach.

by the Sea on May 12, 1948. (He is buried in El Encinal Cemetery in Monterey.) After the ceremony, the mourners walked to the Point Pinos Lighthouse, located on the northern tip of the peninsula.

Dating to 1855, ⓭ Point Pinos Lighthouse is the oldest continuously working lighthouse on the West Coast. The building, lenses, and prisms are all original. For Steinbeck's characters, the lighthouse is a somber, contemplative place. Several walk from Pacific Grove out to the lighthouse, among them the bouncer William in *Cannery Row*, sad and isolated. Suzy in *Sweet Thursday*, in love with Doc, "mooned away on the path that leads along the sea to the lighthouse on Point Pinos. She looked in the tide pools, and she picked a bunch of the tiny flowers that grow as close to the ocean as they can." In *Sweet Thursday*, Doc, working in his lab, hearing voices of loneliness, "would leave his work and walk out to the lighthouse to watch the white flail of light strike at the horizons."

Point Pinos Lighthouse.

Lovers Point

On any given summer weekend, a wedding is held at ⓮ **Lovers Point.** And who can blame couples for selecting this lovely spot? Some say it was named for its romantic associations, some for the "Lovers of Jesus" who came for outdoor meetings. At one time there was a Japanese tea garden here, serving cakes and tea, as well as lovely dahlia gardens (mentioned in *Cannery Row*). From the beach below, tourists could float in glass-bottom boats and gaze at intertidal life. In the 1930s, these boats were still "well patronized," noted the WPA guidebook.

Lovers Point, circa 1915.

The "Picturesque and Odoriferous" Chinese Fishing Village

The Chinese fishing village in the 1890s.

Chinese squid boats:
They go out at night and burn fagots attached to the sides of their boats. The squids are attracted by the light, and come to the surface and are fairly ladled up by the fishermen. The catches are brought ashore and skillfully and quickly cleaned and put out in large fields to dry. They are packed down in sacks by tramping them with the bare feet, and shipped to China as delicacies.

"Amazing people, the California Chinese," Steinbeck wrote after he left the state. Steinbeck's fictional tribute to the Chinese may be philosophic Lee in *East of Eden* or savvy Lee Chong in *Cannery Row* or perhaps the mysterious Chinaman in *Cannery Row* who shuffles to the sea at dusk, returns at dawn, regular as the tides. The Chinese fishing village figures in several of Steinbeck's recollections, this one in 1948:

The wind is ashore tonight and I can hear the sea lions and the surf and the whistling buoy and the bell buoy at Point Joe and China Point respectively. China Point is now called Cabrillo Point. Phooey—any fool knows it was China Point until certain foreigners became enamored of our almost non-existent history.

Today, Stanford University's Hopkins Marine Station stands where a Chinese fishing village once tipped toward the sea. Some fifty or sixty Chinese men and women came to this beach in the 1850s to harvest abalone. Later, they bleached and sold sea urchins and caught and dried squid. Drying and shipping squid proved to be the most lucrative enterprise, an industry that netted tidy profits at its height in 1930. During his years on the peninsula, Won Yee (Lee Chong in *Cannery Row*) became the local squid boss, his grocery a clearinghouse for all local fishermen. Drying squid, however, also created a much-noted unpopular odor. One late-nineteenth-century observer described the

Cabrillo may or may not have first sighted this point, but them [Chinese] raised hell on it for fifty years, yes, and even buried their people there until the meat fell off and they could ship them cheaper to China. Mary and I used to watch them dig up the skeletons and we stole the punks and paper flowers off the new graves too. I used to like that graveyard. It was so rocky that some of the bodies had to be slipped in almost horizontally under the big rocks.

And, in 1957, writing for the *Monterey Peninsula Herald*, he noted rather cynically that Cannery Row redevelopment might consider re-creating the "old old" on Cannery Row:

I remember it well, shacks built of scraps of wood, matting, pieces of tin. The district known as Chinatown, a street free of sewage disposal and very romantic. In it the Chinese kept alive the arts of gambling, prostitution, and the opium pipe. I remember the night the whole thing burned to the ground. We felt that a way of life was gone forever. The purchasers [of Cannery Row land] could re-create this pylon of the past with the help of Hollywood scene designers.

On the back of the photo is written, "The Chinese fishermen supplied Monterey with freshly caught fish—delivering them while still flapping in baskets slung over the shoulders with bamboo pole."

Hopkins Marine Station of Stanford University

With his lifelong passion for science, it's not surprising that Steinbeck had a close association with ⑮ the Hopkins Marine Station. John and his sister Mary attended summer classes here in 1923, both taking general zoology and English composition. Both Steinbeck and Ricketts knew Hopkins scientists. Director W. K. Fisher let John and Carol park their skiff *Yancy* overnight at the "no parking" zone and drop nets for fish.

Hopkins is nearly as old as Stanford University. Timothy Hopkins, treasurer of the Southern Pacific Railroad, was on the Stanford University Board of Trustees. A man of vision and scientific curiosity, he had "visited Dohrn's Marine Station at Naples," writes David Starr Jordan, the university's first president, "and was very much impressed." Hopkins and Jordan wanted a marine station for the newly formed Stanford University, where students could study marine zoology and botany. A site at Point Aulon—now Lovers Point —and $500 were donated by the Pacific Improvement Company; another $300 was given by the town of Pacific Grove; and an additional $1,000 was donated by Hopkins—who later gave more money for buildings, books, and equipment. The Hopkins Seaside Laboratory of Stanford University opened its doors officially in 1892 with thirteen students: "It proves a perfect paradise for the marine biologist," wrote a founding professor. Many women came to Hopkins in the early years, schoolteachers whose only avenue to biological study was the marine laboratory.

When the station moved to its present location in 1917, the remarkable Dr. W. K. Fisher became director, a post he held for twenty-six years. His ecological, holistic approach to marine biology was progressive, and it was perhaps this quality that drew both Steinbeck and Ricketts to the station and to the man in the 1920s and 1930s. Fisher wrote a statement in 1919 that heralds the station's ecological interests: "It is within the scope of a marine station to find out everything possible about the animals and plants of the ocean, as well as about the physical characteristics of the ocean itself. . . . One phase of the instruction at the station will cover the relation of all these facts to the welfare of man."

Certainly this would be the direction that Steinbeck's and Ricketts's ecological and holistic thought turned in the 1930s and 1940s. In 1919, Fisher suggested that the sardine population "bears a very definite relation" to plankton levels—another insight that would take decades for scientists and fishermen to fully appreciate. The Monterey Bay sardine, caught directly in front of the station, engaged Hopkins scientists who conducted a "little known research project," a local paper reported, and concluded in 1941 that sardines in the bay were decreasing in size.

In 1945, Steinbeck struck a deal with Hopkins's director and the president of Stanford, and in August,

First marine laboratory, 1890s.

Sea Otters

Sea otter mural, Pacific Grove bike trail.

For almost a century, the southern sea otter, slaughtered for its thick fur, was thought to be extinct. But in March 1938, a small herd, heretofore known only to locals, was reported in a Big Sur cove. Scientists at Hopkins Marine Station told local papers that only two other herds of sea otters were known to exist at that time: one in the Aleutians and one under Japanese protection in the Kurile Islands. Due to the remote location of the Big Sur coast, a few otters managed to survive centuries of slaughter—living on the fringe in a de facto refuge. Protected today by the Endangered Species Act, the otter population has recovered—in the bay and at Moss Landing—and the plump creatures can readily be seen floating, bellies to the sky, as they crack open an assortment of benthic invertebrates they place on their stomachs.

Steinbeck's agents, McIntosh & Otis, drafted an agreement: John would donate $6,000–$9,000 for a proposed John Steinbeck Aquarium on the Hopkins grounds, provided that the marine station would lease Ricketts, for one dollar a year, about a third of an acre for a new lab. The aquarium, Steinbeck wrote, would be "largely for scientific purposes (research and teaching) and secondarily for public attendance." Director Lawrence Blinks loved the idea and wrote the university president, "Quite aside from the aquarium aspect, Ricketts is a good scientific worker and his expeditions with Steinbeck will probably yield many valuable specimens for the Marine Station, so the tie-up would be desirable in any case." To fund his part of the deal, Ricketts had to sell his Cannery Row lab for at least $18,000 to finance the new lab building; apparently the cannery that had offered to buy his lab, acknowledging the end of sardine runs, backed out of the deal. Although the John Steinbeck Aquarium never came to be, the Monterey Bay Aquarium is modeled on Ricketts's ecological principles set forth in his groundbreaking 1939 work, *Between Pacific Tides*.

Today, the Hopkins Marine Station still funds holistic investigations into tuna, sharks, whales, and squid as well as interconnections among pelagic creatures and their environment, carrying on the work of Fisher and many other dedicated scientists.

Cannery Row today.

New Monterey is liminal space on the peninsula—not Spanish Monterey, not Methodist Pacific Grove, but the shoreline and sloping wooded hills between these places, where fishermen and immigrants established roots. It's a place between two communities with clearly demarcated boundaries and histories. In New Monterey, industries took hold, flourished, and vanished, only to be replaced by other ventures, much like waves of ecological succession in the rich waters just offshore. The Chinese dried squid in New Monterey. Sicilian fishermen came here. Beginning early in the twentieth century, canneries and reduction plants were built in New Monterey, and the area supported the region's lucrative sardine industry until the the late 1940s, when sardines disappeared. In 1945, John Steinbeck put this in-between land on the map, so that the fame of Cannery Row would eclipse that of all other peninsula locales.

Cannery Row in Monterey in California is a poem, a stink, a grating noise, a quality of light, a tone, a habit, a nostalgia, a dream. Cannery Row is the gathered and scattered, tin and iron and rust and splintered wood, chipped pavement and weedy lots and junk heaps, sardine canneries of corrugated iron, honky tonks, restaurants and whore houses, and little crowded groceries, and laboratories and flophouses.

Cannery Row made a hero of Doc, the novel's central character, who was, in life, Edward Flanders Ricketts, a marine biologist who operated a small marine biological lab in New Monterey. He was John Steinbeck's closest friend for eighteen years, and their friendship was essential to Steinbeck's thinking and his art. Beginning in 1930, when they met—either in a dentist's office (Steinbeck's version) or at a Carmel party (more likely)—Ricketts was a touchstone for Steinbeck. "Everyone found himself in Ed," Steinbeck wrote, and that everyone included Steinbeck himself. It was arguably the most vital connection of Steinbeck's life—fulfilling some deep

Ed Ricketts inside his lab, 1945.

collaborators. They discussed any and all subjects—the mathematics of music, observations of animal behavior, interpretations of modern art, the philosophy of Carl Jung. If Pacific Grove was Steinbeck's home and writerly retreat, the lab in New Monterey was where ideas were forged. In the little laboratory by the sea, John Steinbeck's mind moved outward. There one of the peninsula's most beloved residents, Edward Ricketts, and one of its most famous, John Steinbeck, forged perhaps the most unusual and significant collaborative relationship of the twentieth century. To map Ricketts's influence on Steinbeck and vice versa is to trace interweaving threads that bind together science, metaphysics, and holistic thought.

Edward F. Ricketts: A Scientist First

Ricketts made his life's work the intertidal zone. Born in 1897 in Chicago, he came west in 1923 with fellow marine biologist and business partner Albert E. Galigher. At the University of Chicago, both men had been students of Warder Clyde Allee, whose theory of "mutual interdependence or automatic cooperation among organisms" helped Ed formulate his own beliefs about cooperation, both in animals and in humans. Their life in the West began as a joint effort: Ed's wife, Anna, recalled that the men "decided that it would be best if the two families lived together on a share basis, sharing car, house and food. We could all benefit that way and put most of the monies into the firm"—a biological supplies lab in Pacific Grove. For a year, that mutual effort (all four collecting marine specimens) helped establish one of the first biological supply houses on the West Coast. The 1925 catalogue offered for sale marine creatures from microscopic organisms to rays, octopuses, hagfish, starfish, and jellyfish, as well as rats, frogs, and cats. But establishing a business was tough going, and in 1925 Galigher departed for Berkeley. For most of Ricketts's

psychic need more completely than any other relationship, including those with his three wives. In nearly every one of his novels, a male character offers to another male solace, wisdom, insight, and the "toto picture," to borrow a favorite phrase of Ed's. These men, always solitary but generally embedded in a social maelstrom, are intimate friends and mentors to Steinbeck's protagonists—characters Doc Burton, Jim Casy, Slim, Lee, and others. Their significance is relational, for the bonds forged are marked by honesty, commitment, companionship, even love. Male friendship is more deeply satisfying, more complex, and more significant than any other union in his fiction.

For eighteen years, Ricketts and Steinbeck were intellectual sparring partners, soul mates, and twenty-five-year career on the peninsula, his business bumped along, rarely prosperous though never insolvent, thanks in part to Steinbeck's significant investments and in part to Ed's own quirky business practices—leaving bills unopened, according to friends. But Ricketts cast a wide net of economic goodwill by paying local kids to collect eels (two cents), frogs (five cents), cats (twenty-five cents), and rattlesnakes (price varied). Ricketts was most certainly scientist first, businessman last.

If business practices were never Ed's forte, innovative thought about ecology was. Ecology is the science of connections between and among organisms and their environment. Ricketts's ecological sensibilities focused on interactions among invertebrates—"little beasties" was his phrase—in different intertidal habitats, a holistic viewpoint hardly appreciated by marine scientists in the

1930s. This ecological foundation led Ricketts to be a great generalist—he never specialized in any particular group of animals or specific subject like anatomy or physiology or embryology. Indeed, it's impossible to peruse Ricketts's papers (held at Stanford University, his letters collected in *The Renaissance Man of Cannery Row*, his essays in *Breaking Through*) and not be dazzled by the range of his scientific interests, the extensive scientific bibliographies he prepared, and the volume of his epistolary exchanges with other scientists. Ricketts read widely in scientific literature and observed the natural world with full "participation," a favorite word of both Ricketts and Steinbeck—meaning, for both, full engagement of the mind and senses, noting the interdependence of species.

Ricketts's range was broad. He considered ideas about "four levels of ecology." He wrote a textbook on

Edward Flanders Ricketts "had more fun than anyone I've ever known," wrote Steinbeck in 1951.

Ricketts's lab.

invertebrates, *Between Pacific Tides* (1939). He composed an essay on wave shock, noting that marine animals thrive in different intertidal zones. He planned a handbook on the intertidal life of San Francisco Bay (with Steinbeck in 1940), compiled the phyletic catalogue of invertebrates for *Sea of Cortez* (1941), and was planning a similar intertidal study of the "Outer Shores" of British Columbia the year he died (1948).

This breadth of marine interests was the scientific side of the holistic view of life that Ricketts cherished, one that guided his attempts to synthesize complex interconnected biological phenomena. He spent hours compiling data on fluctuating plankton levels measured in sea water—his own measurements as well as those from marine stations in La Jolla and the Aleutian Islands. He concluded in a 1947 letter to Joseph Campbell that there was "a primitive biological rhythm operative over the whole of the north Pacific." (He shared that insight with scientists at nearby Hopkins Marine Station, who, ten years earlier, had published findings on "a predictable rhythm in the changes in temperature of water in the bay.") Ricketts combined these observations with data on declining sardine populations of the 1940s in a series of newspaper articles that viewed the problem holistically as one involving changing ocean temperatures, plankton supplies, and overfishing. His prescient view continues to be one that marine scientists of today struggle to develop.

Much of Ricketts's scientific passion, some assert, is muted in Steinbeck's accounts of the affable but detached Doc in *Cannery Row*, *Sweet Thursday*, and "The Snake," a story set in the Cannery Row lab. The fictional Doc embalms cats, prepares invertebrate specimens, mounts developing starfish eggs on microscope slides at precise times, collects at low tide, and struggles with writing a

scientific paper. Ricketts himself did all these things. Although Ricketts didn't write with Steinbeck's fluidity, he tirelessly revised a series of essays on science and human psychology, working hard to articulate complex ideas—as does Doc in *Sweet Thursday*.

Between Pacific Tides

Ricketts produced his seminal work, *Between Pacific Tides*, coauthored by Jack Calvin, the same year that Steinbeck published *The Grapes of Wrath*, 1939. Published by Stanford University Press and now in its fifth edition, *Between Pacific Tides* is historically important and remains a valuable text on intertidal ecology. It was the first work to classify the sea life of the Pacific coast by specific zones of the intertidal environment, stressing interconnections among the different species that inhabited the "protected outer coast," the "open coast," and the "bay and estuary." To Ricketts, the important unifying theme was the community of organisms—how the different species interacted with each other, and how the specific habitat type determined the structure of its own community. This was a radical departure from the traditional approach of classifying organisms by taxonomic groupings, or phyla. Ricketts's handbook is practical, and easily readable by the nonscientist.

Frontispiece from *Between Pacific Tides*, second edition (1948).

Ricketts and Steinbeck: Water-Gazers

"I am a water fiend. I think that is why I need these fish bowls. Water is everything to me."

During the years that Steinbeck lived in his family's 11th Street house in Pacific Grove, (1930–36), he would usually work until late afternoon and then often walk two blocks down the hill toward the bay, turn right along Ocean View Avenue, and end up at Ed Ricketts's marine supply lab, snug against the sea on what was then simply "cannery row" in New Monterey. Walking this path allows one to feel the allure of water, to sense that humans are, as Herman Melville reminds us at the beginning of *Moby Dick*, essentially "water-gazers." For water-gazers, the sea suggests

John Steinbeck, circa 1938.

all that is elusive in human experience, what Melville calls "mystical vibrations." Steinbeck felt these vibrations. He had "a spiritual streak," said Elaine, his third wife. He was a water-gazer.

Certainly he loved living near the ocean. "I don't like Yosemite at all," he wrote his godmother in 1935. "Came out of there with a rush. I don't know what it was but I was miserable there. Much happier sailing on the bay." Friends say that young John, something of a loner, took long walks on the beach when his family came to Pacific Grove each summer. On a trip to New York City in 1937, reported his agent Elizabeth Otis, John and Carol "went up and down the escalator at a major department store, and every time he got to the sporting goods section he'd go over and touch a boat." When he moved permanently to New York in 1949, it took him only a few years to buy a house near the sea, in Sag Harbor. Even before he and Elaine moved in, he built himself a small boat, later bought bigger boats, and regularly sailed and fished in the estuary around his point of land. The sport of fishing, he wrote to Harry Guggenheim in 1966, "I consider the last of the truly civilized pursuits. Surely I find it a most restful thing. And if you don't bait the hook, even fish will not disturb you."

Undoubtedly much of his fishing time was spent water-gazing. "Modern sanity and religion are a curious delusion," he wrote in 1930. "Yesterday I went out in a fishing boat—out in the ocean. By looking over the side into the blue water, I could quite easily see the shell of the turtle who supports the world." An American Indian

Salinas mural of Indian creation myth.

Ricketts was talking about, think of the mystical moments in *Cannery Row*: the old Chinaman's eyes, the vision of the drowned girl in the La Jolla tide pool. In each passage, the reader is asked to comprehend experience beyond physical reality.

For both men, philosophic inquiry was as fundamental to the human condition as was investigative journalism or collecting marine animals. "Man is related to the whole thing, related inextricably to all reality, known as well as unknowable," Steinbeck writes in *Sea of Cortez*. To live fully, that book conveys, humans must look from "the tide pool to the stars and back again." It was not simply a theoretical position but a frame of mind that they shared throughout the 1930s—Steinbeck as both gritty realist and symbolist, Ricketts as marine biologist and philosopher.

creation myth was as real to Steinbeck as the water itself, as he moved easily from facts to symbols all his life. "Always prone to the metaphysical," Steinbeck wrote several months into his relationship with Ricketts, "I have headed more and more in that direction."

Ricketts was also a water-gazer, long intrigued by metaphysics, prone to the abstract. Walt Whitman had been his favorite poet since childhood—and there was much of Whitman's yeasty grounding and spiritual ache in him. Like Whitman, Ed was a spiritual nomad and sparked in all who came to the lab a yearning to "break through," one of his favorite notions, to mental fields beyond the physical. Ricketts was drawn to the "true things," in his words, an "alignment of 'acceptance' (= being) with 'breaking thru' (= becoming)." He found wholeness in Bach's music and in the poetry of William Blake, Walt Whitman, and Robinson Jeffers, all of whom embraced "not only the 'beauty' of ugliness, but the 'beauty' of beauty, even more important, the 'beauty' of the deadly desultory . . . the beauty of all things as vehicles for breaking through." To get a sense of what

At the Lab

In 1928, Ricketts moved his business and then gradually his home life to Cannery Row. If in the daytime scientific work got done at ❶ **Ricketts's lab,** at 800 **Cannery Row,** at night the space was given over to conversation and drinking. Ricketts's lab was New Monterey's salon, a tiny bohemian enclave of artists, writers, and musicians who were invited for parties and dinners or simply dropped by in the evenings to see what was happening. "There were great parties at the laboratory," Steinbeck recalled, "some of which went on for days." The group was committed to rollicking good times, companionship, intellectual sparring, and the *New Yorker*, a magazine that brought East Coast sophistication to the shores of the Pacific. What happened at the lab was the kind of relaxation and friendship that Steinbeck assigns to the paisanos in *Tortilla Flat* or Mack and the boys in *Cannery Row*. In Ed's presence people became the best of themselves, if tales told are true. And leavening it all was always the commitment to a good time: "People who are concerned with 'the eternal verities,'" Ed wrote, "would do well to remember that fun is one of them."

The real Ed and the fictional Doc are conflated in nearly everyone's mind, and what emerges is a nearly legendary figure who embraced in life and embodied in fiction acceptance, relaxation, camaraderie, and conversation. "Everyone near him was influenced by him," Steinbeck writes in a long essay about his friend, "About Ed Ricketts," "deeply and permanently. Some he taught how to think, others how to see or hear." Rolf Bolin, director of the Hopkins Marine Station in the 1940s, said, "I went over there for the purpose of feeling better." Ed would listen with great sensitivity and compassion. He would play liturgical music. Before the lab burned in 1936 (rebuilt on the same spot), his walls were covered in charts that traced the history of world music, art, and history.

On April 24, 1948, Steinbeck wrote in his journal that he felt close to "some kind of release of the spirit. I don't know how this is going to happen. I just know it is so. Maybe through the book maybe through sorrow or pain or something. Anyway it is near and I must be ready for it." On May 5, he wrote, "No word from Ed. I have a feeling that something is wrong with him." Three days later, Ed Ricketts was struck by a train as he drove across the tracks at Drake Avenue and Cannery Row (now marked by a bust of Ricketts). Having eerily anticipated the loss, Steinbeck was numb. After Ricketts's funeral, he wrote to Ritch and Tal Lovejoy, "Wouldn't it be interesting if Ed *was* us and that now there wasn't any such thing or that he created out of his own mind something that went away with him. I've wondered a lot about that. How much was Ed and how much was me and which was which."

In January 1949, John destroyed many of Ed's letters and notebooks. He then spent the better part of the next six years laying to rest the ghost of Ricketts and the siren call of his own past—in *East of Eden* (there is much of Ricketts in Lee); in the marvelous essay "About Ed Ricketts," the preface to the *Log from the Sea of Cortez*, published in 1951; and in the wacky novel *Sweet Thursday* (1954).

Ricketts's spirit endured in Monterey as well. In 1956, another group took over the space that had sheltered Ed. For more than fifty years, the "lab group" held weekly stag parties at Ed's lab on Wednesday nights. These businessmen, lawyers, and artists helped found the Monterey Jazz Festival. In

Ed Ricketts inside the lab, 1948.

Joseph Campbell at the Lab

One year, 1932, clarifies the vital importance of metaphysical speculation at the lab. Early that year a footloose young Joseph Campbell—later in life a famed mythologist—came to the peninsula at the suggestion of Carol Steinbeck's sister, Idell, and spent several months in the company of Ricketts and Steinbeck. It would be a seminal year, "our year of crazy beginnings," recalled Campbell in a 1939 letter to Ricketts. Campbell reflected on the significance of their interaction: "Since my last letter I have been pushing slowly forward, as through a swamp, toward that great synthesizing middle-point which we all glimpsed those days of the great intuitions." Those days included nights, when the group would gather at the lab, Ricketts wrestling with the notion of breaking through physical sensations to some greater truth; Steinbeck revising *To a God Unknown*, his pantheistic novel; and Campbell seeking a "synthesis of Spengler and Jung. . . . Joyce's new work *Finnegans Wake* is the closest thing I have found to a complete resolution of the problem." The problem, for Campbell, was to trace underlying cultural patterns, the "hero with a thousand faces."

The prevailing ideals were to defy conventional thinking, to find meaning in music and nature and spirituality and philosophy, to sift for unity, to see the "whole picture," as Ed termed it. For Ricketts, the "problem" of unity was resolved by a group of writers and philosophers he called "Extra-humanists, the breaking-thru gang: Whitman, Nietzsche, Jeffers, Jung, Krishnamurti, Stevenson . . . Emerson's oversoul. James Stephens knew it. Conrad Youth and Heart of Darkness. Steinbeck To a God Unknown, and In Dubious Battle." All were willing to grasp a sense of the whole. "You and your life-way," Campbell wrote Ricketts, "stand close to the source of [my] enlightenment." "Enlightenment" is not a bad word to describe what happened to all three of them in 1932, water-gazers all.

Yet, what might have been a historical triad was disrupted by affairs of the heart. Campbell fancied Steinbeck's feisty wife Carol. Carol fancied Campbell. John, tormented, went off into the Sierra Nevadas—departing to excite "profound pity," thought a disgusted Campbell (whose "job" it was to "disappear," as he and Carol had agreed, although the two continued to write one another). Campbell joined Ricketts on a collecting trip in British Columbia and up to Sitka, Alaska.

Years later, Steinbeck exacted his gentle revenge, apparently casting Campbell as the effete and pretentious Joe Elegant in *Sweet Thursday*, a writer who explains to brothel owner Fauna "the myth and the symbol" of his book and the "reality below reality." She isn't impressed: "Listen, Joe, whyn't you write a story about something real?"

Joseph Campbell (second from right) joined Ed Ricketts (center) on a collecting trip to Sitka, Alaska, in 1932.

1993, the group ensured the small building's future when they deeded it to the City of Monterey for a California pittance, $170,000. Although the building has hardly changed since 1936, the city has long struggled with the problem of how to preserve this fragile wood structure. The city opens the lab to the public once a month, and the Cannery Row Foundation also gives themed tours of the lab.

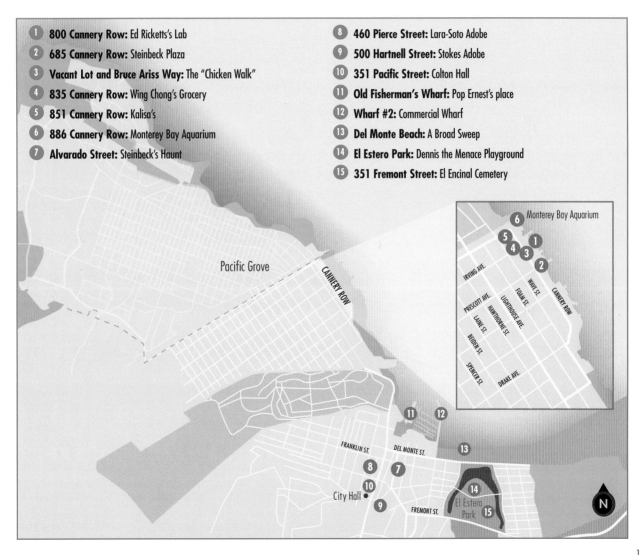

1. **800 Cannery Row:** Ed Ricketts's Lab
2. **685 Cannery Row:** Steinbeck Plaza
3. **Vacant Lot and Bruce Ariss Way:** The "Chicken Walk"
4. **835 Cannery Row:** Wing Chong's Grocery
5. **851 Cannery Row:** Kalisa's
6. **886 Cannery Row:** Monterey Bay Aquarium
7. **Alvarado Street:** Steinbeck's Haunt
8. **460 Pierce Street:** Lara-Soto Adobe
9. **500 Hartnell Street:** Stokes Adobe
10. **351 Pacific Street:** Colton Hall
11. **Old Fisherman's Wharf:** Pop Ernest's place
12. **Wharf #2:** Commercial Wharf
13. **Del Monte Beach:** A Broad Sweep
14. **El Estero Park:** Dennis the Menace Playground
15. **351 Fremont Street:** El Encinal Cemetery

The Sardine Industry

For more than forty years, the eight- to ten-inch Monterey Bay sardine, packed six to eight to an oval can in oil or tomato sauce, gave life to Monterey's cannery row. Each night during the season, from mid-August to mid-February, fishermen went out in boats—first lamparas, and by 1926, purse seiners—to scoop up tons of sardines and dump their catches in hoppers a hundred yards out in the bay. From the hoppers, the sardines were sucked into the canneries through underwater pipes.

In the early twentieth century demand for fish came from the East, Europe, and Asia, and fresh fish could not be shipped that far. Only drying—the Chinese method—and canning—the American method—could ensure solid profits.

The abundant sardine promised a reliable source of revenue, so after an early salmon cannery closed, sardine canneries were built on Monterey's shores. Initially, fish offal was tossed into the bay, until the Chinese taught cannery owners that this too was a valuable resource. The first fish reduction plant was built in 1915, processing not only offal but whole fish into the much more lucrative fish oil and fish meal—fed to chickens, cows, and pigs.

Sicilian, Italian, and Portuguese men fished, and their wives and daughters packed, making about thirty-three cents an hour at cannery work until unions came in 1936 and wages rose. Conditions in the canneries were rugged—smelly and cold, workers sometimes standing in water up to their knees—but far from oppressive. Only women worked the lines. One of the biggest problems these women reported was daycare. They had to report for work whenever full boats came in after a night of fishing—large canneries owned a couple of boats and leased several more for the season. Whistle codes announced the start of the workday—at 3:00 a.m., 4:00 a.m., and 5:00 a.m. What to do with sleeping children if you were a cutter, called to work first, or a packer, allowed to arrive a little later, perhaps at 8:00 in the morning?

Women in the canneries, 1930s.

A Fitting Tribute?

Midway along Cannery Row at ❷ Steinbeck Plaza, a bust of John Steinbeck stands near the sidewalk. A story about that bust explains much about Steinbeck's relationship with his first wife, Carol Henning Steinbeck.

Unveiled in February 1973, the bust is signed "Carol Brown, Sculptress." The identifying label is perhaps meant to distinguish between artist Carol Brown and her sister-in-law, Carol Steinbeck Brown. Married to brothers, both Carols lived in Monterey in the early 1970s. John's former wife loved ceramics and, noted the sculptress, "that's how we became interested in the bust. I don't remember whose idea it was." When work on the Steinbeck bust began, Carol Steinbeck Brown brought her sister-in-law lots of photos of John and scraps of paper with notes John had written. Together they went over memorabilia. Even though she harbored ill will toward her former husband, Carol wanted to make sure this bust was a true likeness. As the sculptress worked, every couple of weeks Carol Steinbeck Brown would visit, telling the artist to "Make his head bigger" and then swearing at the bust, venting her anger at the man who had left her for a much younger woman. Carol's visits unsettled the artist. Indeed, the first bust "collapsed because she said to make it so big." When the project finally neared completion, Carol Steinbeck Brown considered the bust a collaborative effort and wanted recognition, her own name listed with the artist's under the final work of art. She felt "so confident in editing or interpreting," said the artist. "She felt she collaborated with John in the sense that she was secure in being a critic." But neither John nor her artist sister-in-law gave Carol the recognition she craved. The artist signed only her own name to the bust. According to the sculptress, Carol Steinbeck Brown felt a "sense of being left out. She had collaborated with me on the bust and I had failed her. She had collaborated with John and he failed her."

Flora Woods: Monterey's Notorious Madam

Stately Flora Woods appears in Steinbeck's novels as Fauna in *Sweet Thursday* and Dora Flood in *Cannery Row*, "a great woman, a great big woman with flaming orange hair and a taste for Nile green evening dresses." Some have said that Steinbeck sentimentalized prostitution, created stereotypical whores with hearts of gold. But Flora Woods was, in life and art, the Ethel Merman of Monterey, cutting a wide swath.

During her three decades as madame, Flora owned several brothels on the peninsula. The Quick Lunch opened in 1917 and offered patrons a hearty lunch and a roll in the sack. (Steinbeck was surely thinking of this establishment when he wrote about Rosa and Maria's restaurant in *The Pastures of Heaven*.) Flora's other houses included the Golden Stairs and one located near the baseball park, which competed "for

the attention and patronage of youth." Flora's most infamous establishment was the Lone Star Café, Steinbeck's Bear Flag, across the street from Ricketts's lab (the original building was torn down).

"Notorious" Flora made the news regularly throughout the 1930s. When fire destroyed Ricketts's lab in 1936, the front page of the *Monterey Peninsula Herald* ran both a large photo of the burning lab (Ricketts lost everything) and a small column: "Firemen save Flora Woods."

Others were less eager to save her properties. In the mid-1930s, a local judge launched a campaign to wipe out Monterey County prostitution and Chinese gambling houses, most of which were in Salinas and Monterey. "Can Monterey Find an Honest and Sensible Way to Regulate Prostitution?" queried the *Monterey Trader* on January 17, 1936. "The state law bans prostitution . . . but the public puts up with various compromises," particularly in Monterey, where "a lax and apathetic public," the article complained, "has handed control of municipal affairs over to a 'wideopen town' majority" and thus the problem "gets out of hand." The state of things made it "possible for Flora Woods to run her business to suit herself and to dictate to the public, or rather to the public's officers, just where and how she will operate. And inasmuch as Madame Woods gets away with it, the increasing smaller fry follow suit."

Flora's Girls, a mural once on Cannery Row, by Eldon Dedini.

She seems to have gotten away with quite a bit. Bowing to public pressure in 1936, she did close her ballpark location—but one suspects that deals were struck, allowing the Lone Star to stay open. In 1942, all brothels were closed by the army. Ricketts wrote to Sparky Enea, the cook on the *Sea of Cortez* trip, about the "sad story of the Lone Star. Everything was moved out, including of course all the beds—and boy were there a lot of them! The front of the building was torn off, and now the place is being used to store fish meal. What a fate!"

A Steinbeck Theater?

In 1959, the city of Monterey proposed that the theater on Cannery Row be named the Steinbeck Theater. He wrote back,

> Your suggestion . . . is of course flattering. I can only warn you that my own success in the theater has not been all rosy. You may be taking on a jinx. Having one's name on an institution smells slightly of the epitaph and I can only assure you, but perhaps not prove, that I am not dead, certain pronouncements of critics to the contrary. . . .

> I could not stop you from using my name if I wished, since it is probably in the public domain. Would it be out of order in view of our long association, and because he was one of the greatest humans I ever knew, that Ed Ricketts' name be substituted for mine, or if because his name is not yet as widely known as it deserves, that our names be used together?

> Rodgers and Hammerstein, Buck and Bubbles, Mike and Ike, Mr. Gallagher and Mr. Shean, Cohn and Schine, Aucassin and Nicolette, corned beef and cabbage—these seem not to suffer from a duality. If your projected theater could be named the Ricketts and Steinbeck, any reservations of mine, self-conscious or sentimental, would instantly disappear, and a name that deserves remembering could be at least proposed. Thank you for the compliment. Could you, however, among the cultural clutter, sometimes put a little gut-bucket in the theater? I would feel safer if Pee Wee Russell has some small niche in the world of Bach and Rene Clair.

The theater did open, and Barnaby Conrad's film *Flight*, based on Steinbeck's short story, had its world premiere there.

Cannery Row

In *Cannery Row*, John Steinbeck devotes about a page to the canning industry. Steinbeck's terrain is not commercial Cannery Row but after-hours Cannery Row, when the habitat "became itself again," quiet and magical. In the half-light of sunset or dawn, "the hour of pearl," the little enclave is, for Steinbeck, a human tide pool. His characters are "specimens." The book traces little fragmented histories of Monterey denizens and shows how a community forges bonds on a frog hunt or at a raucous party. Steinbeck enigmatically remarked that *Cannery Row* was written on four levels, levels that book critics missed. Perhaps his four levels parallel Ricketts's own ideas about four approaches to the study of ecological complexity: first, name and characterize the species present in a particular habitat; second, determine community interactions; third, consider the complex life histories of each species; and fourth, recognize a "niche concept" by which similar invertebrate communities are found in widely different geographical areas.

Hauling sardines, circa 1940.

119

Steinbeck's dedication of the novel ("For Ed Ricketts who knows why or should") says it all.

Cannery Row also maps Steinbeck's memories. Stand in front of the lab, book in hand, facing the street, and read the opening paragraphs of chapters 3 and 5 to look at Cannery Row through Ricketts's eyes, sharing his vista— "participating" fully, as Steinbeck wants his readers to do in this little novel. Today that may seem impossible in a Cannery Row that is chockablock with restaurants, T-shirt shops, and bars. Many feel that Steinbeck's and Ricketts's spirits have evaporated in the zeal for commercial development. Indeed, when Steinbeck came through the area in the 1960s, long before Cannery Row became a tourist mecca, he was glum at changes made—as most of us are when returning to places of the heart, enclaves of the spirit, spaces lost to time. But an aura lingers.

"Chicken walk" on Cannery Row, 1945.

Other Cannery Row Sites

Next to the building that was once the Lone Star brothel is Cannery Row's "vacant lot," once full of abandoned pipes, where Mack and the boys took the "chicken walk" up the hill.

The walk is now paved and renamed ❸ Bruce Ariss Way, and the lot is home to three little fishermen's houses—moved here in the mid-1990s—each furnished to reflect workers' ethnic diversity. Ariss was a local artist, editor, friend of Steinbeck and Ricketts, and, for more than sixty years, a legend in the community. A 1989 mural panel (one of several painted by local artists to hide a Cannery Row construction site) was

The Wing Chong grocery.

Writing about Cannery Row

Typically, Steinbeck did not revisit old work. The exception is the Cannery Row material, stories that engaged him for more than fifteen years, from 1938, when he had in mind a "magnificent story about Monterey," to 1955, when he finally got the whole of that story out of his head.

After finishing *The Grapes of Wrath*, he started and then abandoned a satiric play he thought "might be fun," "The God in the Pipes." It tells of a man leaving Salinas—where the "people [are] so wise naturally that they need never read nor study"—to consult a Monterey prophet, the "Boss" living in a cannery pipe. Steinbeck was airing some of his rancor toward Salinas.

He wrote *Cannery Row* in 1944, immediately after he returned to the United States after a 1943 stint overseas as a war correspondent. Nostalgia for what he'd left behind found its way into *Cannery Row*, a complex little book about the bums and whores, the flotsam and jetsam edging in around Doc's marine laboratory. It is one of his best novels, a must-read for anyone visiting the peninsula and anyone wishing to understand Steinbeck's and Ricketts's holistic vision.

The book and its hero, Doc, were beloved by many. In 1947, Burgess Meredith wanted to work with Steinbeck on a play or film of *Cannery Row*, with Meredith as the charismatic Doc and with, he said, "Humphrey Bogart standing by." In 1948, Steinbeck came to California to scout locations for a film of *Cannery Row*. He thought about an opera. In 1953, he started work on a libretto for a musical based on *Cannery Row*.

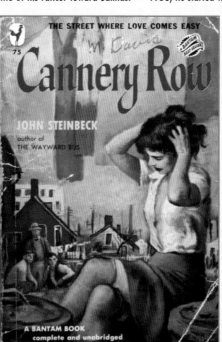

He ended up with a consciously extravagant novel, *Sweet Thursday* (1954), intended for the musical theater. Rodgers and Hammerstein used this novel for one of their only musical missteps, the rarely performed *Pipe Dream* (1955).

Whimsical *Sweet Thursday* is Steinbeck's swan song to California. It lacks the heft of *Cannery Row*, consciously so. Steinbeck's last California novel is a wry and frothy creation: "The playful sun picked up the doings of Cannery Row, pushed them through the pinhole, turned them upside down, and projected them in full color on the wall of Fauna's bedroom." Anyone picking up the novel should keep that perspective in mind. It's a cockeyed book, maybe a fictional wake as well. In it Steinbeck scatters the ashes of his best friend, writing Ricketts into a crazy little love story, and then sending him and his girl into the setting sun that shines briefly on Doc's "laughing face, his gay and eager face."

moved here, and another one of his paintings of 1930s Cannery Row is at the group entrance to the aquarium.

The two-story building at ❹ 835 Cannery Row once housed the Wing Chong, or "glorious, successful," grocery, which opened on November 16, 1918. Five years earlier, Won Yee had immigrated to America, where he saved money and moved to Monterey to open his market, one of about a dozen Chinese residences or businesses along a two-block stretch of Cannery Row. In *Cannery Row* he is Lee Chong, whose

The Queen of Cannery Row, Kalisa Moore.

"position in the community surprised him as much as he could be surprised," writes Steinbeck—perhaps a wry comment. In the back of his store, the real Won Yee ran gambling tables and sold bootleg liquor during Prohibition and opium at other times. If police raided, patrons escaped through a tunnel that came out behind the Hovden warehouse.

Cannery Row Development: Steinbeck's Advice

Asked in 1957 by the *Monterey Peninsula Herald* what his advice for development of Cannery Row would be, Steinbeck noted with playful exaggeration that developers could consider several possibilities: one solution might be to re-create the "new-old" of the cannery days:

> A number of these buildings still stand. The purchasers might keep them as national monuments. Their tendency to rust could be halted by spraying them with plastics. Maintenance of this reminder of our historic past would, however, require that the rocks and beaches be stocked with artificial fish guts and scales. Reproducing the billions of flies that once added beauty to the scene would be difficult and costly.

> But with strides in chemistry and with wind machines, the odor of rotting fish and the indescribable smell of fish meal could be wafted over the town on feast days. Perhaps this era should be kept as a monument to American know-how. For it was this forward-looking intelligence which killed all the fish, cut all the timber, thereby lowering the rainfall.

His honest solution was far better:

> I suggest that these creators be allowed to look at the lovely coastline, and to design something new in the world, but something that will add to the exciting beauty rather than cancel it out. . . . Then tourists would not come to see a celebration of a history that never happened, an imitation of limitations, but rather a speculation on the future.

Perhaps his vision was realized in the Monterey Bay Aquarium.

In a 1953 interview, members of the Yee family, who continued to run the store until 1954 (and still own the building), were asked what question was most often put to them by tourists. Their answer: queries about Steinbeck's Old Tennis Shoes whiskey. "We could have made a fortune if there had been a brand of whiskey named Old Tennis Shoes," said Frances Yee.

Next to Lee Chong's, at ❺ 851 Cannery Row, there was once a brothel, Steinbeck's "La Ida's" and in fact La Ida Cafe. Later it became Kalisa's La Ida Cafe, a half-century restaurant business operated by "the Queen of Cannery Row," Kalisa Moore. She met Steinbeck when he came through the area in 1960 on his trip with Charley and is memorialized with a bronze bust by Jesse Corsaut on Bruce Ariss Way.

The Monterey Bay Aquarium, 886 Cannery Row.

Matchbook cover.

The modern anchor of Cannery Row is ❻ the Monterey Bay Aquarium, located at 886 Cannery Row. On this site was the Hovden Cannery, one of the first canneries to open and the last to cease operation, in 1973. With a ten-boat fleet in the halcyon years of the sardine industry in the late 1930s and early 1940s, it was one of the largest of the area's sixteen canneries. Stanford University bought the site—to prevent a luxury hotel from going up across from Hopkins Marine Station—and later sold it to the Packard Foundation for the aquarium that the Foundation funded, and which opened in 1984. Cannery history is eloquently and briefly told near the entrance (a free exhibit), and the aquarium itself is a fabulous place, exhibiting marine life of Monterey Bay and beyond.

Past the aquarium, along the bike and walking path that parallels Ocean View Avenue (and covers the tracks of the old Del Monte Express), the sweep of the bay overwhelms any strolling visitor. Walk here and you may become a water-gazer.

Alvarado Street at Franklin, circa 1946.

holes have been replaced by the Monterey Plaza Hotel. The Keg, Johnny Garcia's place, draws Steinbeck for a mournful drink in *Travels with Charley*. In 1940, he wrote part of *Sea of Cortez* from an office above the Wells Fargo Bank at 399 Alvarado Street. Before Doc leaves town on a collecting trip in *Cannery Row*, he stops to eat at Hermann's, at 380 Alvarado, a burger joint that was open twenty-four hours a day, seven days a week. Doc orders a hamburger (fifteen cents) and a beer (ten cents) and thinks about what a beer milkshake might taste like.

Steinbeck briefly owned one of Monterey's adobes, ❽ the Lara-Soto Adobe at 460 Pierce Street. In 1945, the year *Cannery Row* was published, Steinbeck brought his second wife, Gwyn, and baby Thom to live here. He wrote *The Pearl* in the back garden. Steinbeck wrote to his editor, Pat Covici, on October 24, 1944:

Steinbeck's Monterey

Several spots in Monterey retain the Steinbeck mark, and one way to see the town Steinbeck haunted is to take a walk on the "Path of History," as indicated on maps available at the Monterey Chamber of Commerce offices in Custom House Plaza and insets in the sidewalks. The Monterey Old Town Historic District was declared a National Historic Landmark in 1970.

Most of Steinbeck's ❼ Alvarado Street watering

Evelyn McCormick, "Casa Jesus Soto," circa 1920. By 1944, when Steinbeck purchased the house, it was the Lara-Soto Adobe.

We bought a house in Monterey. You may think this precipitate but it is a house I have wanted since I was a little kid. It is one of the oldest and nicest adobes in town—with a huge garden—two blocks from the main street and yet unpaved and no traffic. Four blocks from the piers. It was built in the late thirties before the gold rush and is in perfect shape . . . it is a laughing house.

❾ The Adobe at **500 Hartnell Street,** behind the Monterey Public Library, was once the home of Hattie Gragg. Steinbeck loved talking to longtime residents of any community where he lived, and Hattie, one of the oldest in Monterey, loved telling him stories. She told him the true story about Josh Billings, California humorist, who died at the Hotel Del Monte—her narrative became a chapter in *Cannery Row.* Dr. J. P. Heintz from Luxembourg had an office near Hattie's, as Steinbeck describes: "Where the new post office is, there used to be a deep gulch with water flowing in it and a little foot bridge over it. On one side of the gulch was a fine old adobe and on the other the house of the doctor who handled all the sickness, birth, and death in the town."

Across the street from the Monterey Public Library, at **❿ 351 Pacific Street** (with its fine Monterey history archive housed in the California Room), is **Colton Hall,** where California's first constitution was debated in 1848. Adjacent to Colton Hall is the old Monterey Jail, where Danny in *Tortilla Flat* languished for a month, smashing bedbugs on the wall.

⓫ Old Fisherman's Wharf, off Del Monte Boulevard, is a good place to stroll, listen to sea lions, and eat fried Monterey squid (a splendid snack) or clam chowder (samples along the wharf). Take a whale watching cruise to see humpbacks and blues, dolphins and seabirds. Here "Pop" Ernest Doelter taught American diners how to eat abalone. He pounded the tough muscle into steaks for his restaurant on the Monterey wharf (and at the 1915 Pan Pacific Exposition in San Francisco). Suzy and Doc eat there in *Sweet Thursday* ("Pop" is Sonny Boy). A menu from about 1932 notes, "Nectar of Abalone" for twenty-five cents and "All fish (fresh daily) for $.50." Lobsters were fifty cents, seventy-five cents, and one dollar.

⓬ Wharf #2 is the commercial wharf, where commercial fishing boats still unload their catches. Close to the end of the pier are two unloading stations

Pop Ernest's menu.

Cannery Row: Fact or Fiction?

When *Cannery Row* was published in 1945, Steinbeck's friend Ritch Lovejoy wrote a review of the book for the *Monterey Herald,* claiming in his headline that "Cannery Row is Monterey's." "It may be that the dreamlike quality of Steinbeck's writing, although vivid, just cannot strike even the remotest chord of reality in the mind of a city dweller or to go a step farther, anyone as far east as the Nevada border."

For proof of this all we have to do is to glance at the dust-cover of the book, which shows a cannery-row composed of New England landscape dotted with vague ash trees (or something) and some small skiff-piers over a lake or river where maybe men catch trout on strings with bent pin hooks, and process them in the little three story buildings along the banks.

The eastern magazines suffer a little from the same—shall we call it malady? Time magazine shows a picture of fisherman's wharf, with a strong indication that they believe this to be "cannery row." Newsweek magazine says that the story is about a "snug little settlement on the coast of Monterey country . . . inhabited by a casual assortment of human beings such as only Steinbeck could create. . . .

You and I in Monterey . . . cannot well consider either fiction or fabrication Red Williams's service station, Holman's department story, Tom Work, Excelentisima Maria Antonia Field, Tiny Colletti (whose name is merely misspelled), "Sparky" Enea, and a few other people.

In 1934, Red Williams opened a gas station at Lighthouse and Fountain in Pacific Grove, next to Holman's department store. Tom Work owned a lumberyard as well as many other Monterey properties. Excelentisima Maria Antonio Field, daughter of a Mexican landowner, and her brother Stevie (a friend of Steinbeck's, mentioned in *Travels with Charley*) inherited a rancho on the Monterey Salinas highway, the Laguna Seca section. Maria Antonio was recognized by the King of Spain in 1933 for her work perpetuating Spanish California history. And Tiny and Sparky, fishermen, went with Steinbeck on the *Sea of Cortez* voyage.

Indeed, much in *Cannery Row* is thinly masked fact. In the novel, Dora Flood's bouncer, William, commits suicide by plunging an ice pick through his chest. On March 6, 1933, a small piece ran in the *Monterey Herald:* "Self-Inflicted Wound Is Fatal." "Plunging an ordinary ice pick into his chest just above the heart, Henry Wojciechowski, 45, former soldier, last night committed suicide at the home of Flora Woods, local night life figure."

The handwritten manuscript of *Cannery Row* was composed in the present tense and changed to past tense in the typescript (both are housed at Stanford's Special Collection). The place, Cannery Row, and the time, the 1930s, lived, vividly, in his mind and heart.

Shortly after the novel was published, *Life* magazine photographer Peter Stackpole was sent on assignment to photograph the "real" Cannery Row. Afterwards, Stackpole remarked to his editor: "But Steinbeck wrote the real Cannery Row."

as well as a seafood market. When Monterey Bay squid are in the area (hauls are irregular because squid numbers have decreased), some boats unload at this pier (others at Moss Landing), and early mornings reveal the operations that transfer tons of squid from the boats, through the weighing houses, and into waiting trucks. Today, most of the squid catch is shipped to Asia for processing, then back to America for eating.

Near the wharf is the Municipal Beach, now Window on the Bay—locally known by its former name, ⓭ Del Monte Beach—a wide sweep of sand where sandpipers run "as though on little wheels." A wooden walk and then a bike path lead to the railroad stop for the Hotel Del Monte; only the platform remains. Where ladies once detrained, the descendants of Mack and the boys lounge on low walls.

Across from Municipal Beach is peaceful ⓮ El Estero Park and Dennis the Menace playground. Dennis's creator, Hank Ketchum, was a member of the lab group from mid-century on. The statue of Dennis, alas, was stolen from the playground. Many of Steinbeck's friends and characters are buried at ⓯ El Encinal Cemetery at 351 Fremont Street: Ed Ricketts, Flora Woods,

Horace Bicknell (Mack), Tiny Colletto, paisanos Eduardo P. Martin (Danny) and Eduardo Romero (Pilon), Hattie Gragg, "Pop" Ernest Doelter, and Johnny Garcia.

"Change was everywhere," Steinbeck writes at the beginning of *Sweet Thursday*, a novel set immediately after World War II. But that melancholic strain is balanced by lighter notes; the book finds exuberance in adaptation. This is a good way to approach today's Cannery Row: peel the veneer to glimpse the Cannery Row that existed for Steinbeck.

Steinbeck (third from left) and friends, Del Monte pier, circa 1910.

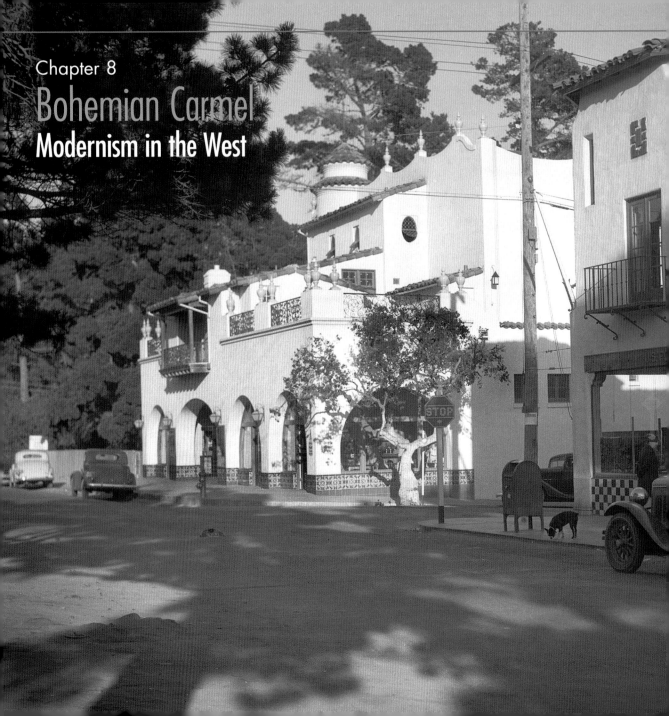

Chapter 8

Bohemian Carmel
Modernism in the West

Hills covered with Monterey pine and live-oak forests, now owned by the Pebble Beach Company, stand between old Monterey and picturesque Carmel-by-the-Sea. A wall might as well separate these diverse communities. Spanish Monterey, the site of the military presidio and Colton Hall, place of preserved Spanish and Mexican adobes and fishing wharves, is layered with two and a half centuries of California history, whereas Carmel has been burnishing its charm only since 1903. The difference is also cultural. From its inception, Carmel was a mecca for artists and bohemians. However briefly, creative individualism was Carmel's clarion call.

Although Steinbeck maintained a wary distance from Carmel, the town affected him profoundly. Many like-minded peninsula liberals lived or worked in Carmel at some point, and Steinbeck's career was shaped by the political radicalism and artistic ferment that was Carmel in the 1930s.

Carmel in the Early Years

In the late nineteenth century, attempts to create a town near the white Carmel Beach and its famous mission were blocked by the area's inaccessibility. In 1888, developers envisioned a Catholic retreat, Carmel City, similar to Pacific Grove's Methodist enclave, but plots didn't sell—even at twenty-five dollars—largely because the road to Carmel was a long and dusty hour from Monterey. Fifteen years later, however, two experienced visionaries, James Franklin Devendorf and Frank H. Powers (a real estate planner and a lawyer, respectively), were more successful. Carmel-by-the-Sea was marketed as an ecologically sensitive "village" designed to attract artists and writers: "Teachers and Brain Workers at Indoor

Employment," announced a 1903 brochure. "The settlement," Devendorf wrote in 1913, "has been built on the theory that people of aesthetic (as broadly defined) taste would settle in a town of Carmel's naturally aesthetic beauties provided all public enterprises were addressed toward preventing man and his civilized ways from unnecessarily marring the natural beauty so lavishly displayed here." With better roads and better plans than those of Carmel City, Devendorf's colony drew iconoclasts, creative spirits, liberals, Stanford professors, and the ecologically inclined.

For a century, Carmel's development has been marked by a fierce commitment to rusticity, intimacy, and the natural environment, sometimes to the point of arguable extremism. Carmel has prided itself on a low-key atmosphere, rather like Taos, New Mexico, or Woodstock, New York, where the arts are cultivated amid sylvan ease. The town had no

electricity until 1914 and has never had a jail or cemetery. To this day, side streets do not have sidewalks or streetlights and houses lack house numbers. Mail is picked up at the post office, not delivered. Carmel has banned neon signs, chain restaurants, billboards, hotdog stands, and, briefly, ice cream cones eaten in public. From its inception, Carmel defined itself against unsightly mainstream culture, against, noted the local paper during Steinbeck's years on the peninsula, "thousands of standardized towns extending from coast to coast."

Early on, many "brain workers" were indeed drawn to this idyll—"starving writers and unwanted painters," Steinbeck writes in *Travels with Charley*— and a few refugees from the 1906 San Francisco earthquake. Jack London

Statue of Father Serra by Jo Mora.

John Steinbeck fell in love with his third wife, Elaine, in 1949 when they met for dinner at ❶ the Pine Inn, on Ocean Avenue between Lincoln and Monte Verde Streets, up the street from the beach. Their connection was immediate, electric. When they finally returned to their respective rooms, neither could sleep.

Mary Austin's wikiup.

and his wife came for extended visits in 1906 and 1910, experiences that made their way into *The Valley of the Moon.* Writer Sinclair Lewis came in 1909 to serve as a secretary for two sisters. Upton Sinclair, muckraking novelist and, later, candidate for governor of California, moved to Carmel for a few months after his socialist experiment, Helicon Hall in New Jersey, burned to the ground in 1907. Environmental writer Mary Austin discovered Carmel Bay in the summer of 1904 and returned in 1906 to write in her wikiup in a tree near the Pine Inn. "Mecca" was the Carmel house of lyric poet George Sterling, to which came satirist H. L. Mencken, novelist Theodore Dreiser, and critic and Stanford professor Van Wyck Brooks. Conversations there, reported Mary Austin, were "ambrosial." Poet Robinson Jeffers, who arrived on the peninsula in 1914, would call those early years "The Carnival time when wine was as common as tears/The fabulous dawn. . . ."

Such early denizens were serious writers, and during their months or years in Carmel they relished their camaraderie and the region's serene beauty. Their heightened sensibilities stamped Carmel as the ultimate western bohemian retreat. Sterling, Austin, and others would regularly picnic on the beach, feast on abalone chowder, and fashion new verses of the abalone song ("Oh! Some folks boast of quail on toast, /Because they think it's tony./But I'm content to owe my rent/And live on abalone").

From the earliest years, Carmel was plagued by a feeling of unreality. Self-conscious primitivism—life devoted to simplicity, health, and art—both attracted and repelled intellectuals. Critic and writer Van Wyck Brooks, for one, was uncomfortable in Carmel during his 1911 summer visit: residents were, in his eyes, artistic pretenders and idlers. Their existence ran counter to the prevailing American ideal of self-determination and energetic work habits. Brooks wrote:

> *Others who had come from the East to write novels in this paradise found themselves there becalmed and supine. They gave themselves over to day-dreams while their minds ran down like clocks, as if they had lost the keys to wind them up with, and they turned into beachcombers, listlessly reading books they had read ten times before and searching the rocks for abalones. For this Arcadia lay, one felt, outside the world in which thought evolves and which came to seem insubstantial in the bland sunny air.*

> *I often felt in Carmel that I was immobilized . . . for there was something Theocritean, something Sicilian or Greek, in this afternoon land of olive trees, honey-bees and shepherds.*

This was also Steinbeck's view. Life was simply too easy, the setting too beautiful, the literary output not chastened by suffering, struggle, and woe.

Carmel in the 1930s

By the 1930s, many thought that Carmel's artistic identity was set: the place did not nourish serious work. In his 1930 survey of California writing, Carey McWilliams notes that "there are several volumes of 'exquisite' verse published annually in Carmel of which the least said the more charitable." John and Carol Steinbeck agreed. She collected bad seagull poetry published in local papers. He wrote a friend in 1929 that he had seen a Carmel writer, "H. Pease, and his shopkeeper's attitude—his wrapping up stories in butcher paper and delivering them to a hungry public—horrifies me." To Steinbeck's mind, literary pretenders lived in Carmel. "We have literary acquaintances in Carmel," he wrote to a friend in 1931, "writers of paper pulp and juvenilia. They hate me, despise me because I can't 'sell' anything." He socialized with Jack Calvin, who had published two boys' adventure books on the salmon fishery of Alaska and had worked with Ricketts on the manuscript that became *Between Pacific Tides*. In another letter, Steinbeck describes a party that he and Carol attended shortly after settling on the peninsula.

> *We went to a party at John Calvin's in Carmel last week. These writers of juveniles . . . wring the English language, to squeeze pennies out of it. They don't even pretend that there is any dignity in craftsmanship. A conversation with them sounds like an afternoon spent with a pawnbroker. Says John Calvin, "I long ago ceased to take anything I write seriously." I retorted, "I take everything I write seriously; unless one does take his work seriously there is very little chance of its ever being good work." And the whole company was a little ashamed of me as though I had three legs or was an albino.*

This was the face of Carmel that John and Carol emphatically and vocally rejected.

But another side to Carmel drew in the Steinbecks—and many other serious artists. Carmel fostered individualism. It was and still is artistically inclined. Although the town became more conservative in the 1930s, when real estate and business interests lobbied for control, Carmel continued to nurture a vigorous and outspoken liberal core. Local papers like the *Carmel Pine Cone* and the short-lived but sophisticated *Carmel Cymbal* give ample evidence of keen cultural awareness throughout the 1920s and 1930s. In a 1926 edition of the *Cymbal*, for example, poet and librarian Dora Hagemeyer reviewed Countee Cullen's poems, discussed "The Trend of Modern Fiction," and analyzed Bertrand Russell's views on education. In the same year, the paper announced a series of lectures on "Five Approaches to Modern

Carmel-by-the-Sea on a sunny day.

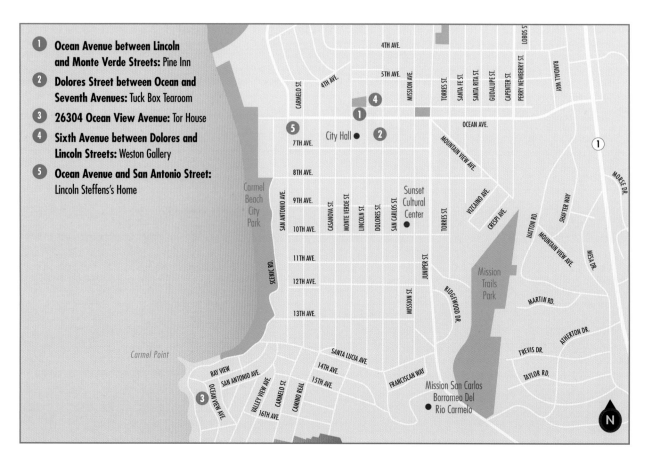

1 **Ocean Avenue between Lincoln and Monte Verde Streets:** Pine Inn

2 **Dolores Street between Ocean and Seventh Avenues:** Tuck Box Tearoom

3 **26304 Ocean View Avenue:** Tor House

4 **Sixth Avenue between Dolores and Lincoln Streets:** Weston Gallery

5 **Ocean Avenue and San Antonio Street:** Lincoln Steffens's Home

Music" and a talk on abstract painting. It reprinted Dorothy Parker's poems from the *New Yorker*, Hayward Broun's column from the *New York World*, and Ernest L. Blumenschein's article on "The Taos Art Colony." Wit marked each issue: a series on "Prominent Citizens of Carmel" featured pet dogs.

From Lake Tahoe, Steinbeck wrote his parents in dismay when hearing of owner Bassett's financial difficulties with the *Cymbal*: "It is the only paper of its kind, and a really interesting sheet with legitimate

pretensions of individuality and cleverness. . . . Bassett says what he pleases, and that is a joy no matter how you may disagree with him." In short, Carmel of the 1920s and 1930s was a sophisticated community.

An Artists' Enclave

Throughout the years, many serious artists and intellectuals have gravitated to Carmel. In the 1930s, the community was remarkably varied. Joseph

Why Pixie Houses?

Carmel's most beloved bungalow is the ❷ **Tuck Box Tearoom** on **Dolores Street between Ocean and Seventh Avenues**, a shop designed by Hugh W. Comstock. The story behind this and other

Comstock houses in the town is as charming as the cottages themselves.

In the 1920s, Carmel resident Mayotta Brown made popular felt and rag dolls, "Otsy Totsys." When she married Hugh W. Comstock, a Midwestern farmer's son with no training in architecture, he built in their backyard (on Torres near Sixth Avenue) a doll house showroom that he called "Gretel" for the Otsy Totsys. The next year he built "Hansel." Demand ran high for "fairy tale houses," as the Comstock cottages were first called. They were constructed of chalk rock, bent pitched roofs, and whimsical leaded glass windows. He built with native materials—rock from the Carmel Valley, hand-carved timbers, hand-cut redwood shingles, and hand-forged fixtures. Built between 1924 and 1930, the little houses were originally painted grey with olive trim.

The Tuck Box Tearoom.

Campbell came through in 1932: "At last," Campbell wrote " . . . a world of my contemporaries. I don't know why, but suddenly I felt that this was exactly what I had lacked—this being one of a world of my own age." Langston Hughes lived in Carmel in 1933. Ed Ricketts lived there in the early 1930s, as did Francis Whitaker, artist blacksmith and founder of the John Reed Club (a communist organization), and Mary Bulkley, feminist and poet, who often played music for Steinbeck when he came to her home to talk. "Miss hearing the music so much," he wrote her from Los Gatos. "It was a good thing. I wish I could have some right now." He inscribed a copy of *Tortilla Flat* to her: "To Miss Mary Bulkley: Pablo said—'Mrs. Palochico has given Danny a harmonica.' 'This may not be a good thing,' Pilon

observed. 'For music brings more out of a man than was ever in him.' JS" The man who wrote his books based on the "mathematics of music," structured novels on Bach's chords, and listened to Tchaikovsky must have found Mary Bulkley's musical sensibilities soothing.

Four Carmel artists and writers in particular helped shape Steinbeck's art—two he knew well personally, two he knew through their work: Beth Ingels, journalist; Lincoln Steffens, journalist and muckraker; Edward Weston, photographer; and Robinson Jeffers, poet. All four were bound intimately to the landscape and sensibility of the region. Their clear-eyed and vivid sense of place and culture tallied with Steinbeck's own.

Breaking Through: Robinson Jeffers

Robinson Jeffers wrote "the most powerful, the most challenging poetry in this generation," declared the *New York Herald Tribune* in 1928. Four years later, he was on the cover of *Time* magazine. That same year, Edward Ricketts, John and Carol Steinbeck, and Joseph Campbell pored over Jeffers's poetry. According to Campbell, Carol came into the lab one day exclaiming, "Really, I've got the message of 'Roan Stallion'—and she recited parts."

> . . . *Humanity is the start of the race; I say*
> *Humanity is the mold to break away from, the crust to break*
> *through, the coal to break into fire,*
> *The atom to be split.*
>
> *Tragedy that breaks man's face and a white*
> *fire flies out of it; vision that fools him*
> *Out of his limits, desire that fools him out of his limits . . .*

For Ricketts, the Steinbecks, and Campbell, a poet who talked about breaking cultural and humanitarian boundaries was a revolutionary voice, a kindred soul. This poet of "inhumanism" wrote about a natural world that was not human-centered. In his verse, Jeffers cultivated what he called a "reasonable detachment" that allowed for "transhuman magnificence." His poetry concerned permanent things—the sea, the cliffs of Big Sur, the fierce hawk that was his personal symbol. He claimed the rugged terrain of Big Sur as his poetic landscape. Jeffers's ideas made their way into the book Steinbeck was writing at the time, *To a God Unknown*. "The whole book was an attempt to get away from the particular form of fantasy which goes by the name of realism," Steinbeck wrote a friend in 1933. Campbell reported that he read and reread lines from "The Roan Stallion" on his 1932 journey to Sitka with Ricketts. And Ricketts used Jeffers's poem to articulate his notions of transcendence: "modern soul movements," he wrote, see "not dirt for dirt's sake, or grief merely for the sake of grief, but dirt and grief

wholly accepted if necessary as struggle vehicles of an emergent joy—achieving things which are not transient by means of things which are."

Jeffers's "inhumanism" is closely aligned with what Steinbeck was getting at in his own fictional stance—to see humans as part of a larger whole, to acknowledge that humans don't control nature but are one species living among others. In 1936, Jeffers said in an interview: "People have always taken themselves too seriously. They don't realize what a tremendous lot there is outside themselves. After all, man is just an animal which has developed."

Oddly enough, for all their appreciation, neither John nor Carol Steinbeck met Jeffers during their peninsula years. In 1938, when they were living in Los Gatos, the Steinbecks were finally introduced to Jeffers by Bennet Cerf. Jeffers's reclusive lifestyle reflected his fierce individualism. Sculptor Gordon Newell tells of offering to help Jeffers

Robinson Jeffers near Tor House, looking at a hawk statue.

build ❸ **Tor House**, at **26304 Ocean View Avenue**, on the Carmel coast. Jeffers refused Newell's assistance: "He wanted to do it himself," Newell reflected. His wife, Una, concurred: "I think he realized some kinship with [the granite] and became aware of strengths in himself unknown before." This insularity kept him aloof from many in the town—literally up in "Hawk Tower," built in the early 1920s for Una and modeled on Yeats's tower in Ireland.

Although Tor House is now surrounded by houses worth millions of dollars, it retains a feeling of isolation and independence. Jeffers's granite presence remains in rooms furnished as he left them. Tours are offered Fridays and Saturdays.

Robinson Jeffers.

Regionalism: Beth Ingels

Beth Ingels was Carol's staunch buddy. She reportedly read several books nightly, and, like Carol, had a dry wit and an unconventional manner. Beth became friends with John as well, and she was a more significant influence on his prose than anyone might guess. Like John, she loved local history and stories. Beth and Carol helped turn Steinbeck's gaze from the mythic (*Cup of Gold*) to the regional.

In 1930, Beth penned a column for the *Carmel Pine Cone*, "Carmel's Beginnings." One piece that year concerned the "hiding place" of bandit Tiburcio Vasquez in Corral de Tierra. "Cabins still stand there that were occupied by him and his men," she wrote—a historical note that makes its way into Steinbeck's *The Pastures of Heaven*, in which teacher Molly Morgan goes in search of Vasquez's cabin. Indeed, it was Beth who told Steinbeck the family stories of Corral de Tierra, her childhood home. She had considered writing a book about the area herself: in one of her notebooks is a list of possible tales about Corral de Tierra, her outline for a novel. Another notebook page lists stories entitled "Romance on Tortilla Flat"—including a reference to "the Pirate," a local character who owned several dogs. Beth's unpublished stories and proposals are eerily close to Steinbeck's own. She also kept a dog notebook in order to write "a

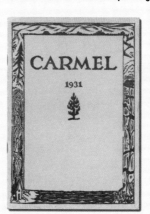

parody of serious dog books, with photos of dogs doing things they shouldn't." And she completed a manuscript titled "Cannery Row" about women cannery workers. Beth Ingels mined the local terrain in which Steinbeck would strike pay dirt.

Carol and Beth created Carmel's first directory in 1930.

Modernism: Edward Weston

To many critics of twentieth-century literature, John Steinbeck is hardly a modernist writer. For them, he is not experimental ("make it new" is one modernist cry) but a man working consciously in a realistic mode. Others see him as a naturalist, a writer who insists that human lives are shaped by forces outside human control. Or they classify him as a regionalist, a writer recording the disharmonies, traditions, and patterns of a specific place and time. But Steinbeck can also be understood as a modernist, a man of the West experimenting with unfettered language, photo-sharp realism, and an unsentimental, scientifically detached view of human lives. "The only advantage I can see about writing at all," he wrote to a friend in 1931, "is to try to overturn precedent. All of my work has been built on plans more or less unused. . . . Personally I think publishers never give the reader credit for enough intelligence." Steinbeck shared with other modernists a distrust of realism. If his prose is often journalistic in its precision, it is also suggestive, layered. Perhaps the vision of Edward Weston, modernist photographer, was closest to Steinbeck's own.

Certainly Weston was an acquaintance of Steinbeck's; in the mid-1930s, Weston's assistant, Sonya Noskowiack, took one of the only formal photographs Steinbeck permitted during the decade. And Steinbeck would have known Weston's photographs, mostly landscapes with a close eye for natural objects. Rejecting the sentimental photography known as pictorialism, the f.64 group, which Weston helped organize in 1932, advocated sharp realism in treatment of commonplace subjects and precise rendering of detail. The f.64 photographers imposed no "qualities foreign to the actual quality of the subject" in order to capture "the life force within the form." Their photographs were a visual rendering of Steinbeck's nonteleological acceptance of what "is." Equally committed to natural expression, Steinbeck spent the early 1930s mastering the taut sentence, stripping his prose of archaic and Latinate words, ornate phrases, and heavy symbolism. Weston's art, like Steinbeck's until 1935, was staunchly apolitical, focusing instead on the California landscape. For Weston, beauty was itself an end.

Weston and Steinbeck suffered at the hands of the East Coast establishment that hardly recognized the modernity of works that seemed to self-proclaimed avant-garde critics mere vestiges of realism, harkening more to a rural past than to a complex future. ❹ **The Weston Gallery** is on **Sixth Avenue between Dolores and Lincoln**. It carries the work of Edward Weston, Ansel Adams, and other photographers.

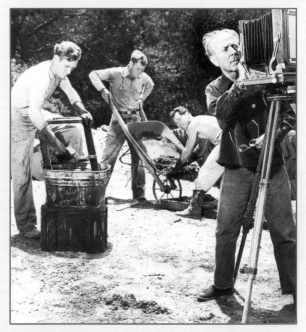

Edward Weston at the camera, with sons (l-r) Cole, Neill, and Chan building Weston's adobe house on Wildcat Hill, Carmel Highlands, 1948.

Political Activism: Lincoln Steffens

"In the 1930s if you weren't a radical, you were a hunk of protoplasm."—Caroline Decker, labor organizer

Not all who came to ❺ **Lincoln Steffens's home** at **Ocean Avenue and San Antonio Street** between 1927 and 1936 agreed with the radical politics of the ailing muckraker: "they came because there was greatness, kindliness, wit, knowledge, rich experience and sympathy in Lincoln Steffens," reported the *Monterey Peninsula Herald* when he died on October 8, 1936. They came because Steffens, like Arthur Miller decades later, stood for something essential to the liberal tradition: the free exchange of ideas, sympathy for the underdog, and scorn for rigid ideologies. "A lot of social things were happening," observed 1930s activist Richard Criley, "currents that centered on Steffens's household." His Carmel home was a beacon for young journalism students from Stanford, liberal politicians, actors, artists, scholars, and writers.

In 1931, Steffens had published his autobiography, and his fame grew with its wide reception: there was a long waiting list for the book at the Carmel library. He became Carmel's liberal conscience, a public defender of communism, the presence behind—if not a member of—the local John Reed Club, a few liberal spirits who would gather to discuss socialism and communism. "I am not a Communist," he explained to a Harvard undergraduate. "I merely think that the next order of society will be socialist and that the Communists will bring it in and lead it." From 1932 on, California liberals became more deeply involved with labor situations, largely because of the widely publicized 1933 cotton strike, the 1934 waterfront strike, and the 1936 Salinas lettuce strike. Steffens and his spirited wife, Ella Winter,

Lincoln Steffens.

hosted radicals and communists at their home, donated to striking workers, and sheltered fugitive organizers. Steinbeck's political radicalism took root in Steffens's home.

Initially reluctant to take sides in the labor dispute, Steinbeck attended a few meetings of the John Reed Club—just watching—and was then urged by Carol, Steffens, and Winter to interview strike organizers hiding out in Seaside, a few miles up the coast. Steinbeck began with the idea of writing a biography of an organizer; he ended up writing *In Dubious Battle*, a novel, wrote Steffens, that was a "stunning, straight, correct narrative about things as they happen." Without Steffens and Winter, Steinbeck may never have written his labor trilogy of the late 1930s: *In Dubious Battle*, *Of Mice and Men*, and *The Grapes of Wrath*. Steffens, wrote Martin Flavin Jr., "made people believe not in ideas but in themselves, and that is why they came to him."

Lincoln Steffens's home, Ocean Avenue and San Antonio Street.

Chapter 9
Los Gatos
A Place to Write

...try and part of the grey country of Okla
they
~~It~~ did not cut the scarred earth. The plow
marks. The last rams lifted the corn quickly
...so along the sides of the roads so that the
...began to disappear under a green cover.
...ew pale and the clouds that had hung in h...
...were dissipated. The sun flared down on the
...a line of brown spread along the edge of each...
...and went away and in a while they did...
...darker green to protect themselves and they...
...e surface of the earth crusted, a thin hard c...
...pale so the earth became pale, pink in...
...e grey country ⊬ In the water cut gul...

In the Valley of the Sun

Los Gatos
CALIFORNIA

I n May 1936, John and Carol Steinbeck left the Monterey Peninsula for Los Gatos, a small town at the southern end of the Santa Clara Valley, sixty miles north of Monterey. Settled in the nineteenth century by Italians, Yugoslavs, and Anglos, this warm valley, with its mild, Mediterranean climate, was ideal for growing apricots and almonds and plums. By the 1930s, it was the "Valley of Heart's Delight," carpeted by orchard blossoms in early March. "There is no fruit that surpasses that which is grown along our foothills for fineness of grain, flavor, and amount of sugar," declared the Los Gatos Chamber of Commerce in the early 1900s. Plums dried to prunes in the sun. Apricots and peaches were canned in Los Gatos and throughout the valley. John and Carol purchased a hillside lot above town, one and a half acres covered with oaks that provided a sweeping view of the valley. In Los Gatos, the Steinbecks met creative and forceful people: a winemaker, a socialist, an artist. For Carol, perhaps, it was paradise—she had hated the Pacific Grove summer fog. For John, it was simply a place to write.

During his Los Gatos years, Steinbeck's imagination was on the road, restlessly absent from home. Sometimes with Carol, sometimes alone, he drove south on Highway 99 into Kern County to interview farmworkers, southwestern migrants, and the men and women who tried to help them. He worked with these people. He may well have traveled Route 66 with them. In those four Los Gatos years, he wrote his signature works—*Of Mice and Men* and *The Grapes of Wrath*—and published his first significant journalistic essays, "The Harvest Gypsies." During his first year there, 1936, he conceived all three projects, and that one year may well be his annus mirabilis. In Los Gatos, John Steinbeck found his stride as an engaged artist, a man who recorded the fervor of the times. Ten years later, he recalled those months working on *The Grapes of Wrath*: "A few times I have in work heard the thundering and seen the flash which must have been the universe at work. In that participation there was a glory that shadows everything else."

For Steinbeck, Los Gatos was primarily a tiny work-room, six feet on each side, with a cot, gun rack,

Los Gatos today.

window, and desk. Detaching himself from the places of his heart—the Salinas Valley and the Monterey Peninsula—may have freed his imagination to merge fully with his new subject, migrant woe, and his new characters, the dispossessed.

An Engaged Artist

With the publication of *In Dubious Battle* in 1936, Steinbeck cemented his reputation as proletarian writer. This label stuck with him throughout the Depression, indeed throughout his career. From the 1930s on, many critics, book reviewers, and a worldwide reading public—certainly those with liberal or socialist leanings—wanted this 1930s spokesman for the plight of working people to continue publishing a certain kind of fiction, novels of social protest. Steinbeck strenuously resisted consistency in his career and would not be placed on a procrustean bed of artistic partisanship. Even when writing his labor trilogy in the last half of the 1930s, he often said that his role was that of the detached observer. The "intent of the book" *In Dubious Battle*, he wrote his agent, was to present "an unbiased picture." To his mind, any writer of social commentary must "stand clear": "I haven't gone proletarian or anything else," he wrote to his first biographer, Harry Thornton Moore, in 1936. *In Dubious Battle*

is just a story and an attempt to do the thing honestly . . . [and] to make some kind of pattern out of the half articulate men . . . I tried to have little sympathy if anything . . . but if you know enough about any man you like him . . . I have no position . . . I am like the doctor—I want to see. One cannot see very much if he looks through the narrow glass of political or economic preconceptions.

The book remains one of the most searing accounts of a labor strike in American literature and raises the question of workers' rights—when will field-workers get a fair shake? In spite of his reluctance to be tagged a proletarian writer, Steinbeck is America's troubadour of the common man and woman.

The late 1930s found Steinbeck in full-throated outrage. Though he stood a firmly "detached" observer of California's uneasy labor situation when he moved to Los Gatos, during his four years there he would become the voice for suffering humanity more fully than he likely thought possible. Two years after asserting his detachment, he replied vehemently to an invitation to appear at a local "nonpartisan" forum:

Your card alarms me . . . I am afraid of that word non-partisan. . . . The Associated Farmers are non-partisan. In fact, the word non-partisan describes one of two kinds of people: 1. Those who through lack of understanding or interest have not taken a side, and 2. those who use the term to conceal a malevolent partisanship. I am completely partisan. Every effort I can bring to bear is and has been the call of the common working people to the end that they may have what they raise, wear what they weave, use what they produce and in every way and in completeness share in the works of their hands and heads. And the reverse is true. I am actively opposed to any man or group who, through financial or political control of means of production and distribution, is able to control and dominate the lives of workers. I hope this statement is complete enough so that my position is not equivocal. . . . I am writing this once formally to put an end to any supposition that I am non-partisan.

With a world at war against fascism, John Steinbeck waged his campaign in California, using the pen as his weapon of choice.

Of Mice and Men

Of Mice and Men, the novella Steinbeck had partially written before moving to Los Gatos, is a partisan novel. George and Lennie barely have a chance—ever on the road, always controlled by ranch owners, doomed to scant wages, and tormented by bus drivers who "Didn't wanta stop at the ranch gate" and "kicks us out" miles from their destination. George's angry outburst at the beginning of this novel defines their place on the American landscape: these two are

"Woman at the Dump," by Dorothea Lange.

riffraff. The bus driver doesn't want to be seen carrying such men, invisible American workers, and he wants to exert his power, however slight, over the unhomed. Steinbeck's partisanship is evident in his ability to make readers see Lennie and George's huddled stature. Their simple story of friendship, of dreams made and lost, wins hearts. It is, perhaps, the book that makes readers out of more high school students than any other American novel. And it is the book more frequently censored than nearly any other because the brutal language of the working class offends many. Written in an experimental form that Steinbeck created for this story, the "play-novelette," the text serves as both novel and script. The work cracks open the fissure between power and powerlessness at the core of American culture.

The book's gestation mirrors that of Steinbeck's other Los Gatos novel, *The Grapes of Wrath*. When his political sensibilities were acutely tuned, conception of subject and character preceded structure and style. The subject of *Of Mice and Men* was an incident occurring a dozen years earlier: In the mid-1920s, Steinbeck had seen a troubled man kill a straw boss, and he told a New York reporter that this gave him the story. Characters most likely emerged from his past as well: Lennie is one of several "unfinished people" in Steinbeck's canon, those with the sensibilities of a child. He knew one such boy in Salinas, a child most often

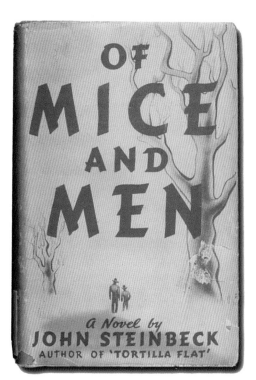

seen outside Bell's Candy Store in Salinas. Each Easter the boy was given a rabbit, and in the week following he would pet the rabbit to death.

But story and character needed context, "the wall of background" he found necessary for fictional resonance. Steinbeck, a natural storyteller, wrote searingly about marginalized Americans because he took such care to create resonant lives. Before he left Pacific Grove, he asked friends if they remembered the name for someone who cleaned out a bunkhouse—"swamper" was the word he wanted, Candy's position. His dialogue is razor sharp: "For too long the language of books was different from the language of men. To the men I write about profanity is adornment and ornament and is never vulgar and I try to write it so." And the enclosed spaces of *Of Mice and Men*—clearing, bunkhouse, and barn, each exactly described—re-enact the shuttered lives of working stiffs.

"The Harvest Gypsies"

Steinbeck's partisanship took on a messianic edge in the late summer of 1936, when George West, editorial page editor of the liberal *San Francisco News*, asked him to write about the miserable housing conditions of dust-bowl migrants pouring into California to pick crops. Numbers are estimated at over half a million during the decade of the 1930s, all envisioning California as the

A photograph by Dorothea Lange of the Arvin migrant camp, near Bakersfield, circa 1938. Lange worked as a photographer for the Farm Security Administration during the Great Depression. She documented the same conditions that Steinbeck wrote about in his journalism and fiction; her photos accompanied Steinbeck's articles for the *San Francisco News* that were published as "The Harvest Gypsies." Those articles were later collected and published as *Their Blood Is Strong.*

promised land, most finding only seasonal work, substandard or no housing, and great antagonism on the part of resident Californians, wary of the migrants' poverty, southern drawl, "hard-lookin'" appearance, and mostly Baptist fervor. Steinbeck's imprimatur on a six-part exposé on available housing, the line of thinking went, would help garner support for the recently launched federal camp program for migrants.

As reporter and witness, Steinbeck left Los Gatos in August 1936 for the Kern County Hoovervilles,

makeshift roadside settlements, and then toured one of the new federal camps set up near Bakersfield, the second such federally funded camp established in California. (Eventually, fifteen would be constructed around the state. The Arvin camp is still open.) He read camp manager Tom Collins's detailed reports of the migrants' woes and spoke to destitute Oklahomans. In October 1936, the *News* published his series of six articles, called "The Harvest Gypsies." He said he used the word gypsies ironically: "It seemed to me an irony that people like these should be forced to live the life of gypsies," he wrote to Tom Collins, apologizing if he hurt people's feelings with his title. Those lucid exposés ask that the reader participate in the actuality of gypsy life. His prose nudges readers on a visual tour of makeshift houses built "by driving willow branches into the ground and wattling weeds, tin, old paper and strips of carpet against them. A few branches are placed over the top to keep out the noonday sun. It would not turn water at all. There is no bed."

That first investigative journey, from Los Gatos through Salinas to Bakersfield and back, altered Steinbeck's life and career. On the way home, he saw his hometown of Salinas arming itself for one of the nastiest California labor strikes of the late 1930s. What he'd witnessed on the road realigned his sensibilities, giving him a new subject, a new cast of characters, and an altered sense of place. He wrote to his agent immediately after the trip:

> I've seen such terrific things in the squatters' camps that I can't think out of them right now. There's Civil War making right under my nose. I've got to see it and feel it. I have a lot now . . . I start on another play tomorrow and I think it will be a good one. It is to be laid in a squatter camp in Kern County. Instead of stage direction I'll furnish photographs. This thing is happening now and it's incredibly rich dramatically.

This urgent letter taps issues at the core of Steinbeck's documentary imagination: the journalist's need to witness events firsthand, the documentary artist's ability to emotionally grip life as lived, and the writer's search for a pattern of expression. The migrant play was never written—it was not the proper vehicle for his story. But *The Grapes of Wrath* had its gestation in

Tom Collins, manager of the Arvin camp near Bakersfield, photographed by Dorothea Lange.

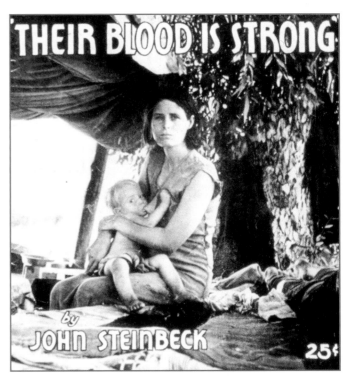

The cover of *Their Blood Is Strong*, photo by Dorothea Lange.

that journalistic assignment, the novel's soul laid out in that letter to his agent. To tell the migrant story accurately, he'd meld his life and art with theirs.

The writer who resided in Los Gatos, who depended heavily on Carol to edit his prose, and who enjoyed Los Gatos friends who solaced him with food and wine was nonetheless imaginatively absent. His became a gypsy existence. A writer can't write about "the Proletariat," he wrote Henry Thornton Moore, "whatever they are, unless you have lived with them and worked and lifted things and fought and drank with them. . . . All the terms are phony—proletarian—bourgeois . . . it's all just people. Write about people not classes." That Steinbeck would do. During the fall and winter of 1937–38, he visited migrant camps; he may have gone back to Oklahoma and come West with the migrants (as his friend Joseph Henry Jackson claimed), or he may have established himself as a laborer and worked with the migrants, as the Los Gatos paper claimed. Steinbeck kept his gypsy life, his research, under wraps.

The Grapes of Wrath

The Grapes of Wrath is Steinbeck's quintessential California fiction. In what many claim is his greatest novel, he shook free his imagination to embrace the state itself. More than any other novel he wrote, place is movement through space, migrants dreaming of California for more than a third of the novel, living across California for the rest. This novel pits Oklahoma entropy against Western fecundity, as migrants journey from "a place of sadness and worry and defeat" to California, "a new mysterious place."

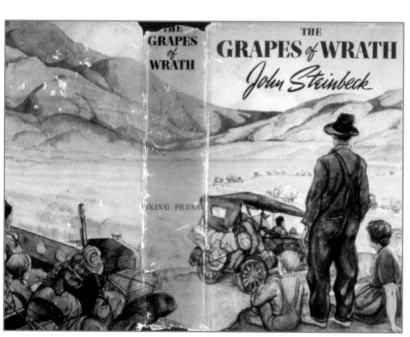

As the Joads near California, they give voice to the state's allure, its legendary status. In California they hear that a "fella near the coast" (William Randolph Hearst, no doubt) "got a million acres," holdings so vast and unimaginable that it inspires a sermon from Casy. Steinbeck's migrants confront the authoritative blue mountains that guard the state, the "jagged ramparts" depicted on the stunning cover of the first edition. The majestic Colorado River cuts a boundary that several characters in the novel can't pass. A "terrible" desert, "bones ever'place," tests resolve as carloads of dreamers pass from Needles to Bakersfield. In Steinbeck's hands, the migrants' journey is a mythic passage to a land

The 1936 Salinas Lettuce Strike

Between 1930 and 1938, more than 150 strikes took place in rural California. Wages were low, housing for migrant workers was miserable, and civil liberties were abused by organizations such as California's Associated Farmers—businessmen, chambers of commerce, growers, and shippers—determined to crush labor unrest. Abuses were documented thoroughly by several individuals, including economist Paul Taylor from Berkeley, photographer Dorothea Lange, and lawyer and activist Carey McWilliams from Los Angeles—and John Steinbeck.

In the fall of 1936, Steinbeck wrote, "There are riots in Salinas and killings in the streets of that dear little town where I was born. I shouldn't wonder if the thing had begun. I don't mean any general revolt but an active beginning aimed toward it, the smoldering."

From 1920 to 1930, annual American consumption of lettuce went from 2.3 pounds to 8.3 pounds per person. Growing and shipping lettuce—"green gold," as it came to be known—made fortunes for Salinas farmers who were, in fact, running industrial operations. For workers who packed lettuce for shipping, it was a wet, cold, demanding job. One worker recalled in an interview,

They used to get the 300-pound blocks of ice . . . they didn't have crushers like now. . . . They had these ice picks, you know, and they'd shave it, you know, they'd keep chopping. . . . At that time they used to put it in a wheelbarrow . . . and then you'd wheel the wheelbarrow to the packers there who were packing the lettuce, and then they would pack one layer of lettuce, and get a scoop of ice, and put the scoop of ice in the crate . . . then one layer of lettuce, scoop of ice, another layer of lettuce, and another scoop of ice. Then they would

put the lid on, the paper, they had a paper there that would hold the ice in, and lid the crate. Then they would load the crates [about 70 pounds each] into a refrigerated car . . . and then the loader . . . he would chop the ice into little blocks . . . he would pick the ice and throw it on top. He would put the ice on top of the crates.

Wages paid for this work, as for picking crops, slipped steadily during the 1930s. In 1936, shed workers were requesting exclusive representation by their union, the Fruit and Vegetable Workers Union, an affiliate of the moderate American Federation of Labor. Unlike field-workers, who were Filipino or Mexican in the mid-1930s, shed workers were largely white.

The growers and shippers of Salinas were ready for a battle—no compromises considered in demands for recognizing unions. They consolidated shipping to one packing operation in Salinas and one in

Tear gassing during the Salinas lettuce strike, 1936.

Watsonville and built ten-foot-high barbed fences around each, importing scab workers and guarding the areas with squads armed with tear gas, clubs, and firearms.

The "battle of Salinas" was a large, vicious strike. It pitted white migrants, "the red menace," against "embattled farmers," the latter a well-oiled cooperative effort involving the powerful Grower-Shipper Vegetable Association of Central California (a newly formed citizens association), armed Salinas citizenry, and the California Highway Patrol. Joining them in the most bitter moments was a visiting self-styled "coordinator"—Steinbeck called him "the General"—who urged Salinas citizens to take up arms, fulminating that this was war, reds against patriotic Americans. Newspapers in California, as well as across the country, covered the strike: "For a full fortnight the 'constituted authorities' of Salinas have been but the helpless pawns of sinister fascist forces which have operated from a barricaded hotel floor in the center of town," reported the *San Francisco Chronicle*. ("Now what happened would not be believable," writes Steinbeck, "if it were not verified by the Salinas papers of the time.")

This nasty strike may well have been the basis for Steinbeck's quickly written, angry 1938 diatribe against "Salinas fat cats," "L'Affaire Lettuceberg." The satiric manuscript was a "job," "a vicious book, a mean book," he wrote his agent, that "has a lot of poison in it that I have to get out of my system." A month later he destroyed it, turning once again to his more tempered novel about migrant workers, *The Grapes of Wrath*.

of tall tales and visionary acres. The Joads's first vista after Tehachapi Pass seems to encompass the whole of that mythical land: "The vineyards, the orchards, the great flat valley, green and beautiful, the trees set in rows, and the farm houses. . . . The distant cities, the little towns in the orchard land, and the morning sun, golden on the valley."

That vista midway through *The Grapes of Wrath* hovers over the whole novel—California as an agricultural paradise supporting human endeavor. "The spring is beautiful in California," Steinbeck writes in chapter 25, where visionary California collides with starvation California. "The prunes lengthen like little green bird's eggs, and the limbs sag down against the crutches under the weight." But fruit rots because industrialized agriculture can't make enough money if they bring surplus crops to market. "And children dying of pellagra must die because a profit cannot be taken from an orange." For migrants, Cali-fornia is an endless road, temporary shelters, scant food, and brutal advice to keep on moving. Steinbeck's great achievement in *The Grapes of Wrath* is to keep his readers' gaze steadily on the state's two great truths: its panoramic promise and its brutal realities.

It took Steinbeck months to contain his anger at what he saw on his investigative trips, months casting about for tone and a pattern for the migrant story. He planned a "four pound book," he told his agent late in 1936, "a devil of a long hard book." Eighteen months later he wrote her again, "Yes, I've been writing on the novel but I've had to destroy it several times." During those eighteen months he had considered other artistic patterns for the material: a play with photographs, a satire on Salinas "fat cats." In between those aborted projects he apparently agreed to a collaboration with Horace Bristol and to edit camp manager Tom Collins's weekly reports on migrant conditions near Bakersfield, writing a preface for the book. In the months when *The*

Grapes of Wrath was taking form, his imagination was in overdrive. None of the collaborative projects, nor the nasty satire, bore fruit, but a letter to Collins about editing his reports is a fine example of how Steinbeck bridged the terrain between reportorial and fictive prose. It's one of his most telling statements of the artistic process generating *The Grapes of Wrath*, turning fact into fiction.

I've worked out a plan for presenting this material, but it doesn't depart much from your plan. The dialect in this human side must be worked over because it is the hardest thing in the world to get over. . . . Above all we need songs, as many as we can get. For songs are the direct and true expression of a people. Maybe we can get them to bring them to us in their own spelling. That would be the best of all. . . .

We'll put the songs in and of course the histories. They are fine. Throughout the thing will be more on the human side than on any other. Then there is the one other thing I want to mention. In all of the stories there is no personal description. I have seen the people enough so that I could describe the speaker and it wouldn't be the real person who spoke but enough like him or her so that it would be essentially true. Do you think that is all right? But they do have to be described. If this works out as I hope it will I should like to include photographs of people, of the place of the activities.

The letter suggests how closely linked fiction and nonfiction were for Steinbeck. Collins composed painstakingly accurate reports, but they needed the context of the fiction writer's gaze to bring the people to life. They needed the impact of documentary realism—art relying on the interplay among photographs, music, dialogue, reportage—to make the people real; the documentary impulse of the 1930s was didactic art that moved people's sensibilities through visual commentary, the mind bound to the heart. A commitment to the personal and evocative is evident in all that Steinbeck and other documentary artists created in the 1930s.

For Steinbeck, gone was the artistic detachment of *In Dubious Battle*. His fiction and his nonfiction during his Los Gatos years measure the human toll of struggling for "a better kinder life." The difference between his fiction and his journalism is a matter of "levels," one of his favorite words to describe the depth of his fiction. Rooted in journalistic precision, Steinbeck's fiction is nonetheless just that, fiction and not historical fact—a distinction that was missed by countless reviewers of *The Grapes of Wrath*, who took Steinbeck to task for the color of Sallisaw dirt and the Joads's balance book and the accuracy of Associated Farmers burning migrant camps. The book is historical, fictive, ecological (land

The back of this photo, by Dorothea Lange, reads, "Nipomo, California. March 1936. Migrant agricultural worker's family. Seven hungry children and their mother, aged 32. The father is a native Californian."

and water use), and mythic, its pattern a quilt, a patched-together narrative of dialogue, freeze-frame visuals, musical intonations, and panoramic vistas.

During Steinbeck's era of partisanship, the late 1930s, he committed himself fully to the task of finding a novelistic "pattern" that honored migrants and, more broadly, the enduring American belief in "a new life." He insisted that the lyrics of Julia Ward Howe's Civil War anthem, the "Battle Hymn of the Republic," be printed in the endpapers of the first edition of *The Grapes of Wrath*. He insisted on the book's American heart—on the eve of attacks that would accuse him of communist leanings.

Once the novel was complete, Steinbeck moved on from his position as migrant partisan and spokesman—although never ceasing to champion ordinary Americans. In the months following the April 1939 publication of *The Grapes of Wrath*, Steinbeck left behind the migrant material, Los Gatos, and Carol, his wife of a decade.

Los Gatos: Gem City of the Foothills

Founded in the mid-nineteenth century, Los Gatos was, from its inception, a California idyll, a pastoral retreat without Carmel's pretensions to art, without Pacific Grove's Methodists, without Monterey's Spanish roots or Salinas's incredibly fertile soil. Located at the base of the Santa Cruz Mountains, it became a

locus of trade and transportation, a thriving market town. Los Gatos was a town of lumber mills and vineyards, orchards, and farms. Chickens were raised here; French prunes and apricots were grown in the town and on the nearby Santa Cruz mountains. A stream, Los Gatos Creek, tumbled from those mountains and was once full of trout and a spawning ground for salmon. For twenty square miles to the north of town, fruit trees bloomed and flourished in the Santa Clara Valley. At the south of the town, a winding road climbed and dipped its way to Santa Cruz over the steep coastal range.

Like Salinas, Los Gatos is relatively close to the sea,

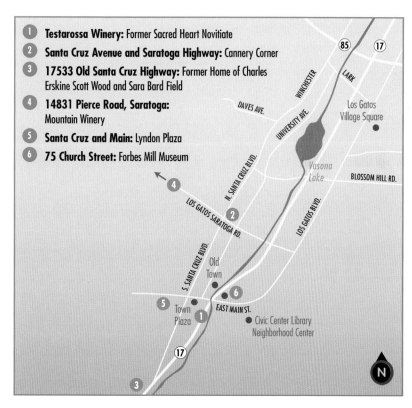

1. **Testarossa Winery:** Former Sacred Heart Novitiate
2. **Santa Cruz Avenue and Saratoga Highway:** Cannery Corner
3. **17533 Old Santa Cruz Highway:** Former Home of Charles Erskine Scott Wood and Sara Bard Field
4. **14831 Pierce Road, Saratoga:** Mountain Winery
5. **Santa Cruz and Main:** Lyndon Plaza
6. **75 Church Street:** Forbes Mill Museum

Gwyn Conger

Steinbeck met Gwyn Conger in the summer of 1939, when he went to Los Angeles to escape the publicity over *The Grapes of Wrath*. The attraction was electric and immediate. Nearly twenty years younger than Steinbeck, sensual and fun-loving, Gwyn seemed everything that tough, witty, hard-drinking, and pragmatic Carol was not. Gwyn was "luscious," said one male friend, feminine, tractable, and witty. She shared John's romanticism and his sense of the whimsical. When he first met her, she was a lounge singer in Los Angeles with a "very pretty, Irish kind of voice," her voice teacher noted, but hardly an ambitious performer. Whenever he was in town—or when she spent a few weeks in San Francisco singing for the 1939 World's Fair—Gwyn found plenty of time to cavort with Steinbeck.

They married in 1943, and their marriage lasted five rocky years. She proved to be less winsome and tractable than Steinbeck may have wished. When he went overseas as a war correspondent a few months after their marriage, Gwyn, who had not wanted him to leave, refused to write him letters for weeks. After the war, the two sons born to the couple brought tensions—Steinbeck had never been all that certain he wanted children—and she claimed that one son wasn't his. Gwyn's temperament rankled—the hard-working Steinbeck complained that she coddled herself, stayed late in bed. He tried to build for himself the perfect soundproof room in his basement and experimented with writing in the dark— signs of a marriage gone awry. Gwyn drank heavily. Her flirtations with other men, and finally her acknowledged infidelity, brought about a split. In the terrible summer of 1948, Gwyn left him.

Gwyn and her mother at Gwyn's wedding to John.

Gwyn Conger.

"Valley of Heart's Delight."

twenty-five miles as the crow flies, but unlike Salinas, Los Gatos is cut off from the sea by the steep Santa Cruz Mountains. Thus, the marine influence that makes Salinas foggy and chilly for much of the summer does not affect Los Gatos. Many have been drawn there by its balmy weather. In 1905, the *Lancet*, an English medical journal, asserted that Los Gatos had one of the two "most equable climates in the world," the other being Aswan, Egypt. Visitors came to sanatoriums scattered in the mountains. Horse trails wound through wooded slopes, through manzanita and oak and chaparral, and were used by San Franciscans who had summer homes in the mountains. The climate also drew Jesuits, who built ❶ the Sacred Heart Novitiate above the town, planted vineyards on the sunny foothills, and began harvesting fruit in 1888. By the early 1900s, the winery was the largest bonded ecclesiastical winery in the nation. Although Jesuit production ceased in 1985, wines are produced here today by Testarossa Vineyards, using the Jesuits' stone vaults. Because altar wine was produced during Prohibition, Testarossa is recognized as the fourth-oldest winery in California.

When the Steinbecks moved to the area, the town still enjoyed its nineteenth-century prosperity and its strategic location as gateway to the mountains and the coast—gateway as well to the fragile beauty and fecundity of the Santa Clara Valley. A new four-lane highway to Santa Cruz (now Highway 17) was under construction; the grand opening celebration was held in July 1939. The "Suntan Special," a Southern Pacific rail line connecting the Santa Clara Valley with Santa Cruz, was still running; it closed in 1940 because heavy winter rains caused frequent mud slides on the line. On Cannery Corner, at ❷ Santa Cruz Avenue and Saratoga Highway, stood the Hunt Brothers cannery, where clingstone peaches were canned. All over the Santa Clara Valley, apricots were grown, and farmers brought pits to what is now Vasona Park, where the kernels were dried, cracked, and processed and then shipped to European markets for pastry making. The Depression hardly touched the diverse local economy. The Steinbecks came to a town "free from social art dilettantes," notes a 1936 article in the local paper, "without social art climbers and without the ballyhoo and noise of the most popular centers that use all art as background." Los Gatos did not aim to be Carmel. It was a moderate sort of place—in climate, culture, building, and economy.

Steinbeck's Los Gatos Homes

Although the town of Los Gatos lightly stamped Steinbeck's novelistic sensibilities, place did matter in one important sense during those turbulent years of social engagement. He became a landowner. The serenity of his two Los Gatos homesteads countered the intensity of months spent writing *The Grapes of Wrath*; of imaginatively traveling with "my people," as he called the migrants; of absorbing the outrage that the published novel sparked around the country. Homesteading—creating a place of rest for a weary gypsy—was a counterpoint to creative intensity.

On May 16, 1936, a headline in the Los Gatos paper read, "Noted Author to Join Colony Here of Literary Folk." Even while declaring itself free of "artistic dilettantes," Los Gatos at the same time burnished its reputation for the sophisticated and discriminating: "The property is definitely not a subdivision," read the article. "It merely affords a chance for a few select buyers to obtain a few select building sites." The lot was a wooded hill about a mile from downtown Los Gatos on Greenwood Lane. Secluded, lovely, quiet, it was a writer's paradise. An eight-foot redwood-stake fence protected his privacy. Steinbeck carved a sign for the gate that read, "Steinbeckia"; he later changed this to read, "Arroyo del Ajo" or "Garlic Gulch," since Italian neighbors made good wine and pasta. "The new house is fine," he wrote his agents in the summer of 1936, "built on the plan of an old California ranch house. . . . It overlooks the Santa Clara Valley and it is hidden in an oak forest."

Initially, John and Carol were delighted to escape to their 1.6-acre lot and the 1,452-square-foot house they built on it. The house was snug, only four rooms, one a large living room with a fireplace for entertaining. Interior walls were paneled with hand-rubbed white pine. To play the jazz both of them loved, John had a fine phonographic system installed, built by the same electronic genius who developed a high-fidelity amplifier for Ed's lab, Pol Verbek. Richard Albee made speaker cabinets that looked, Carol yelped, "like baby coffins." She draped serapes over chairs, her color scheme the reds and whites of Mexico,

where they'd traveled on their first trip out of the state a few months before the move. John's workroom was "a little tiny room," he wrote Elizabeth Otis: "Just big enough for a bed and a desk and a gun rack and little book rack. I like to sleep in the room I work in."

Yet the Greenwood Lane house, where he completed *Of Mice and Men* and wrote "The Harvest Gypsies"

The interior of the Greenwood Lane house.

The Biddle Ranch.

articles and *The Grapes of Wrath*, became an uncomfortable skin as he neared completion of the latter novel. He needed to slough it off, as he would slough off so much of his life in the months after finishing *The Grapes of Wrath*. The process was, however, gradual.

When the Steinbecks found the Biddle Ranch off the Santa Cruz Highway in August 1938, he declared it "the most beautiful place I have ever seen." Meanwhile, the novel he was completing took the Joads further into poverty. A little like Faulkner, who restored a southern mansion for himself as his writing deconstructed the Old South, Steinbeck lived, very briefly, in visionary California while he composed a grittier truth. When they moved to the mountain property in October 1938, he described it as "an estate . . . forty-seven acres and has a big spring," in a letter to Carlton Sheffield. "It has forest and orchard and pasture and big trees. It is very old—was first taken up in 1847. The old ranch house was built in 1858 I think." He hired "a staff of servants," a Japanese gardener and cook and an "Okie boy" handyman because he "needs the money so dreadfully. . . . You see it really is an estate," he concluded his letter. It was also home to a one-eyed pig named Connally, a cow, barrels of local wine for visitors to drink, and gardens planted and tended by Carol. They both loved it there—briefly.

Some of Steinbeck's letters read as if the Biddle Ranch is, indeed, the land that the Joads imagined California to be:

It's a beautiful morning and I am just sitting in it and enjoying it. Everything is ripe now apples, pears, grapes, walnuts. Carol has made pickles, and chutney, canned tomatoes. Prunes and raisins are on the drying trays. The cellar smells of apples and wine. The madrone berries are ripe and every bird in the country is here—slightly tipsy and very noisy. The frogs are singing about a rain coming but they can be wrong. It's nice.

This was where Steinbeck recovered from his exhausting pull to write *The Grapes of Wrath* in five months. And it was where he met the fury that the book's publication ignited.

The vitriolic attacks unmoored Steinbeck. "Californians are wrathy over *The Grapes of Wrath*," wrote publicist Frank J. Taylor for *Forum*. "By

Book burning in Bakersfield.

Los Gatos Friends

Although Steinbeck's Los Gatos friends were not as intimate as his Monterey Peninsula buddies, he and Carol certainly discovered the more intriguing local personalities.

Perhaps the most eccentric were Charles Erskine Scott Wood and his wife Sara Bard Field, residents of Los Gatos since 1919, who lived at ❸ **17533 Old Santa Cruz Highway.** The two had moved to the area from Seattle when he was sixty-seven, she thirty-seven. He left behind fame and fortune; she left behind a Baptist minister husband and her children. Wood's long career had sparkled: he had been a famous Indian fighter, a friend to Chief Joseph, and a renowned attorney in Seattle. Field was a staunch suffragette and lyric poet of some note. Their concrete mansion above Los Gatos, completed in 1925 for about $100,000, was a monument to his success as well as to their love and shared intellectual

interests. He took to wearing a toga, as did she. They entertained guests with plays in their own outdoor amphitheater. Guests could hike on trails with benches strategically placed, carved with Field's verses. Art graced the estate: sculptures by Benny Bufano and Robert Stackpole, and, most famously, two stone cats by Robert Trent Paine, completed in 1922, that guard the entrance near today's The Cats Restaurant.

Wood wrote four books during his time in Los Gatos, dialogues in which God, Satan, and Jesus converse with national and international figures. Many people made their way to the estate to discuss philosophy and liberal politics with him, including Lincoln Steffens, Robinson Jeffers, Fremont Older, William Rose Benét, Yehudi Menuhin, and Clarence Darrow. John and Carol, sometimes with Ed Ricketts in tow, went up to see the celebrated couple occasionally, and Ricketts sent Wood vials of shark's liver oil to cure his arthritis.

Martin Ray was no less formidable in his own way. Opinionated, hardworking, and monomaniacal about fine wines, Ray purchased ❹ **the Mountain Winery, at 14831 Pierce Road** in nearby

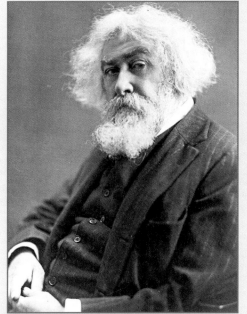

Charles Erskine Wood.

Carol Steinbeck cavorting with Martin and Elsie Ray. "Steinbeck became interested in how we were doing things here," Ray wrote a friend in 1940, "not that he knew much about wine but that we are making wines honestly, as they should be made."

implication, it brands California farmers with unbelievable cruelty in their dealings with refugees from the 'dust bowl.'" Meeting in San Francisco, the Associated Farmers considered a ban: "Although the Associated Farmers will not attempt to have the book banned or suppressed, we would not want our women and children to read so vulgar a book," declared Executive Secretary Harold Pomery. On June 29, 1939, the local newspaper reported "Grapes of Wrath Under Library's Ban at San Jose." The paper explained that the book had been "ruled out as unfit for its patrons." On August 21, the book was "banned from all libraries and schools in Kern County by action of the Board of Supervisors." It was burned in his hometown of Salinas. "A lie, a damned infernal lie," foamed Congressman Lyle Boren of Oklahoma on the floor of the Senate. It was burned in Bakersfield, Saint Louis, Buffalo. The novel was read as fact, as historical record, and many Oklahomans and Californians went out of their way to prove Steinbeck wrong. Others attacked the book's "filthy" language.

Saratoga, from Paul Masson and took it on himself to prove to the world that California's wines could equal those of France. He urged all winemakers in California to do the same, to focus on "fine wines," not always *vin ordinaire*. Ray had the manner of a bulldog, which seemed to suit Steinbeck just fine. The Steinbecks went to the Mountain Winery with some regularity during their Los Gatos years, he to drink good wine, enjoy heated conversations, and even work in the fields with his host or help in the winery itself. Carol probably came up with the title for *The Grapes of Wrath* after a visit to the winery; a card telling his agents of Carol's suggestion is postmarked Saratoga. In 1958, the winery started hosting a concert series; today it is a popular venue for picnicking and enjoying music in a beautiful setting.

For a few brief months in 1939, as protests and praise boiled around him, he enjoyed his "estate" and his many visitors—Lon Chaney Jr., Charlie Chaplin, George and Martha Ford, Joseph Henry Jackson, Burgess Meredith, Pare Lorentz, Ed Ricketts, Spencer Tracy—feeling expansive with the freedom money brought. He took flying lessons in Palo Alto, "an escape into something beautiful"; bought twin Packards for himself and Carol; installed a swimming pool; and bought her a star sapphire ring. But the two were arguing more regularly and drinking heavily. The friends whom he invited to the ranch began to irritate him; he called them "Carol's set." He felt buffeted from within and without. The land that he had relished so briefly was sold in August 1941.

Steinbeck at Work

Steinbeck posed for few photos. He granted few interviews, but here's how he looked to one reporter in 1939: "He was dressed in gray sweatshirt, sailor-like wide bottomed blue jeans, and scarred moccasins. . . . Steinbeck poured a brown paper full of tobacco, and rolled a cigarette."

Steinbeck by the pool he had built for Carol at Biddle Ranch.

Environs of Los Gatos

Because the houses that Steinbeck owned are private and remote, it's advisable to enjoy the town instead. Los Gatos living is California at its best, many claim. It's one of the most sought-after residential areas in the Santa Clara Valley, largely because houses date to the nineteenth century, as so many houses elsewhere in the valley do not.

At the corner of ❺ Santa Cruz and Main Streets was once the Lyndon Hotel, now Lyndon Plaza, where Steinbeck frequently drank with friends—or so claim the locals who remember Steinbeck. Today, you can enjoy a pizza or an ice-cream cone at Lyndon Plaza and consider Steinbeck's preferences.

At ❻ 75 Church Street is a Los Gatos landmark, Forbes Mill Annex, site of the town's first mill. On the other side of Main Street, next to the bridge, a splendid walking trail along Los Gatos Creek winds uphill to the Lexington Reservoir—a popular trail for mountain bikers, dogs, runners, and walkers. If you wish to absorb today's Los Gatos, hike this trail on a balmy Sunday morning, heading to the downtown summer farmers' market afterward.

The road running along the trail, Highway 17, winds to Santa Cruz and meets Highway 1, which runs south to Monterey. Steinbeck took this route when he went back to the peninsula to visit Ed Ricketts and other friends, retreating from the ranch he loved, the wife he would leave, the migrant material, the parties, and the wealth.

The Lyndon Hotel in the 1920s.

Chapter 10

Beyond California

The Lure of Mexico

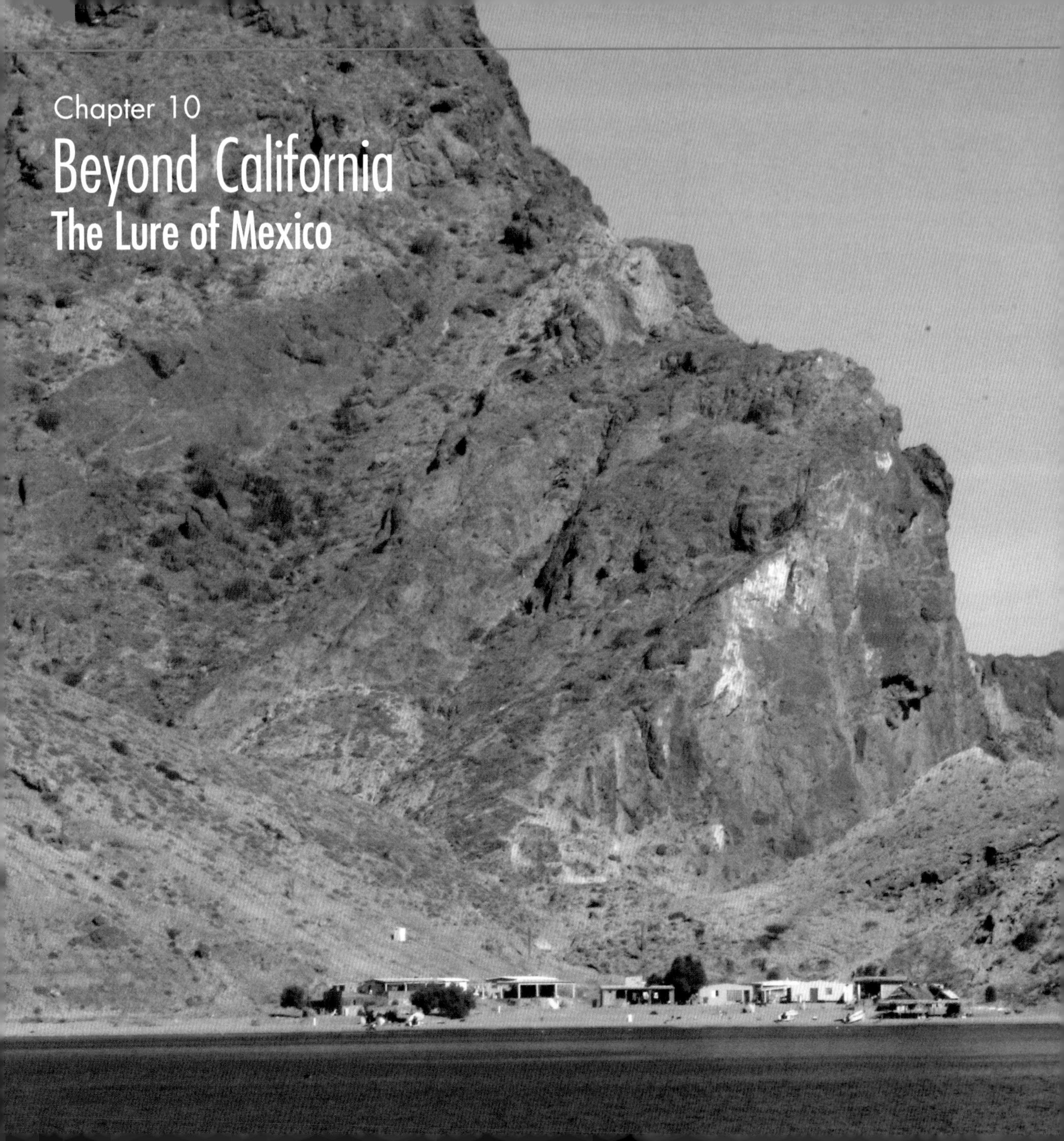

Steinbeck, circa 1960.

A fishing village on the Baja coast—it can be approached only by sea.

Perhaps California could never have contained restless John Steinbeck. Since his early twenties, he had dreamed of other places. His first trip out of the state was to New York City at age twenty-three; his second was to Mexico City at age thirty-three.

Mexico long attracted Steinbeck, and from 1935 to 1949 he made repeated trips south—as tourist, as writer, as filmmaker. "There's an illogic there I need," he said in 1948, after Ed Ricketts's death. For Steinbeck, Mexico seemed an objective correlative of his worldview, a place not primitive —a word having uncomfortable connotations— but primary, having a different set of values from those of his own nation, a simpler, seemingly kinder, more generous approach to life. Nearly a third of his work includes Mexican characters or focuses on Mexican culture—*Tortilla Flat*, *Sea of Cortez*, and *The Pearl* (1947); scripts for *The Forgotten Village* (1941), *A Medal for Benny* (1945), and *Viva Zapata!* (1952); and the short story "The Miracle of Tehepac." He fully embraced the country's history and culture.

Steinbeck in Mexico

Steinbeck absorbed Mexico long before he went there. In Steinbeck's California, the Spanish/Mexican presence was—and remains—everywhere: in Monterey adobes, in tamales sold in cafés, in a large Mexican-American population; in the lilt of Spanish heard and read; in Spanish place-names: Salinas, Soledad, San Juan Batista, Monterey, Corral de Tierra, the Santa Lucia Mountains, and the Gabilans. Young Steinbeck's friends, the Wagners, had fled the Mexican revolution to live in Salinas—Steinbeck loved listening to journalist Edith Wagner's accounts of covering the revolution. A sense of the exotic must have clung to things Mexican for young Steinbeck. In *The Red Pony*, Jody is fascinated with the old paisano's rapier, a sword of dignity that intrigues Jody as much as does old Gitano himself.

The idea of Mexico fired Steinbeck's imagination, but it would take him years to actually visit the country. In 1932, he wrote to his agent Elizabeth Otis that he was going to Mazatlán,

and from there I shall go on horseback in the general direction of Guadalajara . . . [I want] entrée into a number of tiny villages . . . I plan to do a series of little stories on the road—local sagas. . . . Such things might well be done with simplicity, with color and with some charm, if one

San Carlos, Sonora

The Sea of Cortez as it looked to Steinbeck and Ricketts.

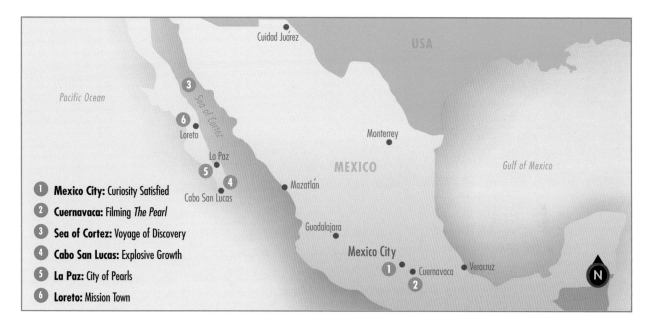

1. **Mexico City:** Curiosity Satisfied
2. **Cuernavaca:** Filming *The Pearl*
3. **Sea of Cortez:** Voyage of Discovery
4. **Cabo San Lucas:** Explosive Growth
5. **La Paz:** City of Pearls
6. **Loreto:** Mission Town

were able to present the incident against its background and at the same time permeate it with the state of mind of its community.

Although financial worries and his mother's stroke prevented that trip, much in the planning of it is pure Steinbeck—that quest for the marrow of a place, seeing the layers of incident, culture, and place as one. A year later he wrote his agent that he wanted to write about "Mexicans and Yuakis taken from jails in Northern Mexico" to work in Spreckels' fields; that book didn't materialize either. The trip he eventually took in 1935, when freed of financial worry, was by car down a newly opened highway to ❶ Mexico City. In 1940, he

Until recently, when squid size diminished considerably, large Humboldt squid were caught and processed in Santa Rosalia.

returned to Baja on a Monterey purse seiner on his expedition with Ed Ricketts. Being drawn to Mexico is part of the mythos of discovery and rebirth Steinbeck enacted in his fiction. His western settlement narratives, which so often end in disappointment, are upended by the possibility of another kind of migration, "southering," looking to another historical, cultural, and ecological frontier.

What kept his interest in Mexico so keen? Curiosity, for one thing. Settled in a Mexico City apartment on that first trip in 1935, he wrote to his agent: "It is impossible for me to do much work here. An insatiable curiosity keeps me on the streets or at the windows. Sometime I'll come back here to live I think." He relished the music,

John and Gwyn in Cuernavaca, 1945.

festivals, and markets of Mexico and included scenes of fiestas, mariachi bands, and harvesting corn in his three Mexican films. Another reason for his love of Mexico was the country's "illogic," a meandering pace that matched his own idiosyncratic ways. His handyman on the Los Gatos ranch, Frank Raineri, noted that Steinbeck asked him about Spanish holidays and celebrations. "John liked to be around Spanish celebrations. . . . He liked Spanish people and liked to be with them. He liked their way of living." Laughter also kept him interested in Mexico. In 1944, having returned from his stint as an overseas correspondent, Steinbeck lived in ❷ Cuernavaca for a few weeks with Gwyn, his young son Thom, and their sheepdog Willie.

Carol Steinbeck on a 1940 trip to the Sea of Cortez with her husband and Ricketts.

Willie the sheepdog, victim of repeated dognappings.

Willie was often dognapped, a friend from that time reported, and held for ransom. Steinbeck concocted a simple solution for Willie's return: "Steinbeck would buy a slide to be projected on the screen at the Cuernavaca movie house, offering a reward for the return of his dog. He called it a racket and in a typically profane manner denounced the thieves, but played the game."

Mexican history drew him. When he was working on the script of *Viva Zapata!*, Steinbeck kept thinking about the Alamo and Santa Ana as the real hero—the subject for another film, he thought. Steinbeck entered into the soul of Mexico as fully as he was able, embracing its traditions, pace, and people—"considerate as only Mexicans can be." The Indians of Mexico—dignified, gracious, poor—engaged his deepest sympathies. He loved the dry soil, the rocky hills, the blue water. The place and the culture tallied with his own sensibilities. *Sea of Cortez* illustrates all of these things.

Sea of Cortez

Baja California is a rugged, mountainous peninsula nearly a thousand miles long that forms the western border of the Gulf of California. Cacti stand sentinel to the sea along its length. In 1940, it was a remote, dry, and unearthly place of tiny fishing villages and a richly diverse sea, a combination that had drawn explorers for centuries. Even though Francisco de Ulloa had circumnavigated the gulf and discovered the mouth of the Colorado River by 1539, a belief that the northern end of the gulf opened into the Pacific persisted well into the seventeenth century.

When Steinbeck and Ricketts sailed on the purse seiner *Western Flyer* to ❸ the Sea of Cortez in March 1940, their intention was clear: to see everything that this place of rich biodiversity had to reveal. Theirs was

Steinbeck (center right) and Ricketts (far right) with two comrades on an expedition described in *Sea of Cortez*. This is the only known photo of the two friends together.

an expedition to collect marine invertebrates, but also became a nearly mythic trip to a legendary place—not so different, really, from the one Steinbeck had imagined for the Joads. Rather than call it the Gulf of California, Steinbeck and Ricketts refer to that body of water by its old name, the Sea of Cortez, after the legendary Spanish conquistador, "a better-sounding and a more exciting name." On their voyage they sailed past "half-mythical places, for they are not only stormy but treacherous, and again that atavistic fear arises—the Scylla-Charybdis fear that made our ancestors people such places with monsters." Again and again, Steinbeck refers to it as a place of mirages, where "the whole surrounding land is unsubstantial and changing," unreal, remote, and exotic. La Paz has "a magic carpet sound to the name," and Puerto Escondido, "the hidden harbor," is a place of magic. Like any legendary place, this one had its heroic past, and Steinbeck and Ricketts repeatedly invoke both the accomplishments and the misconceptions of the explorers and scientists who preceded them and refer to the old histories of "sturdy Jesuit fathers" building missions on the peninsula.

Steinbeck and Ricketts sailed to the Sea of Cortez on the *Western Flyer,* a wooden purse seiner. The Western Flyer Foundation is restoring the boat as an educational vessel equipped with new scientific equipment. When restoration is complete, the *Western Flyer* will stop along the West Coast and cruise to Baja.

It's "the most difficult work I've ever undertaken" he wrote to *New York Herald Tribune* book reviewer Lewis Gannet after completing the manuscript for *Sea of Cortez*, and it clearly was the most hybrid—travelogue, scientific survey, and philosophic narrative. Pages are filled with history, social commentary, environmental observation, conversations, visionary speculation, character sketches, and humor. The book embraces a holistic vision of a biologically rich environment, a place where the sea "swarms with life," the land is dry and forlorn and "burned," and Indians on "lonely little rancherias" seem "to live on remembered things, to be so related to the seashore and the rocky hills and the loneliness that they are these things." In swells of indignant prose, *Sea of Cortez* asks readers to consider that a preoccupation with "external things" may be evidence of human mutation and that a preoccupation with war may be a mutation that "will see us done for," extinct. More gently, the book draws the reader into an amalgamation of physics, metaphysics, Jungian psychology, mysticism, myth, and legend. "And then we talked and speculated, talked and drank beer." This text orchestrates place in a symphonic mode.

Filming Mexico

Steinbeck worked on three films about the native Mexican Indians, each of which considers a problem of adjustment between the Indian culture and a culture of power. His great sense of empathy was touched by the peasants of Mexico, whose land had never been their own. In some ways, the three films mirror the pattern found in Steinbeck's California labor trilogy: *The Forgotten Village*, like *In Dubious Battle* and "The Harvest Gypsies," is reportorial; *The Pearl*, like *Of Mice and Men*, is parabolic; and *Viva Zapata!* like *The Grapes of Wrath*, is an epic.

The answer to why Mexico on film interested him so keenly is found in Steinbeck's holistic sensibilities, reflected in an emblematic incident he notes in *Sea of Cortez*. In Loreto, the crew sees a lovely, admittedly gaudy statue of Our Lady of Loreto in a small, dimly lit chapel of the old mission. "This Lady, of plaster and wood and paint, is one of the strong ecological factors of the town of Loreto, and not to know her and her strength is to fail to know Loreto." Steinbeck appreciated the spiritual longing represented by Our Lady, understood that Mexico's Catholic history was as much a part of the place as the desert and Sally Lightfoot crabs and gay music that he loved. His three films help complete his own ecological embrace of Mexico.

Crew of the *Western Flyer*, including Tony Berry's wife and Carol and John, before departing, March 11, 1940.

167

"The great rocks on the end of the [Cabo] Peninsula are almost literary."

The Sea of Cortez: What Has Changed?

Tourists crowd ❹ Cabo San Lucas beaches to soak up sun and margaritas. High-rise hotels march down the coast in what Steinbeck would have termed "Floridian ugliness." Only the now-abandoned tuna cannery marks the forlorn little town that Steinbeck and Ricketts saw in 1940, one that had been struck by a devastating hurricane the year before: "The tuna cannery against the gathering rocks of the point and a few houses along the edge of the beach were the only habitations visible." But the rugged rocks at the end of the peninsula, resistant to both nature's and man's assaults, have not changed— nor has the color of the water: "Below the Mexican border the water changes color; it takes on a deep ultramarine blue—a washtub bluing blue, intense and seeming to penetrate deep into the water; the fishermen call it 'tuna water.'" Much of the dry, forbidding coast— where cactus and sea are thrown into sharp contrast—has not changed. On this gnarled peninsula, Steinbeck's words still resonate.

Historically, the Mexican government has pinpointed areas of the coast to develop, and when Cabo San Lucas was selected, the land was gobbled up in twenty short years. Although still-lonely coasts are being threatened by ever more hotels and houses—beach lots marked with tiny red flags—much remains untouched on Gulf shores: little rancherias; clusters of tiny fishing shacks; isolated beaches; fishermen going out in pangas to check nets. Up to 2015, squid fisherman in pangas caught Humboldt squid on hand lines out of Guaymas and Santa Rosalia, but since 2005—when this book was first published—the size of squid in the Gulf has decreased by two-thirds. The squid fishery in Santa Rosalia has collapsed because of long-lasting oceanic warming in the Gulf.

Baja California is a place of startling contrasts: high-rises and rancherias, cactus and sea.

❺ La Paz, a fabled city known as the City of Pearls, is still the queen. Although the pearl fishery had been devastated by disease

"The coastline of the Peninsula slid along, brown and desolate and dry with strange flat mountains and rocks torn by dryness, and the heat shimmer hung over the land even in March."

and overharvesting as early as the 1750s and was essentially gone by 1940, the city still burnishes its legendary past. In 2004, a statue, *The Old Man and the Sea,* was added along the city's malecón, the walkway along the harbor. When Steinbeck visited, there was a "broad promenade along the water lined with benches"; those remain. The crew enjoyed a beer in a spacious bar—still possible at La Perla. They wondered why this town had a "home" feeling. "We had never seen a town which even looked like La Paz, and yet coming to it was like returning rather than visiting."

In ❻ Loreto, Steinbeck and Ricketts found "the oldest mission of all,"

crumbling with decay. The Mission of Nuestra Senora de Loreto, built in 1697, has been restored, and a small museum displays artifacts. As in 1940, the town remains "asleep in the sunshine, a lovely town, with gardens in every yard and only the streets white and hot." Development—proceeding slowly—may change that sleepy image.

Many marine animals in the Sea of Cortez remain to delight scuba divers, snorkelers, and tide-pool gazers. Rays leap from the sea,

A Sally Lightfoot crab.

stretching in the sun. Dolphins still jump "out of the water and [seem] to have a very good time." Beneath coastal rocks, Sally Lightfoot crabs, red "with brilliant cloisonné carapaces, walk on their tiptoes." They scurry from human hands, and "everyone who has seen them has been delighted with them." Starfish and brittle stars, urchins, anemones, and shrimp heavily populate rocky coastal waters. When a collector shines a light at night, puffer fish and brittle stars are illuminated, "crawling about like thousands of little snakes. They barely move about in the daylight."

Many who come here wonder about the depletion of coastal resources. It's undeniable that the Sea of Cortez is an altered place, particularly with regard to larger species—Humboldt squid, sperm whales, and vaquita, the latter on the brink of extinction. Perhaps the most dramatic example is the sea turtles that "appeared in numbers" off Magdalena Bay in 1940 and are now depleted there and elsewhere. But today they are protected and in some cases recovering. Hardly any swordfish "play about," leaping out of the sea in the way Steinbeck describes, but one can still witness sailfish and marlin jumping at the right place and time. Schools of yellowfin tuna no longer "beat the water to spray in their millions," and catches have decreased in the last couple of decades. But the protected islands and Cabo Pulmo marine sanctuary (Steinbeck and Ricketts's second stop) are still rich with marine life. In reality, marine ecosystems are dynamic living things that are constantly changing, and we are only beginning to appreciate the complexities involved.

"The abundance of life here gives one an exuberance, a feeling of fullness and richness," Steinbeck wrote. **"Everything ate everything else with a furious exuberance."**

Perhaps the secrets of change lie deeper, beneath the surface of the blue waters. It is here where all marine food chains begin, with lowly planktonic organisms, many invisible to the naked eye. Changes at this foundation level can reverberate throughout the entire ecosystem to the very predators. A holistic problem indeed, and marine scientists today are struggling to understand how such changes might be influenced by long-term climate change (natural or anthropogenic), by artificial fertilization due to agricultural runoff, and by other hidden factors.

Cabo San Lucas today.

Reading *Sea of Cortez* (1941) and *Log from Sea of Cortez* (1951)

Reviewing *Sea of Cortez* (1941), Lewis Gannett of the *New York Herald Tribune* wrote that there is here "more of the whole man, John Steinbeck, than in any of his novels." That is true, but many readers prefer the whole man light, perhaps in a book like *Travels with Charley*. *Sea of Cortez* must be savored, paragraph by paragraph. Thoughts are organic, branching off, bursting forth. And the long "Easter Sunday Sermon" by Ed Ricketts, chapter 14, is tough going for even the most devoted Steinbeck aficionado.

In this book, Steinbeck wanted to capture the quality of his long association with Ed Ricketts, their conversations, shared interests, and scientific curiosity. As he was writing the first draft, Steinbeck wrote his editor that "there are four levels of statement in it and I think very few will follow it down to the fourth. I even think it is a new kind of writing. I told you once that I found a great poetry in scientific thinking."

If the deepest level in *Sea of Cortez* is mythic, another level is scientific, the poetry of the intertidal. Steinbeck, Ricketts, Carol, and the crew collected at numerous intertidal sites in the *Sea of Cortez*, looking at species distribution.

The catalogues of marine invertebrates, both verbal and pictorial (the 1941 edition includes Ricketts's phyletic catalogue), are as crucial to this book as are Whitman's long lists to *Song of Myself*. The particulars of intertidal life are visual snapshots of species in broad distribution patterns, as Steinbeck writes about the first collecting site at Cabo San Lucas:

> We collected down the littoral as the water went down. . . . The uppermost rocks swarmed with Sally Lightfoots, those beautiful and fast and sensitive crabs. With them were white periwinkle snails. Below that, barnacles and Purpura snails; more crabs

Barnacles.

Anemones.

and many limpets. *Below that many serpulids—attached worms in calcareous tubes with beautiful purple floriate heads. Below that, the multi-rayed starfish, Heliaster kubiniji of Xanthus. With Heliaster were a few urchins, but not many, and they were so placed in crevices as to be hard to dislodge. . . . Lower still there were to be seen swaying in the water under the reefs the dark gorgorians, or sea-fans. In the lowest surf levels there was a brilliant gathering of the moss animals known as bryozoa; flatworms; flat crabs; the large sea-cucumber; some anemones; many sponges of two types, a smooth, encrusting purple one, the other erect, white, and calacareous. There were great colonies of tunicates, clusters of tiny individuals joined by a common tunic and looking so like the sponges that even a trained worker must await the specialist's determination to know whether his find is sponge or tunicate. This is annoying, for the sponge being one step above the protozoa, at the bottom of the evolutionary ladder, and the tunicate near the top, bordering the vertebrates, your trained worker is likely to feel that a dirty trick has been played upon him by an entirely too democratic Providence.*

That layered catalogue sways with the retreating water, as intertidal collecting necessarily involves keeping one's eye on retreating and incoming tides. A reader, like a visitor to the region, should gaze attentively at the species hidden in this dry, seemingly barren land, turn rocks carefully in the intertidal to see squirming brittle stars. To look, Steinbeck suggests, is the first step in understanding place, appreciating what is.

Purpura snail.

Heliaster.

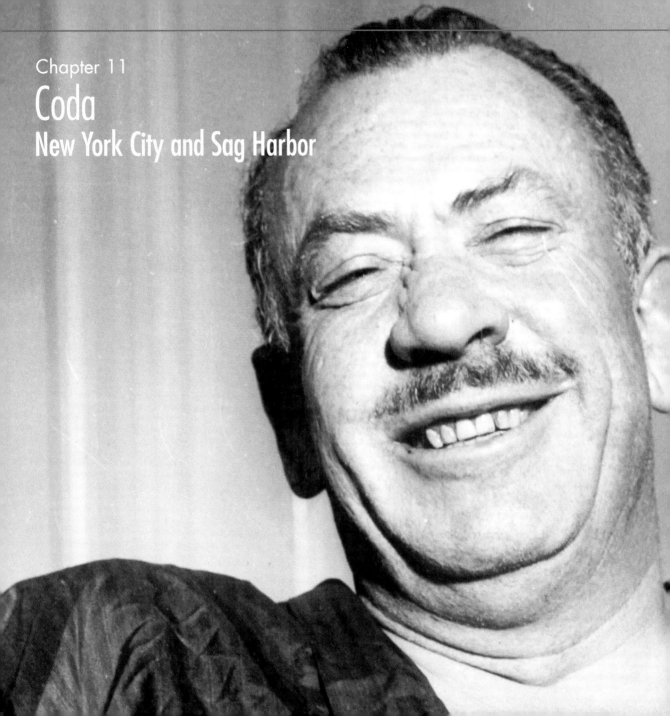

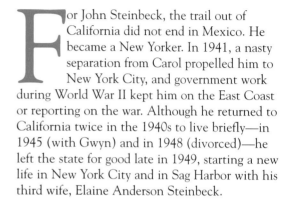

In the concluding pages of his final book, *America and Americans* (1966), Steinbeck considers the restlessness of Americans and, in effect, of himself: "Americans do not lack places to go and new things to find. . . . Far larger experiences are open to our restlessness—the fascinating unknown is everywhere. . . . We have never sat still for long; we have never been content with a place, a building—or with ourselves."

For John Steinbeck, the trail out of California did not end in Mexico. He became a New Yorker. In 1941, a nasty separation from Carol propelled him to New York City, and government work during World War II kept him on the East Coast or reporting on the war. Although he returned to California twice in the 1940s to live briefly—in 1945 (with Gwyn) and in 1948 (divorced)—he left the state for good late in 1949, starting a new life in New York City and in Sag Harbor with his third wife, Elaine Anderson Steinbeck.

Steinbeck's appreciation for New York City would grow slowly. Becoming an urbanite was "rough," he admitted in a 1953 essay, "Making of a New Yorker." And it may be true that the transformation from man of the soil and sea to man of the streets was never quite realized. Certainly the city had chastened him on his 1925 sojourn, when he had worked as a cub reporter. Returning nearly twenty-five years later, he embraced city life with gusto: "New York is the only city I have ever lived in. It is true I have had apartments in San Francisco, Mexico City, Los Angeles, Paris, and sometimes have stayed for months, but that is a very different thing. As far as homes go, there is only a small California town and New York." He loved his East 72nd Street house, where he and Elaine lived for thirteen years, and later the apartment they moved to across the street, with a commanding view of the skyline. He loved New York

neighborhoods—"villages" really—relished the city's energy, its theaters, and nights at the 21 Club.

During the last eighteen years of his life, Steinbeck was sustained by a solid marriage, urbane friends, a summer cottage near the water in Sag Harbor, and the time and money to travel as widely as his restless soul craved.

Critic upon critic has asserted that when Steinbeck left California, he abandoned his subject, the rich soil of the Salinas Valley, the fine clear water of Monterey Bay. In truth, he didn't—he spent much of the 1950s writing about his past. But it also might be said that

Steinbeck's last loop from West Coast to East was to another frontier. He inhabited a kind of psychic West with creative frontiers and satisfying homesteads that sustained and engaged him.

In 1953, the couple bought a cottage in Sag Harbor on a piece of land surrounded by water: "I have a warm and cozy little fishing cottage there, set

John Steinbeck and his dog Charley, 1961. Photo by Hans Namuth.

on a point of land that extends into a protected bay," he wrote in one of his best personal essays, "Conversation at Sag Harbor." In Sag Harbor, he could once again cast down his anchor, throw out his line, dream his dreams, and sing out his prose to the fishes. And in alluring and elusive New York City, married to a Texan, he could relish the swirl of a diverse population and soaring concrete cliffs. If his best fiction did not come from this completion of self, some of his boldest and most inventive works did. John Steinbeck, writer to the end, grasped life and art with the full-bodied grip of a westerner.

John IV, Thom, John, and Elaine.

Timeline

1902 — John Steinbeck is born on February 27 in Salinas, a Northern California agricultural town. On his bedroom wall his mother hangs a picture of George Washington so that her only son might "catch" a bit of presidential greatness.

1919–25 — John enrolls at Stanford University, 100 miles north of Salinas. Away from strict parents and his hometown, John enjoys what Stanford has to offer—freedom, friends, and writing instruction—and, in ROTC training, the opportunity to ride a horse regularly. He drops in and out of university.

1925 — John hops a freighter to New York City, determined to break into the world of published writers.

1926–28 — Unpublished, discouraged, and broke, John returns

John Steinbeck as a teenager. He wrote in later years, "You must know that the story cycle of King Arthur and his knights, particularly in the Malory version, has been my passion since my ninth birthday, when I was given a copy of the 'Morte d'Arthur.' Then my little sister, Mary, and I became knight and squire, and we even used the archaic and obsolete middle English words as a secret language."

home and finds a job as caretaker for a Lake Tahoe estate, spending two long winters holed up in a cabin honing his craft. "No, I am not becoming hand-somer. . . . My face," Steinbeck admitted to a college friend, "gets more and more Irish looking, and I have never heard anyone say that the Irish are a handsome race."

1929 — Steinbeck's swashbuckling first novel, *Cup of Gold—A Life of Henry Morgan, Buccaneer, with Occasional Reference to History,* is published to scant reviews.

1930 — John marries Carol Henning of San Jose, a feisty, witty woman and John's faithful in-house editor during their decade of marriage.

1931 — With the help of college friends, John finds a New York literary agency, McIntosh & Otis, to help place his fiction. The women running the firm become his lifelong friends.

1932 — *The Pastures of Heaven,* Steinbeck's first California fiction, is published. It is a collection of short stories about a meddlesome family who move into what seems an edenic valley.

1933 — In *To a God Unknown,* a novel he had wrestled with for years, Steinbeck writes through his metaphysical notions about humans and place, pantheism, and mysticism. Steinbeck's thinking is profoundly influenced by Joseph Campbell and Robinson Jeffers.

1935 — With *Tortilla Flat*, a wry tale about the paisanos of Monterey, Steinbeck hits pay dirt. Using royalty income, John and Carol visit Mexico; he later writes that he feels "related to Spanish people much more than to Anglo-Saxons."

1936 — *In Dubious Battle*, one of the best strike novels of the twentieth century, is published. His growing reputation as a socially engaged writer catches the attention of the editor of the *San Francisco News*, who sends Steinbeck on a journalistic assignment—to report on the plight of the Okies in California. Steinbeck's hard-hitting articles, "The Harvest Gypsies," are published in October.

1937 — *Of Mice and Men*, one of Steinbeck's finest novels, is published to a widely admiring audience. A few months later, on November 23, George Kaufman opens the play *Of Mice and Men* in New York City. To Kaufman's disappointment, John never comes East to see the play, which wins the New York Drama Critics Circle award the following year.

1938 — Steinbeck's editor, Pascal Covici, brings out a collection of Steinbeck's short stories for Viking Press, *The Long Valley*. Viking remains Steinbeck's publisher for the rest of his career.

1939 — Viking Press spends more on the publicity campaign for *The Grapes of Wrath* than for any other book in its history. But, at the height of his fame, lionized and criticized, Steinbeck wants only to escape the publicity. In Los Angeles he meets Gwyn Conger, who will become his second wife four years later.

1940 — John Steinbeck is a "household name," declares publicity for two superb films: Lewis

***Tortilla Flat*, a painting by Penny Worthington.**

Milestone's *Of Mice and Men*, released in December 1939, and John Ford's *The Grapes of Wrath*, released in January 1940. *The Grapes of Wrath* is awarded the National Book Award and the Pulitzer Prize.

John escapes to the sea in March 1940 on a voyage of discovery with his wife, Carol, and his friend Edward F. Ricketts.

1941 — *Sea of Cortez*, cowritten by Steinbeck and Ricketts, is published a few days before Pearl Harbor. Steinbeck's best work of nonfiction initially receives little notice

***The Grapes of Wrath* was published to worldwide acclaim and controversy in 1939. This is a later Spanish edition.**

Steinbeck depicted writing *Sea of Cortez* in a painting by Judith Diem. Notice how he holds his pencil; he had such large calluses from spending so much time writing that he had to hold his pencil awkwardly.

and less appreciation. *The Forgotten Village*, a documentary film, is released.

1942 — Steinbeck is passionately committed to helping the war effort. In *The Moon Is Down* (a book and a play) he imagines what it must be like to live in an occupied northern European village. He is attacked as being unpatriotic and "soft" on Nazis. In November, *Bombs Away*, a book about training bomber teams, is published.

1943 — Steinbeck's divorce from Carol is finalized in March and a few days later he marries Gwyn Conger in New Orleans. Weeks after the wedding, the restless and committed patriot goes overseas as a war correspondent for the *New York Herald-Tribune*, determined to witness action at the front. He wires eighty-six dispatches to newspapers in the United States and London.

1944 — Son Thom is born on August 2. Steinbeck and Gwyn briefly move back to his home turf, the Monterey Peninsula, where the world-famous author feels out of place: "If I bring good whiskey to a party, I'm elitist; if I bring Dago Red I'm cheap," he reportedly said. Local business interests give this "communist" writer the cold shoulder.

1945 — Steinbeck's nostalgic, humorous, and complex novel about Monterey, *Cannery Row*, is published. Ricketts writes to a friend that the book was written "as an essay on loneliness." Steinbeck returns to New York with Gwyn.

1946 — Son John IV is born on June 12 in New York City. John's marriage to Gwyn is troubled by her suspected infidelity and her taunts—all untrue—that his younger son is not his own.

1947 — *The Wayward Bus* is published. Steinbeck goes to Russia with photographer Robert Capa to interview the people living in postwar Russia—his focus is solidly on people, not politics, he declares. In November *The Pearl* is published, a parable about temptation and power set in Mexico (released as a film the same year).

1948 — *A Russian Journal* is published. This year proves to be one of the writer's worst. His best friend, Ed Ricketts, dies in May, after being hit by a train. Gwyn and John part ways in August.

1950 — John releases some of the rancor he feels toward his divorce and fatherhood in his third and final play-novelette, *Burning Bright*. He marries for the third time, this a happy and stable union with Elaine Anderson Scott, once an assistant stage manager on Broadway. They settle into an apartment on 72nd Street in New York City.

1952 — Elia Kazan's *Viva Zapata!* is released in March. Steinbeck's novel about Salinas, *East of Eden*, is published in September. Steinbeck and Elaine take off for Europe, where they will spend many happy months over the years satisfying his wanderlust and her love of exotic locales. He writes journalistic pieces for various magazines.

1954 — *Sweet Thursday*, a frothy sequel to *Cannery Row* written for the musical theater, is published, a book about "what might have happened" to Ed Ricketts.

1955 — *East of Eden*, featuring James Dean in his first starring role, hits the theaters. John and Elaine buy a summerhouse in Sag Harbor, New York, and begin to split their time between that house and their apartment in Manhattan. The musical *Pipe Dream* by Rodgers and Hammerstein, based on *Sweet Thursday*, opens on Broadway.

1957 — *The Short Reign of Pippin IV*, a satire on French politics, is published. Steinbeck begins research on a beloved project, a modern translation of Malory's *Morte d'Arthur*. (Never completed, his draft was published posthumously as *The Acts of King Arthur and his Noble Knights* in 1976.)

1958 — *Once There Was a War*, a collection of his war journalism, is published.

1960 — After fainting spells that signal a weak heart, John plans a trip across America with the poodle Charley as his only companion. Charley is Elaine's dog, and she urges John to take Charley for protection, to bark for help if he is ill. John tells Elaine that he's "taking Charley, not Lassie!" *Travels with Charley* is published in1962.

1961 — John publishes his twelfth and final novel, *The Winter of Our Discontent*, which is the occasion for his receiving the Nobel Prize in 1962.

1963 — John, Elaine, and Edward Albee travel with the U.S. State Department to Scandinavia, Russia, and Eastern Europe.

1966 — Steinbeck's last book, *America and Americans*, a jeremiad about the country's wavering morality, ecological waste, and ethnic distrust, is published. He travels on assignment with *Newsday* to Vietnam. His admiration for the U.S. soldiers' dedication and his hatred of communism make many think that he supports the unpopular war—in fact, he has grave doubts about Lyndon Johnson's policies. "Letters to Alicia" run in papers around the country.

1968 — John Steinbeck dies of heart failure in New York City, December 20.

Drawing by John Roby for the *Salinas Californian's* 1963 Progress and Rodeo Edition, which honored "Steinbeck as a native son and as the 1962 'Winner of the Nobel Prize for Literature.'"

For Further Reading

Richard Astro, John Steinbeck, and Edward F. Ricketts, *The Shaping of a Novelist* (University of Minnesota Press, 1973; Hemet, CA: Western Flyer Publishing, 2002).

Sanora Babb, *Whose Names Are Unknown* (Norman, University of Oklahoma Press, 2004).

Stephanie Barron, Sheri Bernstein, and Ilene Susan Fort, *Made in California: Art, Image, and Identity, 1900–2000* (Berkeley: University of California Press, 2000).

Susan F. Beegel, Susan Shillinglaw, and Wesley N. Tiffney, Jr., *Steinbeck and the Environment: Interdisciplinary Approaches* (Tuscaloosa: University of Alabama Press, 1997).

Jackson J. Benson, *The Short Novels of John Steinbeck: Critical Essays with a Checklist to Steinbeck Criticism* (Durham, NC: Duke University Press, 1990).

———, *The True Adventures of John Steinbeck, Writer* (New York: Viking, 1984).

Cletus E. Daniel, *Bitter Harvest: A History of California Farmworkers, 1870–1941* (Berkeley: University of California Press, 1982).

Morris Dickstein, *Dancing in the Dark: A Cultural History of the Great Depression* (New York: W.W. Norton, 2009).

Thomas Fensch, *Conversations with John Steinbeck* (Jackson: University Press of Mississippi, 1988).

Albert Gelpi, *The Wild God of the World: An Anthology of Robinson Jeffers* (Palo Alto, CA: Stanford University Press, 2003).

Harold Gilliam and Ann Gilliam, *Creating Carmel: The Enduring Vision* (Salt Lake City, UT: Peregrine Smith Books, 1992).

Charlotte Cook Hadella, *Of Mice and Men: A Kinship of Powerlessness* (New York: Twayne, 1995).

Michael Kenneth Hemp, *Cannery Row: The History of Old Ocean View Avenue* (Pacific Grove, CA: History Company Publishers, 1986).

Neal Hotelling, *Pebble Beach Golf Links: The Official History* (Chelsea, MI, Sleeping Bear Press, 1999).

Anne Loftis, *Witnesses to the Struggle: Imaging the 1930s California Labor Movement* (Reno: University of Nevada Press, 1998).

Sandy Lydon, *Chinese Gold: The Chinese in the Monterey Bay Region* (Capitola, CA: Capitola Book Company, 1985).

———, *The Japanese in the Monterey Bay Region: A Brief History* (Capitola, CA: Capitola Book Company, 1997).

Carol McKibben, *Beyond Cannery Row: Sicilian Women, Immigration, and Community in Monterey California 1915–1999* (Champaign: University of Illinois Press, 2006).

Martha K. Norkunas, *The Politics of Public Memory: Tourism, History, and Ethnicity in Monterey, California* (Albany: State University of New York Press, 1993).

Louis Owens, *John Steinbeck's Re-Vision of America* (Athens: University of Georgia Press, 1985).

Jay Parini, *John Steinbeck: A Biography* (London: Heinemann, 1994).

Katherine A. Rodger, *Breaking Through: Essays, Journals, and Travelogues of Edward F. Ricketts* (Berkeley, University of California Press, 2006).

————, *Renaissance Man of Cannery Row: The Life and Letters of Edward F. Ricketts* (Tuscaloosa: University of Alabama Press, 2002).

Vicki L. Ruiz, *Cannery Women, Cannery Lives: Mexican Women, Unionization, and the California Food Processing Industry, 1930–1950* (Albuquerque: University of New Mexico Press, 1987).

Carlton Sheffield, *Steinbeck: The Good Companion* (Berkeley: Creative Arts Book Company, 2002).

Susan Shillinglaw, *On Reading* The Grapes of Wrath (New York: Penguin, 2014).

————, *Carol and John Steinbeck: Portrait of a Marriage* (Reno: University of Nevada Press, 2013).

Susan Shillinglaw and Jackson J. Benson, *John Steinbeck, America and Americans and Selected Nonfiction* (New York: Viking Press, 2002).

Kevin Starr, *Endangered Dreams: The Great Depression in California* (New York: Oxford University Press, 1996).

Elaine Steinbeck and Robert Wallsten, *Steinbeck: A Life in Letters* (New York: Viking Penguin, 1975).

John Steinbeck, *Journal of a Novel: The* East of Eden *Letters* (New York: Viking Press, 1969).

————, *Working Days: The Journals of* The Grapes of Wrath, edited by Robert DeMott (New York: Viking Press, 1989).

Eric Enno Tamm, *Beyond the Outer Shores: The Untold Odyssey of Ed Ricketts, the Pioneering Ecologist Who Inspired John Steinbeck and Joseph Campbell* (New York: Four Walls Eight Windows, 2004).

Jennie Dennis Verardo and Denzil Verardo, *Salinas Valley: An Illustrated History* (Eugene, OR: Windsor Publications, 1989).

Franklin Walker, *The Seacoast of Bohemia* (Salt Lake City, UT: Peregrine Smith, 1973).

John Walton, *Storied Land: Community and Memory in Monterey* (Berkeley: University of California Press, 2001).

Rick Wartzman, *Obscene in the Extreme: The Burning and Banning of John Steinbeck's* The Grapes of Wrath (New York: Public Affairs, 2008).

WPA Guide to the Monterey Peninsula: Compiled by Workers of the Writers' Program of the Work Projects Administration in Northern California (Stanford, CA: James Ladd Delkin, 1946; Tucson: University of Arizona Press, 1989).

David Wyatt, *The Fall into Eden: Landscape and Imagination in California* (New York: Cambridge University Press, 1986).

————, *Five Fires: Race, Catastrophe, and the Shaping of California* (Reading, MA: Addison-Wesley Publishing Company, 1997).

Notes

Preface

vi: "in Steinbeck's fiction . . .": David Ligare, *Viewpoint: The Pastures of Heaven: An Exhibition oin Celebration of the John Steinbeck Centenary*, April 27–August 4, 2002.

vii: "frantically unenthusiastic": John Steinbeck (JS), *The First Watch* (Los Angeles, Ward Ritchie Press, 1947).

vii: "he savored . . . " Author interview with Elaine Steinbeck, 1998.

viii: "a Don-Quixote-ish . . . ": Elaine Steinbeck to John P. McKnight, 1958, University of Virginia, Folder 6239 V.

viii: "To the stars . . . ": Elaine Steinbeck letter, Center for Steinbeck Studies.

ix: "But it's also true . . . ": Shillinglaw and Benson, *America and Americans*, p. 324.

ix: "Kingdom of despondency . . . ": JS datebook, April 20, 1948 (Pierpont Morgan Library).

ix: "My hunger for there . . . ": JS datebook, April 27, 1948.

Chapter 1

3: "the story of this whole valley . . .": Elaine Steinbeck and Robert Wallsten, *Steinbeck: A Life in Letters (Life in Letters)* (New York: Viking, 1975), p. 73.

3: "My wish is . . .": JS, *Journal of a Novel* (New York: Viking, 1959), p. 61.

3: D. H. Lawrence, *Studies in Classic American Literature* (New York: Doubleday, 1951), pp. 4–5.

4: "On the level vegetable lands . . .": JS, *The Grapes of Wrath* (New York: Penguin, 1992).

4: "My country is different . . .": JS to Robert O. Ballou, 1933, Harry Ransom Humanities Research Center, University of Texas, Austin (University of Texas).

5: "the great word sounds . . .": JS datebook, April 17, 1948, Pierpont Morgan Library (Pierpont Morgan).

5: "and I think very few will follow . . .": JS to Pascal Covici, July 7, 1941, University of Texas.

6: "The floor of the Salinas . . .": JS, *East of Eden* (New York: Penguin, 1992), p. 4.

6: "orange and speckled and fluted nudibranchs . . .": JS, *Cannery Row* (New York: Penguin, 1994).

6: "Each figure is a population . . .": JS, 1932, *To a God Unknown* notebook, Department of Special Collections, Stanford University Libraries (Stanford University).

8: "wall of background . . .": Long Valley Ledger, Center for Steinbeck Studies, San Jose State University (SJSU).

8: "I don't know who the dark watchers . . .": JS to Miss Ridley, 1953, National Steinbeck Center (NSC) archives.

9: "After the valleys were settled . . .": *East of Eden*.

10: "Behind each story, inside it . . .": Joseph R. McElrath, Jr., Jesse S. Crisler, and Susan Shillinglaw, *John Steinbeck: The Contemporary Reviews* (Cambridge: Cambridge University Press, 1996), p. 178.

10: "You know the big pine tree . . . ": *Life in Letters*, p. 31.

10: "Adults haven't the fine clean . . .": JS to Ben Abramson, 1936, University of Texas.

10: "colors more clear than they . . .": Jackson J. Benson, *The True Adventures of John Steinbeck, Writer* (New York, Penguin: 1984), pp. 325–26.

Chapter 2

13: "Strange how I keep . . .": JS datebook, April 24, 1948.

13: "Portuguese and Swiss and Scandinavians": "Always Something To Do in Salinas," Shillinglaw and Benson, *America and Americans*, p. 5.

13: Reports cards are in the family collection.

14: "the richest community . . . ": Shillinglaw and Benson, *America and Americans*, p. 5.

15: "a kind of local competition . . . ": Susan Shillinglaw and Jackson Benson, *America and Americans and Selected Nonfiction* (New York: Viking, 2002), p. 6.

15: "I can remember my mother . . . ": JS to Dorothy Vera, Salinas *Californian*, January 11, 1969.

16: "social structure of Salinas was a strange . . ." and "blackness . . .": Shillinglaw and Benson, *America and Americans*, pp. 6–7.

16: "have condemned the action of Japan . . .": Clifford Lewis, "John Steinbeck's Alternative to Internment Camps: A Policy for the President, December 15, 1941," *Journal of the West*, January 1995, pp. 55–61.

18: "a tough little monkey . . .": "The Summer Before," Kiyoshi Nakayama (ed.), *The Uncollected Stories of John Steinbeck* (Tokyo: Nan'un-Do, 1986).

18: "He loved a sense of home . . .": Terry Grant Halladay, "The Closest Witness: The Autobiographical Reminiscences of Gwendolyn Conger Steinbeck" (M.A. thesis, Stephen F. Austin State University, 1979).

18: "I think no one ever had . . .": JS to Nelson Valjean, March 13, 1953, *Life in Letters*, p. 467.

18: "Wish I had a good farm and a sure crop . . .": Mr. Steinbeck to Esther Steinbeck, January 20, 1911, Stanford University.

19: "In my struggle to be a writer . . .": quoted in Benson, *The True Adventures*, p. 15.

19: "never knows when to quit . . .": Mr. Steinbeck to Esther Steinbeck, October 27, 1910, Stanford University.

20: "Mother stated . . .": JS to parents, March 1926, Stanford University.

20: "I had a cloth hat . . .": JS to Esther Steinbeck, January 9, 1950, Stanford University.

21: "The novel of Salinas . . .": JS to Ted Miller, September 1930, author's collection.

21: "practice poetry": JS datebook, 1948.

21: "while I am talking to the boys . . .": *Journal of a Novel*, p. 8.

22: ""North America's favorite . . .": www.taylorfarms.com/our-story.

23: "was a very good listener . . .": Glenn Graves interviewed by Pauline Pearson, 1969, NSC archives.

26: "a perfect example, inside and out": National Register of Historic Places proposal for historic status, NSC archives.

26: "name a bowling alley after me . . .": JS to Mrs. Radcliffe, December 22, 1957, NSC archives.

26: "Your charming suggestion . . .": JS to Mr. Ward, November 21, 1962, NSC archives.

26: "no town celebrates a writer . . .": JS to "Editors, artists, writers of the Rodeo Edition," July 25, 1963, NSC archives.

27: "I voted against it . . .": quoted in Herb Caen, "Latest from Lettuceland," *San Francisco Chronicle*, March 3, 1969.

27: "Your only weapon is your work": Robert DeMott (ed.), *Your Only Weapon Is Your Work: A Letter by John Steinbeck to Dennis Murphy* (San Jose: Steinbeck Research Center, 1985).

27: "set the cross…": *Winter of Our Discontent*, p. 99. 29: "And do you remember . . .": *East of Eden*.

30: "He set armed guards over . . . ": Shillinglaw and Benson, *America and Americans*, p. 11.

Chapter 3

35: "an execrable place at best . . .": Stephen Powers, *A Walk from Sea to Sea* (Hartford, CT: Columbian Book Co., 1872), p. 305.

36: "the howling wind came through . . .": "Fingers of Cloud," *Stanford Spectator*, February 1924, p. 149.

37: "The surges of the new restless . . .": Shillinglaw and Benson, *America and Americans*, p. 320.

37: "The peak used to be . . .": JS to Carl Wilhelmson, 1920s, Stanford University.

39: "found the old stage road . . .": JS to Gwyn Steinbeck, February 17, 1948, *Life in Letters*, p. 307.

39: "Some workers testified . . .": Court case documents on the short-handled hoe, NSC archives.

40: "Now if you farmers . . ." : Quoted in Jim Conway, "Spreckels Sugar Company: The First Fifty Years," MA thesis, SJSU, December 1999, p. 19.

40: "the greatest of all undertakings . . .": Salinas *Index*, April 27, 1899, quoted in Conway, p. 30.

40: "You'd soak the ground in March . . .": John Vierra, quoted in Conway, p. 59.

42: "worked alongside . . .": Thomas Fensch (ed.), *Conversations with John Steinbeck* (Jackson: University Press of Mississippi, 1988), p. 9.

42–43: "I have usually avoided using . . .": JS to Harry Thornton Moore, March 26, 1939, University of Virginia.

42: "He saw the quail . . .": JS, *The Red Pony* (New York: Penguin, 1994).

43: "And then the summer came . . .": "The Summer Before," Nakayama, *The Uncollected Stories* (New York: Penguin, 1995).

46: "rounded benign mountain": *Travels with Charley*.

47: "I would love to have the old place . . .": JS to Bo Beskow, April 29,1948, *Life in Letters*, p. 311.

Chapter 4

Unless noted otherwise, all letters in this chapter are held at Stanford University.

49: "What I do know . . .": JS to Belle McKenzie, 1939, author's collection.

50: "an institution for the relief . . .": Quoted in David Starr Jordan, *The Days of a Man: Being Memories of a Naturalist, Teacher And A Minor Prophet of Democracy*, Vol. 1 and Vol. 11 (Yonkers-on-Hudson, NY: World Book Company, 1922).

51: "have a sound practical idea . . .": Ibid.

52: "something in the pioneer tradition . . .": Author's collection.

53: "You'll never find . . .": Webster Street to JS, author's collection.

53: "Neither this person . . .": JS to Ruth Carpenter Sheffield, June 1926, *Life in Letters*, p. 13.

54: "My tattoo stands up pretty well . . .": JS to George Mors, February 25, 1964, NSC archives.

55: "One should never miss . . .": Robert De Roos, "Stanford Greats: Edith Mirrielees," *Stanford Observer*, October 1988, p. 19.

56: "monstrous New York . . .": Shillinglaw and Benson, *America and Americans*, pp. 33–34.

56: "I was scared . . .": *Life in Letters*, p. 9.

59: "as a whole, utterly . . .": JS to Sheffield, *Life in Letters*, p. 11.

61: "How beautiful . . .": Shillinglaw and Benson, *America and Americans*, p. 15.

61: "The Caen type of gossip column . . .": JS to Mr. Downie, April 12, 1963, NSC archives.

62: "vague and optimistic . . .": Carlton Sheffield, *John Steinbeck: The Good Companion* (Berkeley, CA: Creative Arts Book Company, 2002), pp. 160–61.

63: "John and Carol enjoyed participating . . .": Sheffield, p. 159.

Chapter 5

67: "were coming back from Palo Alto . . .": Pauline Pearson interview with Toby Street, NSC archives.

68: "There was the great Feast of Lanterns . . .": JS, "This Is the Monterey We Love," *Monterey Peninsula Herald*, July 3, 1946, Sec. 3. p. 1.

68: "I have been planting . . .": Bancroft Library, University of California at Berkeley (UCB).

69: "we found ourselves to be in the best port": Sandy Lydon, *Chinese Gold: The Chinese in the Monterey Bay Region* (Capitola, CA: Capitola Book Company, 1985), pp. 17–18.

70: "minds inflamed by moving pictures . . .": "John Steinbeck States His Views on Cannery Row," *Monterey Peninsula Herald*, March 8, 1957, p. 1.

70: "Hard, dry Spaniards came exploring . . .": *East of Eden*.

71: "The Monterey of last year exists . . .": Robert Louis Stevenson, *Across the Plains* (New York; Scribner's, 1900).

72: "native Californians of Monterey . . .": Lucy Morse, "Monterey, The Old Capital of California," *Noticias del Puerto de Monterey: A Quarterly Bulletin of Historic Monterey*, February 2002.

72: "good people of laughter and kindness . . .": JS, foreword to *Tortilla Flat*, 1937 edition (New York: Penguin, 1997).

72: "a chronic thorn . . ." and "truly an institution . . .": Earl Hofeldt, "Monterey Paisano Dies," *Monterey Peninsula Herald*, November 7, 1957.

72: "Absolutely, Pilon and me . . .": Dudley Towe, "Pilon and Me," *Game and Gossip*, January 20, 1958. p. 14.

72: "I protest Pilon's arrest . . .": JS to Judge Baugh, 1953, California History Room, Monterey Public Library.

73: "There was always available Pilon . . .": "Memoirs of Sal Colleto," Maritime Museum of Monterey.

73: "There are so many . . .": JS to Annie Laurie Williams, December 8, 1937, *Life in Letters*, p. 150.

74: "those in the office representing . . .": Del Monte File, California Room, Monterey Public Library.

75: "These were pretty good people . . .": Dennis Copeland, "Susan Gregory's '*Tortilla Flat*'," *Noticias del Puerto de Monterey: A Quarterly Bulletin of Historic Monterey*, February 2002.

75: "We had a whole lot of fun . . .": Towe, p. 14.

75: "bounded by First and Third Avenue . . .": Emil White (ed.), *Circle of Enchantment: Big Sur, Carmel, Pebble Beach, Monterey, Pacific Grove* (Pacific Grove: Emil White 1964).

76: "we will startle . . .": Ray A. March, "Dali Throws the Party of the Century," *Buying the Best: The Magazine for People Who Love The Monterey Peninsula*, pp. 66–68.

76: "Dali Baffles Best People," *Monterey Peninsula Herald*, September 3, 1941.

78: "splendid gallops . . .": Teddy Roosevelt, 1903, Del Monte File, California Room, Monterey Public Library.

79: "might have grown . . .": Mary Austin, Pebble Beach archives.

81: "There was a great fire last night . . ." JS to Carl Wilhelmson, *Life in Letters*, pp. 30–31.

Chapter 6

83: "I expect to give myself . . .": JS to Kate Beswick, early 1930, Stanford University.

84: "I must have at least one book . . .": JS to Ted Miller, *Life in Letters*, p. 25.

84: "Sometimes I catch eels . . .": JS to Kate Beswick, early 1930, Stanford University.

85: "I Don't Like Mr. Hearst . . .": Carol Steinbeck, *A Slim Volume to End Slim Volumes*, Center for Steinbeck Studies, SJSU.

85: " Nothing mattered but John . . .": Helen Worden, "Mrs. John Steinbeck Fights for Her Man," *San Francisco News*, August 12, 1941.

86: "almost an unconscious state . . .": JS datebook, 1948.

86: "when there is no writing . . ."; "foetus . . ."; "my own children . . ."; "satisfaction . . .": *Life in Letters*, pp. 25, 35, 48, 119.

87: "I think flowers . . .": JS to Pascal Covici, September 1948, *Life in Letters*, pp. 333–34.

87: "It is a gloomy day . . .": JS to Carl Wilhelmson, *Life in Letters*, p. 30.

87: "The little Pacific. . . ": UCB.

88: "We went to PG . . .": JS to Pat Covici, January 1943, University of Texas.

88: "Must have anonymity . . .": JS to Elizabeth Otis and Annie Laurie Williams, March 19, 1937, *Life in Letters*, p. 138.

89: "and planted me . . .": Almira Steinbeck to Esther Steinbeck, April 10, 1905, Stanford University.

89: "very wild and full of weeds . . .": JS to Kate Beswick, February 1929, Stanford University.

89: "My garden is so lovely . . .": JS to Ted Miller, 1931, *Life in Letters*, p. 45.

89: "Pacific Grove and Monterey . . . ": JS, *Sweet Thursday* (New York: Penguin, 1996).

90: "It took . . .": Mary Austin, Carmel *Cymbal*, September 8, 1926, p. 11.

90: "Belgian shepherd puppy . . .": All references to dogs are from *Life in Letters*, pp 21, 24, 42–43, 46, 66, 69.

91: "It wasn't all fun . . .": "A Primer on the Thirties," Shillinglaw and Benson, *America and Americans*, pp. 22–23.

91: "John went completely . . .": Author interview with Marjorie Lloyd, March 1990.

91: "Minor tragedy stalked . . .": JS to Elizabeth Otis, May 27, 1936, *Life in Letters*, p. 124.

92: "Abbott nabs brewery . . ." and all other quotes in this paragraph: *Pacific Grove Tribune*, 1931–32, Pacific Grove Public library.

93: "the one who feels . . .": Benson, *The True Adventures*, p. 477.

94: "mysterious marvel . . .": *Monterey Peninsula Herald*, June 17, 1932, p. 6.

94: "No, I'm afraid it wasn't your man . . .": JS to John S. Coats, *Monterey Peninsula Herald*, February 22, 1964.

95: "Why don't those men . . .": Julia Platt, quoted in *Pacific Grove Tribune*, 1932.

97: "Today I have been thinking . . ." JS to parents, fall 1927, Stanford University.

98: "It was wartime . . . ": Author interview with Red Williams, August 18, 1993.

99: "Among themselves, when . . ." Ricketts, *Between Pacific Tides*.

100: "little trailing glasses . . .": *Sweet Thursday*.

102: "They go out at night and burn fagots . . .": C. B. Wilson, "Hopkins Marine Laboratory: Interesting California Institution" (Hopkins scrapbook 1), p. 10.

102: "The wind is ashore tonight . . .": *Life in Letters*, p. 337.

103: "I remember it well . . .": "John Steinbeck States His View on Cannery Row," *Monterey Peninsula Herald*, March 8, 1957, p. 1.

104: "visited Dohrn's Marine Station . . .": David Starr Jordan to O. L. Elliott, August 13, 1923, Ricketts folder, Miller Library, p. 5.

104: "It proves a perfect paradise . . .": Oliver Peebles Jenkins, "Hopkins Seaside Laboratory," Ricketts folder, Miller Library, p. 58.

104: "It is within the scope . . ." and "bears a very":

W. K. Fisher, "Hopkins Marine Station," *Stanford Review*, 1919.

104: "little known research project": "Scientists at Hopkins Laboratory also prying into Sardines Affairs," *Monterey Peninsula Herald*, February 28, 1941.

105: "largely for scientific purposes . . .": Donation letter, Ricketts folder, Miller Library.

105: "Quite aside from the aquarium . . .": Memo to Mr. Walker from Lawrence Blinks, February 23, 1945, Ricketts folder, Miller Library.

Chapter 7

107: "Everyone found himself . . .": JS, "About Ed Ricketts," preface to *Log from the Sea of Cortez*, 1951 edition (New York: Penguin, 1995).

108: "mutual interdependence . . .": W. C. Allee, *Animal Aggregations: A Study in General Sociology* (Chicago: University of Chicago Press, 1931) and *Cooperation Among Animals: With Human Implications* (New York: Henry Schuman, 1938).

108: "decided that it would be best . . .": "Recollections," Anna Maker Ricketts, Martha Heasley Cox Center for Steinbeck Studies.

109: "had more fun . . .": "About Ed Ricketts."

110: "a primitive biological . . .": Ed Ricketts to Joseph Campbell, April 11, 1947, Stanford University.

110: "a predictable rhythm in the changes . . .": "Marine Station Studies May Aid Local Canneries," *Monterey Peninsula Herald*, July 15, 1937.

111: "I am a water fiend": JS datebook, April 17, 1948.

111: "a spiritual streak": Author interview with Elaine Steinbeck, November 6, 1998.

111: "I don't like Yosemite at all . . .": JS to Elizabeth Baily, May 1935, NSC archives.

111: "went up and down the escalator at a major . . .": Benson, *The True Adventures*, p. 356.

111: "I consider the last of . . .": JS to Harry Guggenheim, April 26, 1966, Harmon collection, SJSU.

111: "Modern sanity and religion . . .": JS to Carl Wilhelmson, *Life in Letters*, p. 31.

112: "Always prone . . .": JS to Carl Wilhelmsen, August 8, 1933, *Life in Letters*, p. 88.

112: "the true things . . .": Ed Ricketts, "2 p ms.," Stanford University.

112: "not only the 'beauty' of ugliness . . .": Ed Ricketts, "Non- Teleological Thinking," Stanford University.

112: "There were great . . .": "About Ed Ricketts."

113: "People who are concerned . . .": Ricketts's diary, December 22, 1942, Stanford University.

113: "I went over there . . .": Rolf Bolin, author's collection.

113: "Some kind of release of the spirit . . .": 1948 notebook, Pierpont Morgan.

113: "Wouldn't it be interesting . . .": JS to Ritch and Tal Lovejoy, *Life in Letters*, p. 316.

114: "our year of crazy beginnings": Joseph Campbell to Ed Ricketts, September 14, 1939, Stanford University.

114: "Since my last letter . . ." and "synthesis of Spengler . . .": Joseph Campbell to Ed Ricketts, August 22, 1939, Stanford University.

114: "Extra-humanists, the breaking-thru gang": Ed Ricketts, "My Literary Classification," Stanford University.

114: "You and your life-way . . .": Joseph Campbell to Ed Ricketts, September 14, 1939, Stanford University.

117: "that's how we became interested in the bust . . .": Author interview with Carol Brown, August 16, 1992.

118: "sad story of the Lone Star . . .": Ed Ricketts to Sparky Enea, September 16, 1942, Stanford University.

119: "Your suggestion . . .": JS to Mr. Adair, May 8, 1959, NSC archives.

119: "niche concept": Edward F. Ricketts, "Zoological introduction to 'The Outer Shores,'" in Katherine Rodger, *Breaking Through: Essays, Journals, and Travelogues of Edward F. Ricketts* (Berkeley: University of California Press, 2006).

121: "magnificent story about Monterey . . .": JS to Annie Laurie Williams, September 11, 1938, Columbia University.

121: "people [are] so wise naturally . . .": "The God in the Pipes" manuscript, published in *The Steinbeck Newsletter* (Fall 1995), pp. 4–9.

122: "A number of these buildings . . .": "John Steinbeck States His View on Cannery Row," *Monterey Peninsula Herald*, March 8, 1957, p. 1.

123: "We could have made . . .": Peggy Rink, "Pilgrimage to Wing Chong's," *Game and Gossip*, May 9, 1953, p. 32.

125: "We bought a house . . .": JS to Pat Covici, University of Texas.

125: "Where the new . . .": *Cannery Row*.

126: "Cannery Row is Monterey's": Ritch Lovejoy, *Monterey Peninsula Herald*, January 3, 1945, p. 9.

127: "as though on little wheels": *Cannery Row*.

Chapter 8

130: "The settlement has been built . . .": Harold Gilliam and Ann Gilliam, *Creating Carmel: The Enduring Vision* (Salt Lake City: Peregrine Smith, 1992), p. 77.

130: "thousands of standardized towns . . .": *Carmel Pine Cone*, November 14, 1930.

131: "The Carnival time . . .": Robinson Jeffers, "To George Sterling," *San Francisco Review*, 1926.

132: "Others who had come . . .": Franklin Walker, *The Seacoast of Bohemia: An Account of Early Carmel* (Santa Barbara: Peregrine Smith, 1973).

132: "there are several volumes . . .": "Carey McWilliams Tells About Carmel Writers," *Carmel Pine Cone*, June 16, 1931.

132: "H. Pease, and his shopkeeper's attitude . . .": JS to A. Grove Day, November 5, 1929, author's collection.

132: "We have literary acquaintances . . .": JS to George Albee, 1931, author's collection.

132: "We went to a party at John Calvin's . . .": JS to Carl Wilhelmson, 1930, *Life in Letters,* p. 30.

134: "It is the only paper of . . .": JS to parents, April 19, 1927, Stanford University.

135: "At last . . .": Stephen Larsen and Robin Larsen, *A Fire in the Mind: The Life of Joseph Campbell* (New York: Doubleday, 1991).

135: "Miss hearing the music . . .": JS to Mary Bulkley, August 17, 1936, Center for Steinbeck Studies, SJSU.

135: "To Miss Mary Bulkley . . .": Inscription to Mary Bulkley, Center for Steinbeck Studies, SJSU.

136: "the most powerful . . .": *New York Herald Tribune,* 1928 as quoted in "Whatever Happened to Robinson Jeffers?" by David Rains Wallace, *Los Angeles Times,* October 29, 2000, p. 1.

136: "Really, I've got the message . . .": Larsen and Larsen, *A Fire in the Mind,* pp. 179–80.

136: "The whole book . . .": Author's collection.

136: "modern soul movements . . .": Ed Ricketts, "The Philosophy of Breaking Through," in Joel Hedgpeth, ed., *The Outer Shores* (Eureka, CA: Mad River Press, 1978), p. 72.

136: "People have always taken themselves . . ." Toni Jackson, "The Hawk and the Rock," *What's Doing,* April 1947, p. 15.

137: "He wanted to do it . . ." and "I think he realized . . .": Author interview with Gordon Newell, 1989.

137: "Cabins still stand there . . .": Beth Ingels, *Carmel Pine Cone,* August 29, 1930.

137: "a parody . . .": Beth Ingels's notebook, author's collection.

138: "The only advantage I can see . . .": JS to Ted Miller, UCB.

138: "qualities foreign to the actual . . .": Naomi Rosenblum, "f. 64 and Modernism," in Terese Heyman (ed.), *Seeing Straight* (Oakland, CA: The Oakland Museum, 1992), pp. 48–49.

139: "In the 1930s if you weren't . . .": Author interview with Caroline Decker, 1989.

139: "A lot of social things . . .": Author interview with Richard Criley, June 20, 1990.

139: "I am not a Communist . . .": Martin Flavin Jr., "Conversations with Lincoln Steffens," *Harvard Advocate,* June 1938.

139: "stunning, straight, correct . . .": Author's collection.

139: "made people believe not in . . .": Justin Kaplan, *Lincoln Steffens: A Biography* (New York: Simon and Schuster, 1974), p. 327.

Chapter 9

142: "A few times I have . . .": JS, 1947, *Wayward Bus Journal,* Pierpont Morgan.

142: "intent of the book . . .": JS to Annie Laurie Williams, April 1936, Columbia University.

142: "I haven't gone proletarian . . .": JS to Harry Thornton Moore, March 1936, University of Virginia.

143: "nonpartisan" and "Your card alarms me . . .": John D. Barry, "Ways of The World . . . With Letters from John Steinbeck That Reflect Labor's Point of View," *San Francisco News,* July 13, 1938, p. 14.

144: "For too long the language . . .": JS to Elizabeth Baily, no date, NSC archives.

145: "It seemed to me an irony . . .": JS to Tom Collins, no date, Benson collection.

146: "by driving willow branches . . .": Shillinglaw and Benson, *America and Americans,* p. 80.

146: "I've seen such terrific things . . .": JS to Elizabeth Otis, fall 1936, Columbia University.

147: "the Proletariat . . .": JS to Harry Thornton Moore, March 1936, University of Virginia.

148: "There are riots in Salinas . . .": JS to George Albee, *Life in Letters,* p. 132.

148: "They used to get the 300-pound blocks . . .": J. J. Crosetti interview, "Pajaro Valley Agriculture, 1927–1977," http://library.ucsc.edu/reg-hist/crosetti.html.

149: "battle of Salinas . . .": Helen Boyden Lamb, "Industrial Relations in the Western Lettuce Industry," (Ph.D. dissertation, Radcliffe College, 1942).

149: "For a full fortnight . . .": Kevin Starr, *Endangered Dreams: The Great Depression in California* (New York: Oxford University Press, 1996), pp. 187–88.

149: "Now what happened . . .": Shillinglaw and Benson, *America and Americans*, p. 11.

149: "a vicious book . . .": JS to Annie Laurie Williams, April 20, 1938, Columbia University.

149: "four pound book . . .": Annie Laurie Williams to JS, January 9, 1937, Columbia University.

149: "Yes, I've been writing . . .": JS to Elizabeth Otis, March 23, 1938, Stanford University.

150: "I've worked out a plan . . .": JS to Tom Collins, no date, Benson collection.

152: "with a very pretty, Irish . . .": Jackson J. Benson interview with Sandy Oliver, Stanford University.

154: "The new house is fine . . .": JS to agents, fall 1936, Columbia University.

154: "a little tiny room . . .": JS to Elizabeth Otis, 1936, Stanford University.

155: "the most beautiful place . . .": Robert DeMott (ed.), *Working Days: The Journals of The Grapes of Wrath* (New York: Viking, 1989), p. 51.

155: "an estate . . . forty-seven acres . . .": Benson, *The True Adventures*, p. 459.

155: "Californians are wrathy . . .": Frank Taylor, "California's Grapes of Wrath," *Forum*, November 19, 1939, pp. 232–38.

157: "Although the Associated Farmers . . .": "Wrath, but No Ban," NSC archives.

157: "banned from all libraries . . .": "Grapes of Wrath Under Library's Ban at San Jose, " *San Jose Mercury News*, June 29, 1939.

157: "A lie, a damned infernal lie . . .": Lyle Boren, Congressional Record, January 10, 1940, pp. 139–40.

158: "He was dressed . . . ": Fensch, *Conversations*, pp. 11–12.

Chapter 10

161: "There's an illogic there . . .": JS to Ritch and Tal Lovejoy, May 27, 1948, Bancroft Library, University of California, Berkeley.

162: "and from there I shall............": JS to Elizabeth Otis, October 2, 1932, Stanford University.

163: "Mexicans and Yuakis ....": JS to Mavis McIntosh, *Life in Letters*, p. 67.

164: "It is impossible for me to ....": JS to Elizabeth Otis, October 12, 1935, Stanford University.

165: "John liked to be around ....": Pauline Pearson interview with Frank Raineri, February 14, 1980, NSC archives.

165: "Steinbeck would buy a slide ....": Jayne Ellison, "Dog Thieves Mourn Steinbeck," *Dayton Daily News*, December 22, 1968.

165: "considerate as only ....": *Sea of Cortez*.

166: "the most difficult work ....": Quoted in Louis Gannett,

"John Steinbeck: Novelist at Work," *Atlantic Monthly*, December 1945, p. 60.

172: "more here…": Lewis Gannett, New York *Herald Tribune*.

172: "there are four…": *Life in Letters*, p. 232.

Timeline

177: "You must know that the . . .": JS, "Letters to Alicia," *The Acts of King Arthur and His Noble Knights: From the Winchester Manuscripts of Thomas Malory & Other Sources* (New York: Farrar, Straus and Giroux, 1993).

177: "No I am not becoming . . .": JS to Katherine Beswick, circa 1930, Stanford University.

178: "related to Spanish people . . .": Pauline Pearson interview with Frank Raineri.

180: "taking Charley . . .": Author interview with Elaine Steinbeck, November 6, 1998.

John and Elaine, circa 1950.

Index

Page numbers in *italics* refer to illustrations or boxed material.

Credits

Art

Cover art, *Landscape from Laguna Seca*, 1999, by David Ligare.

Painting on page vi, *Landscape with Red Pony*, 1999, by David Ligare, Collection Knight Ridder Corporation, San Jose, CA.

Image on page xii ("From the Tide Pools to the Stars") courtesy Ray Troll.

Photo on page 47 (Hamilton Ranch) by Richard Allman, used courtesy of the photographer.

Images on pages 60, 83, 85, 90 (dog), 91 (scrap), 154, and 157 (Carol and friends) and back cover (JS and Carol with duck) courtesy Sharon Brown Bacon.

Image on page 56 courtesy Brown Brothers.

The following images are courtesy of the California Views Collection: page 61 (file 93-46-24; James K. Piggott, photographer), page 64 (file 88-084-0001; photographer unknown), page 114 (file 99-26-06; photographer unknown, summer of 1932), page 128 (file 71-001-0486; Lewis Josselyn, photographer), page 131 (wikiup; file 3183; E. A. Cohen, photographer, April 1908).

Images on pages 126, 152 (Gwyn), 164, and 179 courtesy Martha Heasley Cox Center for Steinbeck Studies, San Jose State University.

Image on page 171 (Cabo San Lucas) courtesy of Linda Cicero.

Images on pages 40 and 41 (Spreckels and Spreckels ad) are from the collection of Jim Conway.

Images on pages 126, 152 (Gwyn), and 179 courtesy Martha Heasley Cox Center for Steinbeck Studies, San Jose State University.

Drawing on page 107 by Walter F. Fisher in Anne B. Fisher, *Salinas, the Upside-Down River* (New York, Ferrar & Rinehart, 1945).

Images on page 162 (Cabo San Lucas) and 163 courtesy of Bill Gilly.

Painting on page 178 by Penny Worthington, courtesy of Steven Hauk Gallery, Pacific Grove, CA.

Image on page 90 (Chautauqua program) courtesy of Miller Library, Hopkins Marine Station.

Images on pages 81, 116 (label), 121, 178 (book cover), and back cover (book cover) from the collection of Jim Johnson. Image on page 59 courtesy of Lake Tahoe Historical Society.

The following images are from the Library of Congress: page 39 (Cesar Chavez), Prints & Photographs Division LC-USZ62-111017]; 139 (Lincoln Steffens), Prints & Photographs Division [LC-DIG-ggbain-05710]; 143 (Woman at the Dump), Prints & Photographs Division [LC-USZ62-122467]; 145 (Arvin migrant camp), Prints & Photographs Division, FSA/OWI Collection [LC-USF34-009892-C]; 146 (Tom Collins), Prints & Photographs Division, FSA/OWI Collection, [LC-USF34-009880-E]; 148 (tear gassing), Prints & Photographs Division [LC-USZ62-122467], 150 (Nipomo), Prints & Photographs Division, FSA/OWI Collection [LC-DIG-ppmsca-03054].

Images on pages 141 and 158 courtesy of Los Gatos Library.

Image on page 146 (cover) is reprinted courtesy of the Simon Lubin Society.

Images on pages 29 and 30 courtesy of Monterey County Historical Society.

The following are courtesy of the Monterey Public Library, California History Room: images on pages 9 (Chinatown, J. K. Oliver, photographer), 66, 69 (visitors on Lovers Point; Morgan Collection), 73 (Morgan Collection), 75 (Ruth Speakman, photographer), 77, 82, 101 (lighthouse; R. J. Arnold, photographer), 102 (Daniel Freeman, photographer), 103, 124 (Rey Ruppel, photographer), 131 (Pine Inn, L. S. Slevin, photographer), 136 (Harbick Collection), 137 (Robinson Jeffers; Morgan Collection), and 138 (George A. Cain, photographer, Harbick Collection)

Photos on pages 11 and 175 (JS with Charley) ©1991 Hans Namuth Estate, courtesy Center for Creative Photography, University of Arizona.

Images on pages 9 (workers; Edwin F. Halloran Collection), 20, 21, 28, 32, 34 (workers; Edwin F. Halloran Collection), 43 (JS and Glenn Graves), 54, 68 (Monterey Harbor), 79, 92, 149 (from the Valley of the World Agriculture Exhibition), 152 (Gwen and mother), 155, 157 (JS), 164 (JS and Gwyn), 165 (Willie), 167 (crew), 174, 175 (JS and family), 177, 180 courtesy of National Steinbeck Center, Salinas.

Photo on page 111 by Sonya Noskowiak, used by permission of Arthur Noskowiak.

Image on page 156 (Wood) courtesy of Oregon Historical Society, #CN023873.

Images on pages 91 (tent cabins), 95, and 101 (Lovers Point), and 104 courtesy of Pacific Grove Heritage Society.

Images on pages 65, 71, 72, 74 (photo by Julian P. Graham), 76 (photo by Julian P. Graham), 78, and 125 courtesy of Pebble Beach Company Lagorio Archives.

Text

Thanks are extended to the following libraries for providing access to and quotations from Steinbeck archives: Department of Special Collections, Stanford University Libraries; Harold A. Miller Library, Hopkins Marine Station of Stanford University; the Annie Laurie Williams Papers, Rare Book and Manuscript Library, Columbia University; Pierpont Morgan Library; National Steinbeck Center, Salinas; Martha Heasley Cox Center for Steinbeck Studies, San Jose State University; Bancroft Library, University of California, Berkeley; Clifton Waller Barrett Library of American Literature, Special Collections, University of Virginia; Harry Ransom Humanities Research Center, University of Texas at Austin.

Nancy Burnett (left) and Susan Shillinglaw (right) in Rocinante, Steinbeck's truck for his *Travels with Charley* trip.

About the Author

Born in Iowa, raised in Colorado, Susan Shillinglaw graduated with a B.A. in English and art from Cornell College and earned a Ph.D. in English from the University of North Carolina, Chapel Hill. Since 1984, she has been a professor of English at San Jose State University, where she was director of the university's Center for Steinbeck Studies for eighteen years. In 2012–13, she was the SJSU President's Scholar. She was also director of the National Steinbeck Center in Salinas from 2015 to 2018.

Dr. Shillinglaw has published widely on John Steinbeck, most recently *Carol and John Steinbeck: Portrait of a Marriage* (University of Nevada Press, 2013) and *On Reading* The Grapes of Wrath (Penguin, 2014). She also has written introductions to several Steinbeck books for Penguin Classics editions. She is working with the Western Flyer Foundation, helping develop educational programs that reflect Steinbeck and Ricketts's holistic perspective for the boat's relaunch in 2020.

About the Photographer

Nancy Burnett has been photographing the California landscape for more than thirty years. She is the producer of *The Shape of Life* and *Strange Days on Planet Earth* for PBS, coproducer of the photographic exhibit *Sea Stars* for the Smithsonian, and coauthor of *The Shape of Life*. She lives in Carmel Valley in California.

About the ArtPlace Series

This book is part of the ArtPlace series published by Roaring Forties Press. Each book in the series explores how a renowned artist and a world-famous city or area helped to define and inspire each other. ArtPlace volumes are intended to stimulate both eye and mind, offering a rich mix of art and photography, history and biography, ideas and information. While the books can be used by tourists to navigate and illuminate their way through cityscapes and landscapes, the volumes can also be read by armchair travelers in search of an engrossing and revealing story.

Visit Roaring Forties Press's website, www.roaringfortiespress.com, for details of these and other titles, as well as to learn about upcoming author tours, readings, media appearances, and all kinds of special events and offers.

A Journey into Steinbeck's California

This book is set in Goudy and Futura; the display type is Futura Condensed. The cover and the interior were designed by Jeff Urbancic. Karen Weldon made up the pages. Kim Rusch designed the maps. Wesley Palmer prepared the index.